GREAT JOBS

FOR

Environmental Studies Majors

Julie DeGalan | Bryon Middlekauff

VGM Career Books

Chicago   New York   San Francisco   Lisbon   London   Madrid   Mexico City
Milan   New Delhi   San Juan   Seoul   Singapore   Sydney   Toronto

Library of Congress Cataloging-in-Publication Data

Middlekauff, Bryon.
    Great jobs for environmental studies majors / Bryon Middlekauff, Julie
DeGalan.
        p.   cm. — (Great jobs for)
    Includes index.
    ISBN 0-658-01652-0
    1. Environmental sciences—Vocational guidance.   I. DeGalan, Julie.
II. Title.   III. Series.

GE60 .M53   2001
363'.0023—dc21   2002016817

VGM Career Books

A Division of The *McGraw·Hill* Companies

2 3 4 5 6 7 8 9 0   LBM/LBM   1 0 9 8 7 6 5 4

ISBN 0-658-01652-0

This book was set in Adobe Garamond by JDA Typesetting Corporation
Printed and bound by Lake Book Manufacturing

McGraw-Hill books are available at special quantity discounts to use as premiums and
sales promotions, or for use in corporate training programs. For more information, please
write to the Director of Special Sales, Professional Publishing, McGraw-Hill, Two Penn
Plaza, New York, NY 10121-2298. Or contact your local bookstore.

This book is printed on acid-free paper.

To Nick, Billy, Beau, Tyler, Olivia, and Hayden, with love.

CONTENTS

ACKNOWLEDGMENTS

Special thanks must go to Denise Betts. We appreciate her guidance and patience as we put together the material for this book and wrote our findings. Denise's encouragement helped us get through the doldrums to find the joy that comes from finishing a work and being happy with the results.

INVESTIGATE THE OPPORTUNITIES

*E*nvironment is the complex of climatic, edaphic, and biotic factors that act upon an organism or an ecological community and ultimately determine its form and survival. The spectacular eruption of Sakurajima in Japan in October 2000 covered the countryside in ash. Infrequent, but spectacular, mudslides in Marin County, California, are produced when highly absorptive soils reach their liquid limit and then begin to move. And the horrific terrorist attack on the World Trade Center Twin Towers on September 11, 2001, spread asbestos dust over an incredibly wide area. All these events resulted in the involvement of knowledgeable and dedicated workers trained in various aspects of environmental studies. From the climatologist determining the impact of the eruption on global climate changes, to the soil geomorphologist trying to learn more about soil behavior on slopes to be able to predict future slides, to the Environmental Protection Agency monitoring technician studying the far-reaching dispersal of asbestos from the Tower explosions—each played an important role in developing an understanding of the impact of both naturally—and purposefully—introduced actions on the earth's ecological system and the resulting consequences for humankind.

EVOLUTION OF ATTITUDES
TOWARD NATURE AND THE ENVIRONMENT

A philosophy that can be traced back to Middle Eastern civilizations that predate Judaism and Christianity teaches that humans are superior to all of the other inhabitants of the planet, and that humans must multiply and subdue and dominate nature. Francis Bacon, a fifteenth-century European philosopher, believed that "man is the center of the world." When Europeans began to populate the New World in the sixteenth century, these beliefs were brought with them. Europeans began to spread throughout the New World in the seventeenth and eighteenth centuries, exploring, exploiting, and eliminating obstacles to their dominion over the land. Manifest Destiny, a mid-nineteenth-century policy designed to justify the domination of all lands on the North American continent, spurred the movement toward and settlement of the west.

Images of this North American western wilderness portrayed in the literature of the time painted a foreboding, dark, haunting environment ruled by wolves and great beasts. The wilderness was seen as a place to be conquered, tamed, transformed, and made fit for people to exploit. Advances in technology and science of that time enabled humankind to understand and control some aspects of nature. In the mind-set of people living then, man had already unraveled the mysteries of the universe and he was ready to conquer his most immediate environment.

THE ENVIRONMENTAL MOVEMENT BEGINS IN THE UNITED STATES

The Need for Wilderness

During the nineteenth century, an awareness of change in the American landscape began to emerge in the writings of early activists like Henry David Thoreau, Ralph Waldo Emerson, and Walt Whitman. They each expressed a reverence for nature in their writings and lamented the demise of the wilderness. It had become apparent to them that the frontier had been pushed very far to the west and that only pockets of unspoiled wilderness remained. These activists knew that wilderness is beautiful and believed that humanity needs beauty because it is good for the soul. Each of these writers believed that some lands needed to be preserved and used as places where people could escape the crowds, noise, smoke, and fast pace of urban life. They acted to make their readers aware of what they knew and felt. The efforts of these three writers formed the basis for the environmental movement in the United States.

Creation of National Parks

Among the men and women who recognized early on the need to preserve wild lands was John Muir, founder of the Sierra Club and an early advocate for the establishment of national parks on public lands. Another early environmentalist was George Caitlin, a traveler and painter of the American West. He recognized the need for preservation of large tracts of land and became instrumental in the initiation of Yellowstone National Park in 1872. These visionaries worked to set aside vast tracts of land to be preserved against development—to retain their pristine condition as a landscape forever devoted to magnificent landforms and scenery, vegetation, and wildlife. Little did Muir and Caitlin know that by 2000, Yellowstone National Park would have 2.84 million visitors a year; Rocky Mountain, 3.2 million; Yosemite, 3.4 million; and Great Smoky Mountain, more than 10 million!

Recognition of the Human Impact on the Environment

Other early activists in the mid-nineteenth century, such as George Perkins Marsh, wrote of the impact humans had upon the environment. The westward expansion, first by wagon, then by train, increased in pace and volume as the railroad tied East to West by 1869. Buffalo were being decimated by the tens of thousands in an effort to exterminate Native Americans by destroying their environment, society, culture, and their means of livelihood.

As the United States became more and more urbanized, the economy boomed. The development of industrial plants led to great concentrations of people in tiny houses and walk-up tenements in tightly packed neighborhoods. Americans were moving in record numbers from rural areas to cities, at first preserving the large family sizes that were needed to successfully maintain a small family farm. Population pressure and provision of water and waste disposal for residences and industry were becoming significant urban problems.

The United States had become a major economy by late in the nineteenth century and population had doubled during the time period of 1860 to around 1900. Factories stamped out millions of pieces of cheap consumer goods for both domestic consumption and export. Factory workers, especially the managerial class, looked for housing outside the confines of the inner city. Interurban rail lines made a commute to the newly emerging suburbs possible, away from and upwind of the smoke-choked air of the factory districts.

Then beginning in about 1925, automobiles began replacing railroads as the primary means of transport and the spread of cities continued. The pace of suburbanization increased greatly after World War II with the emergence of two-worker families and increasing affluence. The nation's population became more tightly knit as the Eisenhower Interstate Highway System was extended across the country and as airline travel became more affordable. People began to move around in their cars and on airplanes as never before.

Now most anyone in the eastern half of the country could travel to Disneyland within two days. This enormous freedom to move about was welcomed by average Americans.

But such freedom had a downside. Affluence caused a tremendous growth in demand for consumer goods. Their production required all sorts of raw materials. Raw materials that needed to be grown, extracted, cut, processed, packaged, moved from one place to another, and retailed. Much more petroleum was used as freight was hauled by truck rather than by rail. As a result of all these changes, environmental hazards increased. The general public's awareness of pollution and species endangerment was heightened.

The EPA Is Established

President Richard Nixon established the Environmental Protection Agency (EPA) in 1970. Its goal was an integrated, coordinated, comprehensive attack upon environmental pollution. The agency was given the charge of identifying, prioritizing, and abating environmental degradation. It was also given the authority to set standards for air and water quality and to establish, monitor, and enforce regulations.

Since 1980, the EPA has identified thousands of contaminated sites to add to a National Priorities List. This list contains Superfund sites, which are uncontrolled or abandoned places where hazardous waste is located, possibly affecting local ecosystems or people. Many of these sites have been remediated, while new sites are continually identified and added to the list. A quick visit to the EPA website reveals a long and geographically widespread list of superfund sites in the United States.

The EPA certainly has its share of detractors, and its speed and effectiveness have been criticized over the last 30 years. But, it does stand as a monument to the people who recognized the need for clean water, clean air, and a healthy environment.

TWO ROOT CAUSES OF TODAY'S ENVIRONMENTAL ISSUES

There are two primary root causes of the environmental issues we face today. They are toxic pollutants and population growth. Both of these issues are discussed in the following sections.

By-Products of Human Activity: Toxins, Pollutants, and Contaminants

Let's begin by defining some terms that are important in environmental studies. Toxic substances are poisons, even in low concentrations, while pollutants are naturally occurring and man-made substances than can cause harm to humans or animals when found in high concentrations. Substances such as lead and arsenic are found naturally in numerous types of rocks and soils. In low concentrations, they aren't usually harmful. If ingested in sufficiently high concentrations, however, they can be fatal. A **contaminant** is a substance whose presence is unexpected in a given setting, such as sulfites or mercury in a water supply. If the contaminant is sufficiently concentrated, it becomes a **pollutant** and can be **toxic**. Although we may use these three terms interchangeably, they do have distinct meanings. In other words, the differences between these words center around the concentration of the substances and their location. A useful substance in its proper place is not a pollutant, but if it is allowed to move into other parts of the environment, it quickly becomes a problem.

An Example of Toxic Pollutants

Water pollution has been taking place for a very long time. The scope and depth of the problem can be made clear by illustrating just a few events that have contributed to the problem.

- Arsenic has been used in the smelting process for iron, as a medicinal (in low doses), and as a means of poisoning undesirable animals and insects. The leftover residue of its production and distribution was a source of contamination for water supplies from its first use, because runoff moved the toxin into surface and groundwater.

- More than 2,000 years ago the Romans built a system of aqueducts to bring water supplies to their cities. Water was distributed around urban areas to and within residences by lead pipes. High lead concentrations in drinking water caused health problems for the Roman population.

- A seventeenth-century bubonic plague outbreak, in a somewhat unusual way, polluted wells in twentieth-century England. Disposal of corpses led to high sulfite concentrations in the watershed. Later residents who depended upon the well water became ill.

- English hat makers in the nineteenth century used mercury nitrate in the felting process and suffered serious health problems as a consequence of their occupation.

- Chromium was long used to coat various automobile parts for aesthetic reasons and to reduce rust. Its manufacture, distribution, and application led to many instances of chromium poisoning.

There are endless examples of historic practices that have left relict pollutants in the environment. And today there are manufacturing techniques that operate similarly, generating toxic and contaminating substances that are purposefully or accidentally disposed of in the environment, creating pollution.

Population Growth Pressures the Environment

The exploitation of nature has become especially critical in recent decades because population pressure makes resources, and, as one of those resources, land, more and more scarce. World population reached about one billion by 1830. Another century was required to add the second billion people. World population had grown to three billion by 1960; only thirty years were required to add that third billion. Although the percentage increase has declined in recent decades, vast numbers of humans are added each year because the population base continues to swell. The earth was supporting four billion people during the 1970s; by 1987, the count was five billion, and sometime during 1999 world population reached six billion. That growth from five to six billion took only twelve years! Numbers this large are difficult to fathom, but consider that approximately ten thousand people are added to the base population every hour of each day.

Many demographers predict that population will stabilize during the next century at about eleven billion. That represents a doubling of the population in the mid-1980s. To support this number of people, technology must improve vastly over current levels to deal with the demands of food supply, energy, and waste disposal, as well as the spread of disease and other related issues. The fact that the earth can successfully feed eleven billion people does not mean that it will allow them to live well.

Population Growth's Impact on the Environment: An Example

In the fascinating BBC and Discovery Channel program series, *Connections I, II,* and *III,* the interaction of events and technological discoveries was explored. The series demonstrated that innovations sometimes create a cascade of unpredictable and negative outcomes. Connections between human activities are not to be viewed as a simple chain linked in a continuum, but rather as a web with tentacles reaching out in uncountable directions, and sometimes in unforeseeable circumstances. Just about every human activity has potential to produce an environmental problem, to which a solution must be sought.

Let's examine just one aspect of population pressure—a global increase over the next few decades in the number of automobiles on the road—and related interactions that will need environmental solutions. In the 1990s, there were about six hundred million cars on roads across the globe. In ten years, that figure was expected to climb to eight hundred million. A dear friend commented recently about the change that had taken place in his home city of Bangalore, India. After living for five years in the United States, he returned there and saw the increase in the number of automobiles on the road. He was amazed at the traffic congestion at each intersection. As developing countries such as India grow their middle class, the number of automobiles will skyrocket.

Cars and Ozone. Continuing with this example, the obvious impacts are an increase in fuel consumption and air pollution. One possible solution would be a transition to hybrid gas/electric cars. They are much more fuel efficient, and they offer the prospect of lowered emissions of ozone and CO_2 levels in the atmosphere. However, these cars are expensive and are being produced only in limited quantities. Even if everyone decided to buy one to replace a current vehicle, it would require about twenty years to replace the "fleet" of cars and trucks on the road today.

Cars and Polluted Water. A number of years ago a gasoline additive, MTBE, was developed and mixed into gasoline supplies in areas of heavy population concentration in the United States. The purpose was to reduce air pollution. It works. However, tiny concentrations of this compound in drinking water have been found to be carcinogenic. Spills of gasoline with MTBE can effectively contaminate a drinking water supply.

Cars and Reductions in Wilderness Areas. You might live in an area where a four-lane highway is being "upgraded" to a six. Additional lanes require more asphalt, a petroleum-based product, which translates to more oil drilling and depletion of our petroleum reserves. At the time of this writing, the Bush Administration advocated opening the National Arctic Wildlife Refuge in Alaska to oil exploration and ultimately to drilling. This will likely impact the caribou herd that migrates through there and detract forever from this wilderness area.

Cars and Manufacturing Energy Use. With more roads come more tollbooths, rest areas, fast-food restaurants, hotels and motels, gasoline stations, and convenience stores. We will then be required to cut more timber, refine additional steel, spin more fiberglass for insulation, craft roll after roll of paper, and manufacture plastics and aluminum to build all of these structures. This activity necessitates the use of more energy, leading to additional petroleum exploration, drilling, and refining.

Cars and Pollution Accidents. More automobiles require the manufacture of more plastics, glass, paint, tires, copper for wiring, and acid for batteries. This means more mining, more chance for accidents and spills, more land to be developed into factories and parking lots, more trees to be cut, more materials to be recycled, and more by-products to be disposed. You get the point. There is little that humans do today that doesn't have huge and widespread impacts on the environment.

SOME ENVIRONMENTAL PROGRESS. ONE EXAMPLE: RECYCLING SODA BOTTLES

In recent decades, we have learned to recycle lots of materials that were once of little value because it was less expensive to begin anew, for example, with raw iron ore than to reprocess steel cans into sheet metal. A recent television program demonstrated the production of carpeting from recycled materials. This technique utilized spent plastic soda bottles. First, the bottles were chipped, melted, and then extruded into fiber. The thread was dyed and spun into yarn. The carpet was then completed in the usual manner. Additionally, used carpeting created from recycled materials can be recycled again. Manufacturers are including bar codes on the carpet so that recycling centers can determine the type of plastic that was used to produce the original carpet. Fortunately, we are doing more and more of this sort of recycling than ever before because consumers are demanding materials with recycled content. But additional methods must be developed and markets identified so that we can use other by-products and consumer wastes in a similar way.

THE NEED FOR ENVIRONMENTAL PROFESSIONALS

What does all of this mean to you, someone who would like to find employment in one of the many environmental fields? It means that governments and individuals have recognized the need to give attention to the environment. People are concerned about air and water quality, soil erosion, wildlife, natural resources, maintaining wilderness areas and open space, recycling, proper disposal of hazardous and nonhazardous waste, and lowering the overall impact of humanity on the environment. If large numbers of people demand that the environment be considered in decision-making, it will become policy. In some cases it already has.

The demand for professionals prepared and trained to educate, plan, administer, and execute will be strong! There are diverse jobs in a range of environmental fields. Some of the jobs that you'll see mentioned in this book will be familiar to you, and some will not. Explore them all because each requires someone with training in some aspect of environmental studies that is critical to the survival of our planet and, thus, all humans.

PART ONE

THE
JOB SEARCH

1

THE
SELF-ASSESSMENT

Self-assessment is the process by which you begin to acknowledge your own particular blend of education, experiences, values, needs, and goals. It provides the foundation for career planning and the entire job search process. Self-assessment involves looking inward and asking yourself what can sometimes prove to be difficult questions. This self-examination should lead to an intimate understanding of your personal traits, your personal values, your consumption patterns and economic needs, your longer-term goals, your skill base, your preferred skills, and your under-developed skills.

You come to the self-assessment process knowing yourself well in some of these areas, but you may still be uncertain about other aspects. You may be well aware of your consumption patterns, but have you spent much time specifically identifying your longer-term goals or your personal values as they relate to work? No matter what level of self-assessment you have undertaken to date, it is now time to clarify all of these issues and questions as they relate to the job search.

The knowledge you gain in the self-assessment process will guide the rest of your job search. In this book, you will learn about all of the following tasks:

- Writing résumés

- Exploring possible job titles

- Identifying employment sites

- Networking

- Interviewing

- Following up

- Evaluating job offers

In each of these steps, you will rely on and often return to the understanding gained through your self-assessment. Any individual seeking employment must be able and willing to express these facets of his or her personality to recruiters and interviewers throughout the job search. This communication allows you to show the world who you are so that together with employers you can determine whether there will be a workable match with a given job or career path.

HOW TO CONDUCT A SELF-ASSESSMENT

The self-assessment process goes on naturally all the time. People ask you to clarify what you mean, you make a purchasing decision, or you begin a new relationship. You react to the world and the world reacts to you. How you understand these interactions and any changes you might make because of them are part of the natural process of self-discovery. There is, however, a more comprehensive and efficient way to approach self-assessment with regard to employment.

Because self-assessment can become a complex exercise, we have distilled it into a seven-step process that provides an effective basis for undertaking a job search. The seven steps include the following:

1. Understanding your personal traits

2. Identifying your personal values

3. Calculating your economic needs

4. Exploring your longer-term goals

5. Enumerating your skill base

6. Recognizing your preferred skills

7. Assessing skills needing further development

As you work through your self-assessment, you might want to create a worksheet similar to the one shown in Exhibit 1.1, starting on the following page. Or you might want to keep a journal of the thoughts you have as you

Exhibit 1.1

SELF-ASSESSMENT WORKSHEET

STEP 1. Understand Your Personal Traits
The personal traits that describe me are:
(Include all of the words that describe you.)

The ten personal traits that most accurately describe me are:
(List these ten traits.)

STEP 2. Identify Your Personal Values
Working conditions that are important to me include:
(List working conditions that would have to exist for you to accept a position.)

The values that go along with my working conditions are:
(Write down the values that correspond to each working condition.)

Some additional values I've decided to include are:
(List those values you identify as you conduct this job search.)

STEP 3. Calculate Your Economic Needs
My estimated minimum annual salary requirement is:
(Write the salary you have calculated based on your budget.)

Starting salaries for the positions I'm considering are:
(List the name of each job you are considering and the associated starting salary.)

STEP 4. Explore Your Longer-Term Goals
My thoughts on longer-term goals right now are:
(Jot down some of your longer-term goals as you know them right now.)

STEP 5. Enumerate Your Skill Base
The general skills I possess are:
(List the skills that underlie tasks you are able to complete.)

The specific skills I possess are:
(List more technical or specific skills that you possess, and indicate your level of expertise.)

General and specific skills that I want to promote to employers for the jobs I'm considering are:
(List general and specific skills for each type of job you are considering.)

STEP 6. Recognize Your Preferred Skills
Skills that I would like to use on the job include:
(List skills that you hope to use on the job, and indicate how often you'd like to use them.)

STEP 7. Assess Skills Needing Further Development
Some skills that I'll need to acquire for the jobs I'm considering include:
(Write down skills listed in job advertisements or job descriptions that you don't currently possess.)

I believe I can build these skills by:
(Describe how you plan to acquire these skills.)

undergo this process. There will be many opportunities to revise your self-assessment as you start down the path of seeking a career.

STEP 1   Understanding Your Personal Traits
Each person has a unique personality that he or she brings to the job search process. Gaining a better understanding of your personal traits can help you evaluate job and career choices. Identifying these traits and then finding employment that allows you to draw on at least some of them can create a rewarding and fulfilling work experience. If potential employment doesn't allow you to use these preferred traits, it is important to decide whether you can find other ways to express them or whether you would be better off not considering this type of job. Interests and hobbies pursued outside of work hours can be one way to use personal traits you don't have an opportunity to draw on in your work. For example, if you consider yourself an outgoing person and the kinds of jobs you are examining allow little contact with other people, you may be able to achieve the level of interaction that is comfortable for you outside of your work setting. If such a compromise seems impractical or otherwise unsatisfactory, you probably should explore only jobs that provide the interaction you want and need on the job.

Many young adults who are not very confident about their attractiveness to employers will downplay their need for income. They will say, "Money is not all that important if I love my work." But if you begin to document exactly what you need for housing, transportation, insurance, clothing, food, and utilities, you will begin to understand that some jobs cannot meet your financial needs and it doesn't matter how wonderful the job is. If you have to worry each payday about bills and other financial obligations, you won't be very effective on the job. Begin now to be honest with yourself about your needs.

Inventorying Your Personal Traits. Begin the self-assessment process by creating an inventory of your personal traits. Using the list in Exhibit 1.2, decide which of these personal traits describe you.

Exhibit 1.2

PERSONAL TRAITS

Accurate	Conservative	Excitable
Active	Considerate	Expressive
Adaptable	Cool	Extroverted
Adventurous	Cooperative	Fair-minded
Affectionate	Courageous	Farsighted
Aggressive	Creative	Feeling
Ambitious	Critical	Firm
Analytical	Curious	Flexible
Appreciative	Daring	Formal
Artistic	Decisive	Friendly
Brave	Deliberate	Future-oriented
Businesslike	Detail-oriented	Generous
Calm	Determined	Gentle
Capable	Discreet	Good-natured
Caring	Dominant	Helpful
Cautious	Eager	Honest
Cheerful	Easygoing	Humorous
Clean	Efficient	Idealistic
Competent	Emotional	Imaginative
Confident	Empathetic	Impersonal
Conscientious	Energetic	Independent

Individualistic	Original	Sedentary
Industrious	Outgoing	Self-confident
Informal	Patient	Self-controlled
Innovative	Peaceable	Self-disciplined
Intellectual	Personable	Sensible
Intelligent	Persuasive	Serious
Introverted	Pleasant	Sincere
Intuitive	Poised	Sociable
Inventive	Polite	Spontaneous
Jovial	Practical	Strong
Just	Precise	Strong-minded
Kind	Principled	Structured
Liberal	Private	Subjective
Likable	Problem solver	Tactful
Logical	Productive	Thorough
Loyal	Progressive	Thoughtful
Mature	Quick	Tolerant
Methodical	Quiet	Trusting
Meticulous	Rational	Trustworthy
Mistrustful	Realistic	Truthful
Modest	Receptive	Understanding
Motivated	Reflective	Unexcitable
Objective	Relaxed	Uninhibited
Observant	Reliable	Verbal
Open-minded	Reserved	Versatile
Opportunistic	Resourceful	Wise
Optimistic	Responsible	
Organized	Reverent	

Focusing on Selected Personal Traits. Of all the traits you identified from the list in Exhibit 1.2, select the ten you believe most accurately describe you. If you are having a difficult time deciding, think about which words people who know you well would use to describe you. Keep track of these ten traits.

Considering Your Personal Traits in the Job Search Process. As you begin exploring jobs and careers, watch for matches between your personal traits and the job descriptions you read. Some jobs will require many personal traits you know you possess, and others will not seem to match those traits.

· ·

> An environmental researcher's work, for example, requires self-discipline, motivation, curiosity, and observation. Researchers usually work alone, with somewhat limited opportunities to interact with others. An environmental project manager, on the other hand, must interact regularly with staff or clients to carry out the mission of the program. Project managers need strong interpersonal and verbal skills, imagination, and a good sense of humor. They must enjoy constant interaction and must become skilled at explaining information using a variety of methods.

· ·

Your ability to respond to changing conditions, your decision-making ability, productivity, creativity, and verbal skills all have a bearing on your success in and enjoyment of your work life. To better guarantee success, be sure to take the time needed to understand these traits in yourself.

STEP 2 Identifying Your Personal Values

Your personal values affect every aspect of your life, including employment, and they develop and change as you move through life. Values can be defined as principles that we hold in high regard, qualities that are important and desirable to us. Some values aren't ordinarily connected to work (love, beauty, color, light, relationships, family, or religion), and others are (autonomy, cooperation, effectiveness, achievement, knowledge, and security). Our values determine, in part, the level of satisfaction we feel in a particular job.

Defining Acceptable Working Conditions. One facet of employment is the set of working conditions that must exist for someone to consider taking a job.

Each of us would probably create a unique list of acceptable working conditions, but items that might be included on many people's lists are the amount of money you would need to be paid, how far you are willing to drive or travel, the amount of freedom you want in determining your own schedule, whether you would be working with people or data or things, and

---

Exhibit 1.3

WORK VALUES

Achievement	Development	Physical activity
Advancement	Effectiveness	Power
Adventure	Excitement	Precision
Attainment	Fast pace	Prestige
Authority	Financial gain	Privacy
Autonomy	Helping	Profit
Belonging	Humor	Recognition
Challenge	Improvisation	Risk
Change	Independence	Security
Communication	Influencing others	Self-expression
Community	Intellectual stimulation	Solitude
Competition	Interaction	Stability
Completion	Knowledge	Status
Contribution	Leading	Structure
Control	Mastery	Supervision
Cooperation	Mobility	Surroundings
Creativity	Moral fulfillment	Time freedom
Decision making	Organization	Variety

---

the types of tasks you would be willing to do. Your conditions might include statements of working conditions you will *not* accept; for example, you might not be willing to work at night or on weekends or holidays.

If you were offered a job tomorrow, what conditions would have to exist for you to realistically consider accepting the position? Take some time and make a list of these conditions.

Realizing Associated Values. Your list of working conditions can be used to create an inventory of your values relating to jobs and careers you are exploring. For example, if one of your conditions stated that you wanted to earn at least $30,000 per year, the associated value would be financial gain. If another condition was that you wanted to work with a friendly group of people, the value that went along with that might be belonging or interaction with people. Exhibit 1.3 provides a list of commonly held values that relate to the work environment; use it to create your own list of personal values.

Relating Your Values to the World of Work. As you read the job descriptions in this book and in other suggested resources, think about the values associated with each position.

....

> For example, the duties of an environmental policy analyst would include researching, and investigating, writing, and editing reports. Associated values are intellectual stimulation and communication.

....

If you were thinking about a career in this field, or any other field you're exploring, at least some of the associated values should match those you extracted from your list of working conditions. Take a second look at any values that don't match up. How important are they to you? What will happen if they are not satisfied on the job? Can you incorporate those personal values elsewhere? Your answers need to be brutally honest. As you continue your exploration, be sure to add to your list any additional values that occur to you.

STEP 3 Calculating Your Economic Needs

Each of us grew up in an environment that provided for certain basic needs, such as food and shelter, and, to varying degrees, other needs that we now consider basic, such as cable television, E-mail, or an automobile. Needs such as privacy, space, and quiet, which at first glance may not appear to be monetary needs, may add to housing expenses and so should be considered as you examine your economic needs. For example, if you place a high value on a large, open living space for yourself, it would be difficult to satisfy that need without an associated high housing cost, especially in a densely populated city environment.

As you prepare to move into the world of work and become responsible for meeting your own basic needs, it is important to consider the salary you will need to be able to afford a satisfying standard of living. The three-step process outlined here will help you plan a budget, which in turn will allow you to evaluate the various career choices and geographic locations you are considering. The steps include (1) developing a realistic budget, (2) examining starting salaries, and (3) using a cost-of-living index.

Developing a Realistic Budget. Each of us has certain expectations for the kind of lifestyle we want to maintain. To begin the process of defining your economic needs, it will be helpful to determine what you expect to spend on routine monthly expenses. These expenses include housing, food, transportation, entertainment, utilities, loan repayments, and revolving charge accounts. A worksheet that details many of these expenses is shown in Exhibit 1.4. You may not currently spend anything for certain items, but you probably will have to once you begin supporting yourself. As you develop this budget, be generous in your estimates, but keep in mind any items that could be reduced or eliminated. If you are not sure about the cost of a certain item, talk with family or friends who would be able to give you a realistic estimate.

If this is new or difficult for you, start to keep a log of expenses right now. You may be surprised at how much you actually spend each month for food or stamps or magazines. Household expenses and personal grooming items can often loom very large in a budget, as can auto repairs or home maintenance.

Income taxes must also be taken into consideration when examining salary requirements. State and local taxes vary, so it is difficult to calculate exactly the effect of taxes on the amount of income you need to generate. To roughly estimate the gross income necessary to generate your minimum annual salary requirement, multiply the minimum salary you have calculated (see Exhibit 1.4) by a factor of 1.35. The resulting figure will be an approximation of what your gross income would need to be, given your estimated expenses.

Examining Starting Salaries. Starting salaries for each of the career tracks are provided throughout this book. These salary figures can be used in conjunction with the cost-of-living index (discussed in the next section) to determine whether you would be able to meet your basic economic needs in a given geographic location.

Using a Cost-of-Living Index. If you are thinking about trying to get a job in a geographic region other than the one where you now live, understanding differences in the cost of living will help you come to a more informed decision about making a move. By using a cost-of-living index, you can compare salaries offered and the cost of living in different locations with what you know about the salaries offered and the cost of living in your present location.

Exhibit 1.4

ESTIMATED MONTHLY EXPENSES WORKSHEET

		Could Reduce Spending? (Yes/No)
Cable	$ _____	_____
Child care	_____	_____
Clothing	_____	_____
Educational loan repayment	_____	_____
Entertainment	_____	_____
Food		
At home	_____	_____
Meals out	_____	_____
Gifts	_____	_____
Housing		
Rent/mortgage	_____	_____
Insurance	_____	_____
Property taxes	_____	_____
Medical insurance	_____	_____
Reading materials		
Newspapers	_____	_____
Magazines	_____	_____
Books	_____	_____
Revolving loans/charges	_____	_____
Savings	_____	_____
Telephone	_____	_____
Transportation	_____	_____
Auto payment	_____	_____
Insurance	_____	_____
Parking	_____	_____
Gasoline	_____	_____
or		
Cab/train/bus fare	_____	_____
Utilities		
Electric	_____	_____
Gas	_____	_____
Water/sewer	_____	_____

	Could Reduce Spending? (Yes/No)
Vacations	_____ _____
Miscellaneous expense 1	
Expense: _____	
Miscellaneous expense 2	_____ _____
Expense: _____	
Miscellaneous expense 3	_____ _____
Expense: _____	

TOTAL MONTHLY EXPENSES: _____

YEARLY EXPENSES (Monthly expenses × 12): _____ _____

INCREASE TO INCLUDE TAXES (Yearly expenses × 1.35): _____ _____ =

MINIMUM ANNUAL SALARY REQUIREMENT: _____

Many variables are used to calculate the cost-of-living index. Often included are housing, groceries, utilities, transportation, health care, clothing, and entertainment expenses. Right now you do not need to worry about the details associated with calculating a given index. The main purpose of this exercise is to help you understand that pay ranges for entry-level positions may not vary greatly, but the cost of living in different locations *can* vary tremendously.

· ·

If you lived in Columbus, Ohio, for example, and you were interested in working as a conservation technician, you would plan on earning $28,750 annually. But let's say you're also thinking about moving to New York, Atlanta, or Phoenix. You know you can live on $28,750 in Columbus, but you want to be able to equal that salary in the other locations you're considering. How much will you have to earn in those locations to do this? Determining the cost of living for each city will show you.

There are many websites like CareerPerfect's (career perfect.com/careerperfect/relocationfs.htm) that can assist you as you undertake this research. Or, use any search engine and enter the keywords *cost-of-living index.* Several choices will appear. Choose one site and look for such options as "cost-of-living analysis" or "cost-of-living comparator." Some sites will ask you to register and/or pay for the information, but most sites are free. Follow the instructions provided and you will be able to create a table of information like the one shown below.

JOB: CONSERVATION TECHNICIAN		
City	Base Amount	Equivalent Salary
Columbus, OH	$28,750	
New York, NY		$34,775
Atlanta, GA		$31,015
Phoenix, AZ		$27,950

At the time this comparison was done, you would have needed to earn $34,775 in New York, $31,015 in Atlanta, and $27,950 in Phoenix to match the buying power of $28,750 in Columbus.

If you would like to determine whether it's financially worthwhile to make any of these moves, one more piece of information is needed: the salaries of conservation technicians in these other cities. The CareerPerfect website also contains job descriptions and salary information for a wide range of positions, including conservation technicians. The website reports the following salaries paid at the 25th percentile earned for the states where the three cities are located. These figures reflect entry-level salaries.

City	25th Percentile Salary	Equivalent Salary Needed	Change in Buying Power
New York, NY	$32,976	$34,775	- $1,799
Atlanta, GA	$28,379	$31,015	- $2,636
Phoenix, AZ	$28,036	$27,950	+ 86

> If you moved to New York City and secured employ-
> ment as a conservation technician you would be earning
> $1,799 less than what it would take to maintain a lifestyle
> similar to the one you lead in Columbus. Moving to
> Atlanta from Columbus would decrease your buying power
> by more than $2,600. Moving to Phoenix would allow you
> to maintain your buying power. Remember, these figures
> change all the time, so be sure to undertake your own cal-
> culations. If you would like to see how these figures were
> calculated you can visit CareerPerfect's website.

....

You can work through a similar exercise for any type of job you are considering and for many locations when current salary information is available. It will be worth your time to undertake this analysis if you are seriously
considering a relocation. By doing so you will be able to make an informed
choice.

STEP 4   Exploring Your Longer-Term Goals

There is no question that when we first begin working, our goals are to use
our skills and education in a job that will reward us with employment, income,
and status relative to the preparation we brought with us to this position. If
we are not being paid as much as we feel we should for our level of education or if job demands don't provide the intellectual stimulation we had hoped
for, we experience unhappiness and as a result often seek other employment.

Most jobs we consider "good" are those that fulfill our basic "lower-level"
needs of security, food, clothing, shelter, income, and productive work. But
even when our basic needs are met and our jobs are secure and productive,
we as individuals are constantly changing. As we change, the demands and
expectations we place on our jobs may change. Fortunately, some jobs grow
and change with us, and this explains why some people are happy throughout many years in a job.

But more often people are bigger than the jobs they fill. We have more
goals and needs than any job could satisfy. These are "higher-level" needs of
self-esteem, companionship, affection, and an increasing desire to feel we are
employing ourselves in the most effective way possible. Not all of these
higher-level needs can be met through employment, but for as long as we
are employed, we increasingly demand that our jobs play their part in moving us along the path to fulfillment.

Another obvious but important fact is that we change as we mature.
Although our jobs also have the potential for change, they may not change

as frequently or as markedly as we do. There are increasingly fewer one-job, one-employer careers; we must think about a work future that may involve voluntary or forced moves from employer to employer. Because of that very real possibility, we need to take advantage of the opportunities in each position we hold. Acquiring skills and competencies associated with will keep us viable and attractive as employees. This is particularly true in a job market that not only is technology/computer dependent, but also is populated with more and more small, self-transforming organizations rather than the large, seemingly stable organizations of the past.

It may be difficult in the early stages of the job search to determine whether the path you are considering can meet these longer-term goals. Reading about career paths and individual career histories in your field can be very helpful in this regard. Meeting and talking with individuals further along in their careers can be enlightening as well. Older workers can provide valuable guidance on "self-managing" your career, which will become an increasingly valuable skill in the future. Some of these ideas may seem remote as you read this now, but you should be able to appreciate the need to ensure that you are growing, developing valuable new skills, and researching other employers who might be interested in your particular skills package.

· ·

If you are considering a position in environmental engineering, for example, you would gain a far better perspective on your potential career if you could talk to an engineer in training (EIT), a more experienced certified engineer, and, finally, an engineering supervisor with a significant work history in environmental consulting. Each will have a different perspective, unique concerns, and an individual set of value priorities.

· ·

STEP 5 Enumerating Your Skill Base

In terms of the job search, skills can be thought of as capabilities that can be developed in school, at work, or by volunteering and then used in specific job settings. Many studies have documented the kinds of skills that employers seek in entry-level applicants. For example, some of the most desired skills for individuals interested in the teaching profession are the ability to interact effectively with students one-on-one, to manage a classroom, to adapt to varying situations as necessary, and to get involved in school activities. Business employers have also identified important qualities, including enthusiasm for the employer's product or service, a businesslike mind, the ability to follow written or oral instructions, the ability to demonstrate self-control, the confidence to suggest new ideas, the ability to communicate with all members of a group, an awareness of cultural differences, and loyalty, to name just a few. You will find that many of these skills are also in the repertoire of qualities demanded in your college major.

To be successful in obtaining any given job, you must be able to demonstrate that you possess a certain mix of skills that will allow you to carry out the duties required by that job. This skill mix will vary a great deal from job to job; to determine the skills necessary for the jobs you are seeking, you can read job advertisements or more generic job descriptions, such as those found later in this book. If you want to be effective in the job search, you must directly show employers that you possess the skills needed to be successful in filling the position. These skills will initially be described on your résumé and then discussed again during the interview process.

Skills are either general or specific. To develop a list of skills relevant to employers, you must first identify the general skills you possess, then list specific skills you have to offer, and, finally, examine which of these skills employers are seeking.

General skills in the scientific and engineering fields are developed through the core curriculum you are required to take at your school. In addition, general skills are also developed through summer internships or co-op assignments. General skills include, but are not limited to, knowledge of math and science, computer programming skills, basic laboratory or engineering design techniques, technical writing, and presentation skills. Specific skills are acquired through the course work in your specific science or engineer major and related work experience in your field. These skills allow you to complete tasks that require specialized knowledge unique to your discipline. Digital design, environmental impact, systems physiology, and hydraulic calculations are just a few examples of specific skills that may relate to a job.

Identifying Your General Skills. Because you possess or will possess a college degree, employers will assume that you can read and write, perform certain basic computations, think critically, and communicate effectively. Employers will want to see that you have acquired these skills, and they will want to know which additional general skills you possess.

One way to begin identifying skills is to write an experiential diary. An experiential diary lists all the tasks you were responsible for completing for each job you've held and then outlines the skills required to do those tasks. You may list several skills for any given task. This diary allows you to distinguish between the tasks you performed and the underlying skills required to complete those tasks. Here's an example:

Tasks	Skills
Answering telephone	Effective use of language, clear diction, ability to direct inquiries, ability to solve problems
Waiting on tables	Poise under conditions of time and pressure, speed, accuracy, good memory, simultaneous completion of tasks, sales skills

For each job or experience you have participated in, develop a worksheet based on the example shown here. On a résumé, you may want to describe these skills rather than simply listing tasks. Skills are easier for the employer to appreciate, especially when your experience is very different from the employment you are seeking. In addition to helping you identify general skills, this experiential diary will prepare you to speak more effectively in an interview about the qualifications you possess.

Identifying Your Specific Skills. It may be easier to identify your specific skills because you can definitely say whether you can speak other languages, program a computer, draft a map or diagram, or edit a document using appropriate symbols and terminology.

Using your experiential diary, identify the points in your history where you learned how to do something very specific, and decide whether you have a beginning, intermediate, or advanced knowledge of how to use that particular skill. Right now, be sure to list *every* specific skill you have, and don't consider whether you like using the skill. Write down a list of specific skills you have acquired and the level of competence you possess—beginning, intermediate, or advanced.

Relating Your Skills to Employers. You probably have thought about a couple of different jobs you might be interested in obtaining, and one way to begin relating the general and specific skills you possess to a potential employer's needs is to read actual advertisements for these types of positions (see Part Two for resources listing actual job openings).

· ·

For example, you might be interested in a career as an environmental planner. Use any one of a number of general resources that describe the job of environmental planner. The *Occupational Outlook Handbook* is one good example. Begin building a comprehensive list of general skills. Then as you read actual job listings, they will reveal an important core of specific skills that are necessary for obtaining the type of work you're interested in.

Following is a sample list of skills you would need to be successful as an environmental planner. These items were extracted from general resources and actual job listings.

JOB : ENVIRONMENTAL PLANNER

General Skills	Related Specific Skill Detailed in Job Announcements
Gather information	Obtain transportation data from state offices of transportation
Disseminate information	Represent organization in public forums
Conduct research	Analyze differences in transportation data among the U.S. states
Be willing to travel	Travel as needed to state offices of transportation
Collaborate on projects	Work with state directors of transportation to obtain data and disseminate study results

---

If you are interested in another type of job in environmental studies, undertake this same activity for at least one job you are considering.

Many of the general skills you develop for one position are transferable to others. This means that the skills can be used in many different kinds of positions. For example, disseminating information is a required general skill for an environmental planner, and it would also be required for an environmental technician or an environmental educator.

....

Now review the list of skills that are required for jobs you are considering, and check off those skills that *you know you possess*. You should refer to these specific skills on the résumé that you write for this type of job. See Chapter 2 for details on résumé writing.

STEP 6   Recognizing Your Preferred Skills

In the previous section you developed a comprehensive list of skills that relate to particular career paths that are of interest to you. You can now relate these to skills that you prefer to use. We all use a wide range of skills (some researchers say individuals have a repertoire of about 500 skills), but we may not particularly be interested in using all of them in our work. There may be some skills that come to us more naturally or that we use successfully time and time again and that we want to continue to use; these are best described as our preferred skills. For this exercise use the list of skills that you created for the previous section, and decide which of them you are *most interested in using* in future work and how often you would like to use them. You might be interested in using some skills only occasionally, while others you would like to use more regularly. You probably also have skills that you hope you can use constantly.

As you examine job announcements, look for matches between this list of preferred skills and the qualifications described in the advertisements. These skills should be highlighted on your résumé and discussed in job interviews.

STEP 7   Assessing Skills Needing Further Development

Previously you compiled a list of general and specific skills required for given positions. You already possess some of these skills; those that remain to be developed are your underdeveloped skills.

If you are just beginning the job search, there may be gaps between the qualifications required for some of the jobs you're considering and skills you possess. The thought of having to admit to and talk about these underdeveloped skills, especially in a job interview, is a frightening one. One way to put a healthy perspective on this subject is to target and relate your exploration of underdeveloped skills to the types of positions you are seeking.

Recognizing these shortcomings and planning to overcome them with either on-the-job training or additional formal education can be a positive way to address the concept of underdeveloped skills.

On your worksheet or in your journal, make a list of up to five general or specific skills required for the positions you're interested in that you *don't currently possess*. For each item list an idea you have for specific action you could take to acquire that skill. Do some brainstorming to come up with possible actions. If you have a hard time generating ideas, talk to people currently working in this type of position, professionals in your college career services office, trusted friends, family members, or members of related professional associations.

If, for example, you are interested in a job for which you don't have some specific required experience, you could locate training opportunities such as classes or workshops offered through a local college or university, community college, or club or association that would help you build the level of expertise you need for the job.

You will notice in this book that many excellent positions for your major demand computer skills. While basic word processing has been something you've done all through college, you may be surprised at the additional computer skills required by employers. Many positions for college graduates will ask for some familiarity with spreadsheet programming, and frequently some database-management software familiarity is a job demand as well. Desktop publishing software, graphics programs, and basic Web-page design also pop up frequently in job ads for college graduates. If your degree program hasn't introduced you to a wide variety of computer applications, what are your options? If you're still in college, take what computer courses you can before you graduate. If you've already graduated, look at evening programs, continuing education courses, or tutorial programs that may be available commercially. Developing a modest level of expertise will encourage you to be more confident in suggesting to potential employers that you can continue to add to your skill base on the job.

In Chapter 5 on interviewing, we will discuss in detail how to effectively address questions about underdeveloped skills. Generally speaking, though, employers want genuine answers to these types of questions. They want you to reveal "the real you," and they also want to see how you answer difficult questions. In taking the positive, targeted approach discussed above, you show the employer that you are willing to continue to learn and that you have a plan for strengthening your job qualifications.

USING YOUR SELF-ASSESSMENT

Exploring entry-level career options can be an exciting experience if you have good resources available and will take the time to use them. Can you effectively complete the following tasks?

1. Understand your personality traits and relate them to career choices

2. Define your personal values

3. Determine your economic needs

4. Explore longer-term goals

5. Understand your skill base

6. Recognize your preferred skills

7. Express a willingness to improve on your underdeveloped skills

If so, then you can more meaningfully participate in the job search process by writing a more effective résumé, finding job titles that represent work you are interested in doing, locating job sites that will provide the opportunity for you to use your strengths and skills, networking in an informed way, participating in focused interviews, getting the most out of follow-up contacts, and evaluating job offers to find those that create a good match between you and the employer. The remaining chapters in Part One guide you through these next steps in the job search process. For many job seekers, this process can take anywhere from three months to a year to implement. The time you will need to put into your job search will depend on the type of job you want and the geographic location where you'd like to work. Think of your effort as a job in itself, requiring you to set aside time each week to complete the needed work. Carefully undertaken efforts may reduce the time you need for your job search.

2

THE RÉSUMÉ AND COVER LETTER

The task of writing a résumé may seem overwhelming if you are unfamiliar with this type of document, but there are some easily understood techniques that can and should be used. This section was written to help you understand the purpose of the résumé, the different types of résumé formats available, and how to write the sections of information traditionally found on a résumé. We will present examples and explanations that address questions frequently posed by people writing their first résumé or updating an old résumé.

Even within the formats and suggestions given, however, there are infinite variations. True, most résumés follow one of the outlines suggested, but you should feel free to adjust the résumé to suit your needs and make it expressive of your life and experience.

WHY WRITE A RÉSUMÉ?

The purpose of a résumé is to convince an employer that you should be interviewed. Whether you're mailing, faxing, or E-mailing this document, you'll want to present enough information to show that you can make an immediate and valuable contribution to an organization. A résumé is not an indepth historical or legal document; later in the job search process you may be asked to document your entire work history on an application form and attest to its validity. The résumé should, instead, highlight relevant information pertaining directly to the organization that will receive the document or to the type of position you are seeking.

23

We will discuss four types of résumés in this chapter: chronological, functional, targeted, and digital. The reasons for using one type of résumé over another and the typical format for each are addressed in the following sections.

THE CHRONOLOGICAL RÉSUMÉ

The chronological résumé is the most common of the various résumé formats and therefore the format that employers are most used to receiving. This type of résumé is easy to read and understand because it details the chronological progression of jobs you have held. (See Exhibit 2.1.) It begins with your most recent employment and works back in time. If you have a solid work history or have experience that provided growth and development in your duties and responsibilities, a chronological résumé will highlight these achievements. The typical elements of a chronological résumé include the heading, a career objective, educational background, employment experience, activities, and references.

The Heading
The heading consists of your name, address, telephone number, and other means of contact. This may include a fax number, E-mail address, and your home-page address. If you are using a shared E-mail account or a parent's business fax, be sure to let others who use these systems know that you may receive important professional correspondence via these systems. You wouldn't want to miss a vital E-mail or fax! Likewise, if your résumé directs readers to a personal home page on the Web, be certain it's a professional personal home page designed to be viewed and appreciated by a prospective employer. This may mean making substantial changes in the home page you currently mount on the Web.

We suggest that you spell out your full name in your résumé heading and type it in all capital letters in bold type. After all, you are the focus of the résumé! If you have a current as well as a permanent address and you include both in the heading, be sure to indicate until what date your current address will be valid. The two-letter state abbreviation should be the only abbreviation that appears in your heading. Don't forget to include the zip code with your address and the area code with your telephone number.

The Objective
As you formulate the wording for this part of your résumé, keep the following points in mind.

Exhibit 2.1

CHRONOLOGICAL RÉSUMÉ

BEAU MIDDLECAUFF

Student Apartment 108
Michigan State University
East Lansing, MI 48824
517-555-1212
bmiddle@xxx.com
(until May 2004)

123 Main Street
Okemos, MI
517-555-7777

Objective

A career in environmental technology, initially as a lab technician and ultimately as a research team leader.

Education

Bachelor of Science in Biology
Michigan State University
May 2004
Minor: Environmental Studies
Overall GPA 3.2 on a 4.0 scale

Honors/Awards

Dean's List, Spring Semester 2004 & Fall Semester 2004
Who's Who Among Universities and Colleges, 2003–2004
The Biology Department Academic Achievement Award, 2002

Related Courses

Analytical Chemistry
Statistics

Computer Science
Lab Safety

Experience

Tutor, Academic Support Services, MSU
Part-time, 2002–2003
Tutored students enrolled in lower-level biology courses.

Switchboard Operator, MSU
Part-time, 2001
Worked on a team of ten operators for a busy campus of 45,000. Used system with sophisticated relay and switching capabilities.

Customer Relations, Quick Print Advertising, E. Lansing, MI
Summers, 2001–2003
Costed jobs, wrote up estimates, made copies, created and placed ads in local papers.

Activities
Outing Club President, 2003; member 2001–2004
Intramural basketball, 2001–2004

References
Personal and professional references are available upon request.

The Objective Focuses the Résumé. Without a doubt this is the most challenging part of the résumé for most writers. Even for individuals who have decided on a career path, it can be difficult to encapsulate all they want to say in one or two brief sentences. For job seekers who are unfocused or unclear about their intentions, trying to write this section can inhibit the entire résumé writing process.

Recruiters tell us time and time again that the objective creates a frame of reference for them. It helps them see how you express your goals and career focus. In addition, the statement may indicate in what ways you can immediately benefit an organization. Given the importance of the objective, every point covered in the résumé should relate to it. If information doesn't relate, it should be omitted. You'll file a number of résumé variations in your computer. There's no excuse for not being able to tailor a résumé to individual employers or specific positions.

Choose an Appropriate Length. Because of the brevity necessary for a résumé, you should keep the objective as short as possible. Although objectives of only four or five words often don't show much direction, objectives that take three full lines could be viewed as too wordy and might possibly be ignored.

Consider Which Type of Objective Statement You Will Use. There are many ways to state an objective, but generally this statement can take four forms: (1) a very general statement; (2) a statement focused on a specific position; (3) a statement focused on a specific industry; or (4) a summary of your qualifications. In our contacts with employers, we often hear that many résumés don't exhibit any direction or career goals, so we suggest avoiding general statements when possible.

1. General Objective Statement. General objective statements look like the following:

- An entry-level educational programming coordinator position

- An entry-level environmental field technician position

This type of objective would be useful if you know what type of job you want but you're not sure which industries interest you.

2. Position-Focused Objective. Following are examples of objectives focusing on a specific position:

- To obtain the position of assistant educational coordinator at State College

- To obtain a position as assistant researcher at *Time* magazine

When a student applies for an advertised job opening, this type of focus can be very effective. The employer knows that the applicant has taken the time to tailor the résumé specifically for this position.

3. Industry-Focused Objective. Focusing on a particular industry in an objective could be stated as follows:

- To begin a career as an environmental engineer in the consulting industry

4. Summary of Qualifications Statement. The summary of qualifications can be used instead of an objective or in conjunction with an objective. The purpose of this type of statement is to highlight relevant qualifications gained through a variety of experiences. This type of statement is often used by individuals with extensive and diversified work experience. An example of a qualifications statement follows:

··

A degree in geography and four years of progressively increasing job responsibility working in the campus library

have prepared me to begin a career as an environmental planner with an organization that values hard work and dedication.

∙∙∙

Support Your Objective. A résumé that contains any one of these types of objective statements should then go on to demonstrate why you are qualified to get the position. Listing academic degrees can be one way to indicate qualifications. Another demonstration would be in the way previous experiences, both volunteer and paid, are described. Without this kind of documentation in the body of the résumé, the objective looks unsupported. Think of the résumé as telling a connected story about you. All the elements should work together to form a coherent picture that ideally should relate to your statement of objective.

Education

This section of your résumé should indicate the exact name of the degree you will receive or have received, spelled out completely with no abbreviations. The degree is generally listed after the objective, followed by the institution name and location, and then the month and year of graduation. This section could also include your academic minor, grade point average (GPA), and appearance on the Dean's List or President's List.

If you have enough space, you might want to include a section listing courses related to the field in which you are seeking work. The best use of a "related courses" section would be to list some course work that is not traditionally associated with the major. Perhaps you took several computer courses outside your degree that will be helpful and related to the job prospects you are entertaining. Several education section examples are shown here:

∙∙∙

- Bachelor of Science Degree in Geology
  State College, Plymouth, NM
  May 2003
  Minor: Environmental Studies

- Bachelor of Science in Chemistry with an Environmental Chemistry Option
  State College, Minneapolis, MN
  May 2004

- Bachelor of Arts in Political Science/Pre-Law, a self-designed program
  State University, Los Angeles, CA
  May 2002

An example of a format for a related courses section follows:

RELATED COURSES

Computer programming	Advanced composition
Systems analysis & design	Business communications
Technical writing	Desktop publishing

Experience

The experience section of your résumé should be the most substantial part and should take up most of the space on the page. Employers want to see what kind of work history you have. They will look at your range of experiences, longevity in jobs, and specific tasks you are able to complete. This section may also be called "work experience," "related experience," "employment history," or "employment." No matter what you call this section, some important points to remember are the following:

1. **Describe your duties** as they relate to the position you are seeking.

2. **Emphasize major responsibilities** and indicate increases in responsibility. Include all relevant employment experiences: summer, part-time, internships, cooperative education, or self-employment.

3. **Emphasize skills**, especially those that transfer from one situation to another. The fact that you coordinated a student organization, chaired meetings, supervised others, and managed a budget leads one to suspect that you could coordinate other things as well.

4. **Use descriptive job titles** that provide information about what you did. A "Student Intern" should be more specifically stated as, for example, "Magazine Operations Intern." "Volunteer" is also too

general; a title such as "Peer Writing Tutor" would be more appropriate.

5. **Create word pictures** by using active verbs to start sentences. Describe *results* you have produced in the work you have done.

A limp description would say something such as the following: "My duties included helping with production, proofreading, and editing. I used a design and page layout program." An action statement would be stated as follows: "Coordinated and assisted in the creative marketing of brochures and seminar promotions, becoming proficient in Quark."

Remember, an accomplishment is simply a result, a final measurable product that people can relate to. A duty is not a result; it is an obligation—every job holder has duties. For an effective résumé, list as many results as you can. To make the most of the limited space you have and to give your description impact, carefully select appropriate and accurate descriptors from the list of action words in Exhibit 2.2.

Exhibit 2.2

RÉSUMÉ ACTION VERBS

Achieved	Conceptualized	Directed
Acted	Condensed	Documented
Administered	Conducted	Drafted
Advised	Consolidated	Edited
Analyzed	Constructed	Eliminated
Assessed	Controlled	Ensured
Assisted	Converted	Established
Attained	Coordinated	Estimated
Balanced	Corrected	Evaluated
Budgeted	Created	Examined
Calculated	Decreased	Explained
Collected	Defined	Facilitated
Communicated	Demonstrated	Finalized
Compiled	Designed	Generated
Completed	Determined	Handled
Composed	Developed	Headed

Helped	Negotiated	Reported
Identified	Observed	Represented
Illustrated	Obtained	Researched
Implemented	Operated	Resolved
Improved	Organized	Reviewed
Increased	Participated	Scheduled
Influenced	Performed	Selected
Informed	Planned	Served
Initiated	Predicted	Showed
Innovated	Prepared	Simplified
Instituted	Presented	Sketched
Instructed	Processed	Sold
Integrated	Produced	Solved
Interpreted	Projected	Staffed
Introduced	Proposed	Streamlined
Learned	Provided	Studied
Lectured	Qualified	Submitted
Led	Quantified	Summarized
Maintained	Questioned	Systematized
Managed	Realized	Tabulated
Mapped	Received	Tested
Marketed	Recommended	Transacted
Met	Recorded	Updated
Modified	Reduced	Verified
Monitored	Reinforced	

Here are some traits that employers tell us they like to see:

■ Teamwork

■ Energy and motivation

■ Learning and using new skills

■ Versatility

■ Critical thinking

■ Understanding how profits are created

■ Organizational acumen

■ Communicating directly and clearly, in both writing and speaking

- Risk taking

- Willingness to admit mistakes

- High personal standards

SOLUTIONS TO FREQUENTLY ENCOUNTERED PROBLEMS

Repetitive Employment with the Same Employer
EMPLOYMENT: The Foot Locker, Portland, Oregon. Summer 2001, 2002, 2003. Initially employed in high school as salesclerk. Due to successful performance, asked to return next two summers at higher pay with added responsibility. Ranked as the #2 salesperson the first summer and #1 the next two summers. Assisted in arranging eye-catching retail displays; served as manager of other summer workers during owner's absence.

A Large Number of Jobs
EMPLOYMENT: Recent Hospitality Industry Experience: Affiliated with four upscale hotel/restaurant complexes (September 2001–February 2004), where I worked part- and full-time as a waiter, bartender, disc jockey, and bookkeeper to produce income for college.

Several Positions with the Same Employer
EMPLOYMENT: Coca-Cola Bottling Co., Burlington, Vermont, 2001–2004. In four years, I received three promotions, each with increased pay and responsibility.

Summer Sales Coordinator: Promoted to hire, train, and direct efforts of add-on staff of fifteen college-age route salespeople hired to meet summer peak demand for product.

Sales Administrator: Promoted to run home office sales desk, managing accounts and associated delivery schedules for professional sales force of ten people. Intensive phone work, daily interaction with all personnel, and strong knowledge of product line required.

Route Salesperson: Summer employment to travel and tourism industry sites that use Coke products. Met specific schedule demands, used good communication skills with wide variety of customers, and demonstrated strong selling skills. Named salesperson of the month for July and August of that year.

QUESTIONS RÉSUMÉ WRITERS OFTEN ASK

How Far Back Should I Go in Terms of Listing Past Jobs?

Usually, listing three or four jobs should suffice. If you did something back in high school that has a bearing on your future aspirations for employment, by all means list the job. As you progress through your college career, high school jobs will be replaced on the résumé by college employment.

Should I Differentiate Between Paid and Nonpaid Employment?

Most employers are not initially concerned about how much you were paid. They are anxious to know how much responsibility you held in your past employment. There is no need to specify that your work was as a volunteer if you had significant responsibilities.

How Should I Represent My Accomplishments or Work-Related Responsibilities?

Succinctly, but fully. In other words, give the employer enough information to arouse curiosity but not so much detail that you leave nothing to the imagination. Besides, some jobs merit more lengthy explanations than others. Be sure to convey any information that can give an employer a better understanding of the depth of your involvement at work. Did you supervise others? How many? Did your efforts result in a more efficient operation? How much did you increase efficiency? Did you handle a budget? How much? Were you promoted in a short time? Did you work two jobs at once or fifteen hours per week after high school? Where appropriate, quantify.

Should the Work Section Always Follow the Education Section on the Résumé?

Always lead with your strengths. If your education closely relates to the employment you now seek, put this section after the objective. If your education does not closely relate but you have a surplus of good work experiences, consider reversing the order of your sections to lead with employment, followed by education.

How Should I Present My Activities, Honors, Awards, Professional Societies, and Affiliations?

This section of the résumé can add valuable information for an employer to consider if used correctly. The rule of thumb for information in this section is to include only those activities that are in some way relevant to the objective stated on your résumé. If you can draw a valid connection between your activities and your objective, include them; if not, leave them out.

Granted, this is hard to do. Playing center on the championship basketball team or serving as coordinator of the biggest homecoming parade ever held are roles that have meaning for you and represent personal accomplishments you'd like to share. But the résumé is a brief document, and the information you provide on it should help the employer make a decision about your job eligibility. Including personal details can be confusing and could hurt your candidacy. Limiting your activity list to a few significant experiences can be very effective.

If you are applying for a position as a safety officer, your certificate in Red Cross lifesaving skills or CPR would be related and valuable. You would want to include it. If, however, you are applying for a job as a junior account executive in an advertising agency, that information would be unrelated and superfluous. Leave it out.

Professional affiliations and honors should all be listed; especially important are those related to your job objective. Social clubs and activities need not be a part of your résumé unless you hold a significant office or you are looking for a position related to your membership. Be aware that most prospective employers' principal concerns are related to your employability, not your social life. If you have any, publications can be included as an addendum to your résumé.

The focus of the résumé is your experience and education. It is not necessary to describe your involvement in activities. However, if your résumé needs to be lengthened, this section provides the freedom either to expand on or mention only briefly the contributions you have made. If you have made significant contributions (e.g., an officer of an organization or a particularly long tenure with a group), you may choose to describe them in more detail. It is not always necessary to include the dates of your memberships with your activities the way you would include job dates.

There are various ways in which to present additional information. You may give this section a number of different titles. Assess what you want to list, and then use an appropriate title. Do not use "extracurricular activities." This terminology is scholastic, not professional, and therefore not appropriate. The following are two examples:

■ ACTIVITIES: Society for Technical Communication, Student Senate, Student Admissions Representative, Senior Class Officer

- ACTIVITIES:
  - Society for Technical Communication Member
  - Student Senator
  - Student Admissions Representative
  - Senior Class Officer

The position you are looking for will determine what you should or should not include. *Always* look for a correlation between the activity and the prospective job.

How Should I Handle References?

The use of references is considered a part of the interview process, and they should never be listed on a résumé. You would always provide references to a potential employer if requested to, so it is not even necessary to include this section on the résumé if space does not permit. If space is available, it is acceptable to include one of the following statements:

- REFERENCES: Furnished upon request.

- REFERENCES: Available upon request.

Individuals used as references must be protected from unnecessary contacts. By including names on your résumé, you leave your references unprotected. Overuse and abuse of your references will lead to less-than-supportive comments. Protect your references by giving out their names only when you are being considered seriously as a candidate for a given position.

THE FUNCTIONAL RÉSUMÉ

The functional résumé departs from a chronological résumé in that it organizes information by specific accomplishments in various settings: previous jobs, volunteer work, associations, and so forth. This type of résumé permits you to stress the substance of your experiences rather than the position titles you have held. (See Exhibit 2.3.) You should consider using a functional résumé if you have held a series of similar jobs that relied on the same skills or abilities.

The Objective

A functional résumé begins with an objective that can be used to focus the contents of the résumé.

Exhibit 2.3

FUNCTIONAL RÉSUMÉ

OLIVIA HAYLOE

Student Apartment 12   12 Cornwall Street
Cleveland State University   Rocky River, OH 44116
Cleveland, OH 44115   215-555-6666
216-555-5555
ohay@xxx.com
(until May 2004)

Objective
An entry-level research assistant position that allows me to use my problem-solving, computing, and communication skills.

Capabilities
• Analytical problem solver
• Experienced software and hardware user
• Effective communicator

Selected Accomplishments
Problem Solving: Researched current and accurate sources of information for on-going research projects. Developed methods and systems for processing survey data results for 23 different projects. Established processing priorities for several overlapping projects; responded to questions and resolved problems for library patrons.

Computing: Used SPSS and SAS software packages to process data; manipulated scanner and graphics software to create graphics for reports; utilized PC hardware; helped implement computerized library security system.

Communicating: Assisted in writing and editing project reports; conducted telephone and door-to-door surveys in the local community; presented research findings to several audiences. Helped library patrons locate materials.

Awards
Awarded outstanding part-time employee of the year certificate
Graduated with honors in Environmental Planning

Employment History

Research Assistant, Center for Urban Studies, Cleveland State University, Cleveland, OH. Summers 2002–2004

Library Worker, CSU Library, Cleveland, OH. 2002–2003

Education

Bachelor of Science in Environmental Planning
Cleveland State University, Cleveland, OH.
May 2003

References

Provided upon request

Specific Accomplishments

Specific accomplishments are listed on this type of résumé. Examples of the types of headings used to describe these capabilities might include research, computer skills, teaching, communication, production, management, marketing, or writing. The headings you choose will directly relate to your experience and the tasks that you carried out. Each accomplishment section contains statements related to your experience in that category, regardless of when or where it occurred. Organize the accomplishments and the related tasks you describe in their order of importance as related to the position you seek.

Experience or Employment History

Your actual work experience is condensed and placed after the specific accomplishments section. It simply lists dates of employment, position titles, and employer names.

Education

The education section of a functional résumé is identical to that of the chronological résumé, but it does not carry the same visual importance because it is placed near the bottom of the page.

References

Because actual reference names are never listed on a résumé, a statement of reference availability is optional.

THE TARGETED RÉSUMÉ

The targeted résumé focuses on specific work-related capabilities you can bring to a given position within an organization. (See Exhibit 2.4.) It should be sent to an individual within the organization who makes hiring decisions about the position you are seeking.

The Objective

The objective on this type of résumé should be targeted to a specific career or position. It should be supported by the capabilities, accomplishments, and achievements documented in the résumé.

Capabilities

Capabilities should be statements that illustrate tasks you believe you are capable of based on your accomplishments, achievements, and work history. Each should relate to your targeted career or position. You can stress your qualifications rather than your employment history. This approach may require research to obtain an understanding of the nature of the work involved and the capabilities necessary to carry out that work.

Accomplishments/Achievements

This section relates the various activities you have been involved in to the job market. These experiences may include previous jobs, extracurricular activities at school, internships, and part-time summer work.

Experience

Your work history should be listed in abbreviated form and may include position title, employer name, and employment dates.

Education

Because this type of résumé is directed toward a specific job target and an individual's related experience, the education section is not prominently located at the top of the résumé as is done on the chronological résumé.

DIGITAL RÉSUMÉS

Today's employers have to manage an enormous number of résumés. One of the most frequent complaints the writers of this series hear from students is the failure of employers to even acknowledge the receipt of a résumé and cover letter. Frequently, the reason for this poor response or nonresponse is

Exhibit 2.4

TARGETED RÉSUMÉ

WILLIAM DAVIDSON

Student Apartment 104B
University of Denver
Denver, CO 80201
303-555-5555
Wdavid@xxx.com
(until May 2004)

12 West 80th Avenue
Denver, CO 80201
303-556-6667

Job Target

Planning assistant with state or regional planning agency

Capabilities

- Provide technical and administrative support
- Work under broad direction of chief planner
- Review and revise reports
- Collect and analyze data
- Use a variety of software and hardware

Achievements

- Edited prize-winning university literary review
- Researched background material for campus author
- Ran successful house painting business
- Maintained an A average throughout college

Work History

2003–present   Research Assistant, City of Denver
Planning Board
- Analyze data to report to city planner

2001–present   Editor, *The Clarion,* campus newspaper
- Responsible for editing entire newspaper

2001–2002   Tutor, Geography Department
- Tutored students enrolled in photogrammetry lab class

2000   Laborer, Facility Services, University of Denver
              • Member of grounds maintenance crew

Education

2004
Bachelor of Arts in Geography
University of Denver
Minor: Planning

---

the volume of applications received for every job. In an attempt to better manage the considerable labor investment involved in processing large numbers of résumés, many employers are requiring digital submission of résumés. There are two types of digital résumés: those that the applicant can E-mail or post to a website, called *electronic résumés*, and those that can be "read" by a computer, commonly called *scannable résumés*. Though the format may be a bit different from the traditional "paper" résumé, the goal of both types of digital résumés is the same—to get you an interview! These résumés must be designed to be "technologically friendly." What that basically means to you is that they should be free of graphics and fancy formatting.

Electronic Résumés

Sometimes referred to as plain-text résumés, electronic résumés are designed to be E-mailed to an employer or posted to a commercial Internet database such as CareerMosaic.com, America's Job Bank (ajb.dni.us), or Monster.com.

Some technical considerations:

- Electronic résumés must be written in American Standard Code for Information Interchange (ASCII), which is simply a plain-text format. These characters are universally recognized so that every computer can accurately read and understand them. To create an ASCII file of your current résumé, open your document, then save it as a text or ASCII file. This will eliminate all formatting. Edit as needed using your computer's text editor application.

- Use a standard-width typeface. Courier is a good choice because it is the font associated with ASCII in most systems.

- Use a font size of 11 to 14 points. A 12-point font is considered standard.

Exhibit 2.5

DIGITAL RÉSUMÉ

TYLER JAMES   ←   Put your name at the
117 Stetson Avenue   top on its own line.
Small School, MA 02459   Put your phone number
859-444-5566   ←   on its own line.
tjames@xxx.com   ←   Use a standard-width
typeface.

KEYWORD SUMMARY
B.S. Biology, 2004
Environment, Biology,   Keywords make your
Lab Equipment,   résumé easier to find in
Lab Work, Lab Testing,   a database.
Water Resources, Water Pollution

EDUCATION   ←   Capital letters emphasize
Bachelor of Science, Biology, 2004   headings.
Small State College, Small School, Nevada
Minor: Environmental Law
G.P.A.: 3.0/4.0

RELATED COURSES
Environmental Chemistry
Ecology   No line should exceed
Current Environmental Issues   sixty-five characters.
Introduction to Environmental Law

SKILL TRAINING   End each line by hitting
Perform and Analyze Genetics Experiments   the ENTER key.
Manipulate DNA

EXPERIENCE
ABC Water Testing, Inc., 2003–2004
 * Numerous lab assignments during   Use a space between
    summer employment   asterisk and text.
 * Worked in state-licensed lab
 * Promoted and increase in salary
 * Staff training with latest equipment

Biology Club Member, 2002–2004
* Participated in local community water cleanup projects
* Participated in local environmental studies projects
* Presented results to local government planning board

House Painting, 2001–2002
* Established business with friends

COLLEGE ATHLETICS
* Played on inter-hall sports teams
* Cocaptain of the football team

REFERENCES
Available upon request.

++ Willing to relocate ++ ◄————————— Asterisks and plus signs
replace bullets.

- Your margin should be left-justified.

- Do not exceed sixty-five characters per line because the word-wrap function doesn't operate in ASCII.

- Do not use boldface, italics, underlining, bullets, or various font sizes. Instead, use asterisks, plus signs, or all capital letters when you want to emphasize something.

- Avoid graphics and shading.

- Use as many "keywords" as you possibly can. These are words or phrases usually relating to skills or experience that either are specifically used in the job announcement or are popular buzzwords in the industry.

- Minimize abbreviations.

- Your name should be the first line of text.

- Conduct a "test run" by E-mailing your résumé to yourself and a friend before you send it to the employer. See how it transmits, and make any changes you need to. Continue to test it until it's exactly how you want it to look.

- Unless an employer specifically requests that you send the résumé in the form of an attachment, don't. Employers can encounter problems opening a document as an attachment, and there are always viruses to consider.

- Don't forget your cover letter. Send it along with your résumé as a single message.

Scannable Résumés

Some companies are relying on technology to narrow the candidate pool for available job openings. Electronic Applicant Tracking uses imaging to scan, sort, and store résumé elements in a database. Then, through OCR (Optical Character Recognition) software, the computer scans the résumés for keywords and phrases. To have the best chance at getting an interview, you want to increase the number of "hits"—matches of your skills, abilities, experience, and education to those the computer is scanning for—your résumé will get. You can see how critical using the right keywords is for this type of résumé.

Technical considerations include:

- Again, do not use boldface (newer systems may read this OK, but many older ones won't), italics, underlining, bullets, shading, graphics, or multiple font sizes. Instead, for emphasis, use asterisks, plus signs, or all capital letters. Minimize abbreviations.

- Use a popular typeface such as Courier, Helvetica, Ariel, or Palatino. Avoid decorative fonts.

- Font size should be between 11 and 14 points.

- Do not compress the spacing between letters.

- Use horizontal and vertical lines sparingly; the computer may misread them as the letters L or I.

- Left-justify the text.

- Do not use parentheses or brackets around telephone numbers, and be sure your phone number is on its own line of text.

- Your name should be the first line of text and on its own line. If your résumé is longer than one page, be sure to put your name on the top of all pages.

- Use a traditional résumé structure. The chronological format may work best.

- Use nouns that are skill-focused, such as *management, writer,* and *programming.* This is different from traditional paper résumés, which use action-oriented verbs.

- Laser printers produce the finest copies. Avoid dot-matrix printers.

- Use standard, light-colored paper with text on one side only. Since the higher the contrast, the better, your best choice is black ink on white paper.

- Always send original copies. If you must fax, set the fax on fine mode, not standard.

- Do not staple or fold your résumé. This can confuse the computer.

- Before you send your scannable résumé, be certain the employer uses this technology. If you can't determine this, you may want to send two versions (scannable and traditional) to be sure your résumé gets considered.

RÉSUMÉ PRODUCTION AND OTHER TIPS

A laser printer is the preferred option for printing your résumé. Begin by printing just a few copies. You may find a small error or you may simply want to make some changes, and it is less frustrating and less expensive if you print in small batches.

Résumé paper color should be carefully chosen. You should consider the types of employers who will receive your résumé and the types of positions for which you are applying. Use white or ivory paper for traditional or conservative employers or for higher-level positions.

Black ink on sharp, white paper can be harsh on the reader's eyes. Think about an ivory or cream paper that will provide less contrast and be easier to read. Pink, green, and blue tints should generally be avoided.

Many résumé writers buy packages of matching envelopes and cover sheet stationery that, although not absolutely necessary, help convey a professional impression.

If you'll be producing many cover letters at home, be sure you have high-quality printing equipment. Learn standard envelope formats for business, and retain a copy of every cover letter you send out. You can use the copies to take notes of any telephone conversations that may occur.

If attending a job fair, either carry a briefcase or place your résumé in a nicely covered legal-size pad holder.

THE COVER LETTER

The cover letter provides you with the opportunity to tailor your résumé by telling the prospective employer how you can be a benefit to the organization. It allows you to highlight aspects of your background that are not already discussed in your résumé and that might be especially relevant to the organization you are contacting or to the position you are seeking. Every résumé should have a cover letter enclosed when you send it out. Unlike the résumé, which may be mass-produced, a cover letter is most effective when it is individually prepared and focused on the particular requirements of the organization in question.

A good cover letter should supplement the résumé and motivate the reader to review the résumé. The format shown in Exhibit 2.6 is only a suggestion to help you decide what information to include in writing a cover letter.

Begin the cover letter with your street address twelve lines down from the top. Leave three to five lines between the date and the name of the person to whom you are addressing the cover letter. Make sure you leave one blank line between the salutation and the body of the letter and between paragraphs. After typing "Sincerely," leave four blank lines and type your name. This should leave plenty of room for your signature. A sample cover letter is shown in Exhibit 2.7.

The following guidelines will help you write good cover letters:

1. Be sure to type your letter neatly; ensure there are no misspellings.

2. Avoid unusual typefaces, such as script.

3. Address the letter to an individual, using the person's name and title. To obtain this information, call the company. If answering a blind newspaper advertisement, address the letter "To Whom It May Concern" or omit the salutation.

4. Be sure your cover letter directly indicates the position you are applying for and tells why you are qualified to fill it.

5. Send the original letter, not a photocopy, with your résumé. Keep a copy for your records.

6. Make your cover letter no more than one page.

Exhibit 2.6

COVER LETTER FORMAT

Your Street Address
Your Town, State, Zip
Phone Number
Fax Number
E-mail

Date

Name
Title
Organization
Address

Dear _____ :

First Paragraph. In this paragraph state the reason for the letter, name the specific position or type of work you are applying for, and indicate from which resource (career services office, website, newspaper, contact, employment service) you learned of this opening. The first paragraph can also be used to inquire about future openings.

Second Paragraph. Indicate why you are interested in this position, the company, or its products or services, and what you can do for the employer. If you are a recent graduate, explain how your academic background makes you a qualified candidate. Try not to repeat the same information found in the résumé.

Third Paragraph. Refer the reader to the enclosed résumé for more detailed information.

Fourth Paragraph. In this paragraph say what you will do to follow up on your letter. For example, state that you will call by a certain date to set up an interview or to find out if the company will be recruiting in your area. Finish by indicating your willingness to answer any questions they may have. Be sure you have provided your phone number.

Sincerely,

Type your name
Enclosure

Exhibit 2.7

SAMPLE COVER LETTER

Hayden Daniels
143 Randon Way
Shreveport, LA 71130
310-555-5555
hdaniels@xxx.com

November 29, 2003

Nicholas Keane
Director of Personnel
Capitol Excavating and Paving
279 Main Street
Shreveport, LA 77130

Dear Mr. Keane:

In May of 2004 I will graduate from Louisiana State University with a Bachelor of Science degree in Urban Planning. I read of your environmental planner opening in *The Times* on Sunday, November 28, and I am very interested in the possibilities it offers. I am writing to explore the opportunity for employment with your company.

The ad indicates that you are looking for enthusiastic individuals with exceptional communication skills. I believe that I possess those qualities. Through my job as a waitperson at a busy diner, I have learned the importance of being energetic and maintaining a positive attitude toward customers. In addition to the various planning classes in my academic program, I felt it important to enroll in some communication courses such as human communication skills, interpersonal communication, and public speaking. These courses helped me become more comfortable interacting with others, and they taught me how to communicate clearly. These characteristics will help me to represent Capitol in a professional and enthusiastic manner.

As you will see by my enclosed résumé, I was an admissions representative for three years of college. This position helped me learn to speak persuasively in that campus tours can be an effective means for attracting new applicants to the college.

I would like to meet with you to discuss how my education and experience would be consistent with your needs. I will contact your office next week to discuss the possibility of an interview. In the meantime, if you have any questions or require additional information, please contact me at home, 310-555-5555.

Sincerely,

Hayden Daniels
Enclosure

7. Include a phone number where you can be reached.

8. Avoid trite language and have someone read the letter over to react to its tone, content, and mechanics.

9. For your own information, record the date you send out each letter and résumé.

3

RESEARCHING CAREERS

One common question a career counselor encounters is "I'm not getting a degree in environmental studies, so can I get a job that relates to the environment?" The answer is yes! Just because you earn a degree that doesn't have the word *environment* in it, you won't be excluded from working in this field. Geography, geology, planning, biology, chemistry, math, computer science—all of these degrees, and others as well, are important to organizations that are involved in environmentally related work.

WHAT DO THEY CALL THE JOB YOU WANT?

There is every reason to be unaware. One reason for confusion is perhaps a mistaken assumption that a college education provides job training. In most cases it does not. Of course, applied fields such as engineering, management, or education provide specific skills for the workplace as well as an education, whereas most liberal arts degrees simply provide an education. Regardless, your overall college education exposes you to numerous fields of study and teaches you quantitative reasoning, critical thinking, writing, and speaking, all of which can be successfully applied to a number of different job fields. But it still remains up to you to choose a job field and to learn how to articulate the benefits of your education in a way the employer will appreciate.

As indicated in Chapter 1 on self-assessment, your first task is to understand and value what parts of that education you enjoyed and were good at and would continue to enjoy in your life's work. Did your writing courses encourage you in your ability to express yourself in writing? Did you enjoy the research process, and did you find that your work was well received? Did you enjoy any of your required quantitative subjects such as algebra or calculus?

The answers to questions such as these provide clues to skills and interests you bring to the employment market over and above the credential of your degree. In fact, it is not an overstatement to suggest that most employers who demand a college degree immediately look beyond that degree to you as a person and your own individual expression of what you like to do and think you can do for them, regardless of your major.

Collecting Job Titles

The world of employment is a big place, and even seasoned veterans of the job hunt can be surprised about what jobs are to be found in what organizations. You need to become a bit of an explorer and adventurer and be willing to try a variety of techniques to begin a list of possible occupations that might use your talents and education. Once you have a list of possibilities that you are interested in and qualified for, you can move on to find out what kinds of organizations have these job titles.

· ·

Many different organizations are involved with the environment. Federal, state, and local governments; consulting firms; nonprofit organizations; private corporations; and schools all hire workers interested in the environment. Each of these employer types presents a different "culture" with respect to the pace of work, the type of environmental effort, and the backgrounds of its employees. Not all employers will present the same "fit" for you.

If you majored in education and enjoyed the in-class presentations you made as part of your degree you might think environmental education is a possible job for you. You could work as a teacher in a traditional setting, the school classroom, or you could work at a state park as a park ranger and present programs to visitors who stop in to see the indoor and outdoor displays. As you research

**careers, be sure to explore the fit that each type of employ-
ment setting presents.**

••

Take training, for example. Trainers write policy and procedural manuals and actively teach to assist all levels of employees in mastering various
tasks and work-related systems. Trainers exist in all large corporations, banks,
consumer goods manufacturers, medical diagnostic equipment firms, sales
organizations, and any organization that has processes or materials that need
to be presented to and learned by the staff.

In reading job descriptions or want ads for any of these positions, you
would find your four-year degree a "must." However, the academic major
might be less important than your own individual skills in critical thinking,
analysis, report writing, public presentations, and interpersonal communication. Even more important than thinking or knowing you have certain skills
are your ability to express those skills concretely and the examples you use
to illustrate them to an employer.

The best beginning to a job search is to create a list of job titles you might
want to pursue, learn more about the nature of the jobs behind those titles,
and then discover what kinds of employers hire for those positions. In the
following section we'll teach you how to build a job title directory to use in
your job search.

Developing a Job Title Directory That Works for You

A job title directory is simply a complete list of all the job titles you are interested in, are intrigued by, or think you are qualified for. After combining the
understanding gained through self-assessment with your own individual interests and the skills and talents you've acquired with your degree, you'll soon
start to read and recognize a number of occupational titles that seem right
for you. There are several resources you can use to develop your list, including computer searches, books, and want ads.

Computerized Interest Inventories. One way to begin your search is to identify a number of jobs that call for your degree and the particular skills and
interests you identified as part of the self-assessment process. There are
excellent interactive career-guidance programs on the market to help you
produce such selected lists of possible job titles. Most of these are available
at high schools and colleges and at some larger town and city libraries. Two
of the industry leaders are *CHOICES* and *DISCOVER*. Both allow you to

enter interests, values, educational background, and other information to produce lists of possible occupations and industries. Each of the resources listed here will produce different job title lists. Some job titles will appear again and again, while others will be unique to a particular source. Investigate all of them!

Reference Sources. Books on the market that may be available through your local library or career counseling office also suggest various occupations related to specific majors. The following are only a few of the many good books on the market: *The College Board Guide to 150 Popular College Majors* by Renee Gernard, *College Majors and Careers: A Resource Guide for Effective Life Planning* by Paul Phifer, and *Kaplan's What to Study: 101 Fields in a Flash*. All of these books list possible job titles within the academic major.

· ·

The *Occupational Thesaurus* is another good resource, which essentially lists job title possibilities under general categories. If you want to become an advertising executive and want to know more specific positions in the field, you can then go to the *Occupational Thesaurus,* which lists scores of jobs under that title. Under "Advertising," there are more than twenty associated job titles listed, including manufacturer's representative and customer relations specialist. If advertising was a suggested job title for you, this source adds some depth by suggesting a number of different occupations within that field.

· ·

Each job title deserves your consideration. Like removing the layers of an onion, the search for job titles can go on and on! As you spend time doing this activity, you are actually learning more about the value of your degree. What's important in your search at this point is not to become critical or selective but rather to develop as long a list of possibilities as you can. Every source used will help you add new and potentially exciting jobs to your growing list.

Classified Ads. It has been well publicized that the classified ad section of the newspaper represents only about 10 to 15 percent of the current job market.

Nevertheless, the weekly classified ads can be a great help to you in your search. Although they may not be the best place to look for a job, they can teach much about the job market. Classified ads provide a good education in job descriptions, duties, responsibilities, and qualifications. In addition, classified ads offer insight into which industries are actively recruiting and some indication of the area's employment market. This is particularly helpful when seeking a position in a specific geographic area and/or a field. For your purposes, classified ads are a good source for job titles to add to your list.

Read the Sunday classified ads in a major market newspaper for several weeks in a row. Cut and paste all the ads that interest you and seem to call for something close to your education, skills, experience, and interests. Remember that classified ads are written for what an organization *hopes* to find, you don't have to meet absolutely every criterion. However, if certain requirements are stated as absolute minimums and you cannot meet them, it's best not to waste your time and that of the employer.

The Sunday want ads exercise is important because these jobs are out in the marketplace. They truly exist, and people with your qualifications are being sought to apply. What's more, many of these advertisements describe the duties and responsibilities of the job advertised and give you a beginning sense of the challenges and opportunities such a position presents. Some will indicate salary, and that will be helpful as well. This information will better define the jobs for you and provide some good material for possible interviews in that field.

Exploring Job Descriptions

Once you've arrived at a solid list of possible job titles that interest you and for which you believe you are somewhat qualified, it's a good idea to do some research on each of these jobs. The preeminent source for such job information is the *Dictionary of Occupational Titles*, or *DOT* (wave.net/upg/immigration/dot_index.html). This directory lists every conceivable job and provides excellent up-to-date information on duties and responsibilities, interactions with associates, and day-to-day assignments and tasks. These descriptions provide a thorough job analysis, but they do not consider the possible employers or the environments in which a job may be performed. So, although a position as environmental engineer officer may be well defined in terms of duties and responsibilities, it does not explain the differences in doing public relations work in a college or a hospital or a factory or a bank. You will need to look somewhere else for work settings.

Learning More About Possible Work Settings

After reading some job descriptions, you may choose to edit and revise your list of job titles once again, discarding those you feel are not suitable and keeping those that continue to hold your interest. Or you may wish to keep your list intact and see where these jobs may be located. For example, if you are interested in public relations and you appear to have those skills and the requisite education, you'll want to know what organizations do public relations. How can you find that out? How much income does someone in public relations make a year and what is the employment potential for the field of public relations?

To answer these and many other questions about your list of job titles, we recommend you try any of the following resources: *Careers Encyclopedia, College to Career: The Guide to Job Opportunities*, the *Occupational Outlook Handbook* (http://stats.bls.gov/ocohome.htm), and the professional societies and resources found throughout this book. Each of these resources, in a different way, will help to put the job titles you have selected into an employer context. Perhaps the most extensive discussion is found in the *Occupational Outlook Handbook*, which gives a thorough presentation of the nature of the work, the working conditions, employment statistics, training, other qualifications, and advancement possibilities as well as job outlook and earnings. Related occupations are also detailed, and a select bibliography is provided to help you find additional information.

Continuing with our public relations example, your search through these reference materials would teach you that the public relations jobs you find attractive are available in larger hospitals, financial institutions, most corporations (both consumer goods and industrial goods), media organizations, and colleges and universities.

Networking to Get the Complete Story

You now have not only a list of job titles but also, for each of these job titles, a description of the work involved and a general list of possible employment settings in which to work. You'll want to do some reading and keep talking to friends, colleagues, teachers, and others about the possibilities. Don't neglect to ask if the career office at your college maintains some kind of alumni network. Often such alumni networks will connect you with another graduate from the college who is working in the job title or industry you are seeking information about. These career networkers offer what assistance they can. For some it is a full day "shadowing" the alumnus as he or she goes about the job. Others offer partial-day visits, tours, informational interviews, résumé reviews, job postings, or, if distance prevents a visit, telephone interviews. As fellow graduates, they'll be frank and informative about their own jobs and prospects in their field.

Take them up on their offer and continue to learn all you can about your own personal list of job titles, descriptions, and employment settings. You'll probably continue to edit and refine this list as you learn more about the realities of the job, the possible salary, advancement opportunities, and supply and demand statistics.

In the next section we'll describe how to find the specific organizations that represent these industries and employers so that you can begin to make contact.

WHERE ARE THESE JOBS, ANYWAY?

Having a list of job titles that you've designed around your own career interests and skills is an excellent beginning. It means you've really thought about who you are and what you are presenting to the employment market. It has caused you to think seriously about the most appealing environments to work in, and you have identified some employer types that represent these environments.

The research and the thinking that you've done thus far will be used again and again. They will be helpful in writing your résumé and cover letters, in talking about yourself on the telephone to prospective employers, and in answering interview questions.

Now is a good time to begin to narrow the field of job titles and employment sites down to some specific employers to initiate the employment contact.

Finding Out Which Employers Hire People Like You

This section will provide tips, techniques, and specific resources for developing an actual list of specific employers that can be used to make contacts. It is only an outline that you must be prepared to tailor to your own particular needs and according to what you bring to the job search. Once again, it is important to communicate with others along the way exactly what you're looking for and what your goals are for the research you're doing. Librarians, employers, career counselors, friends, friends of friends, business contacts, and bookstore staff will all have helpful information on geographically specific and new resources to aid you in locating employers who'll hire you.

Identifying Information Resources

Your interview wardrobe and your new résumé might have put a dent in your wallet, but the resources you'll need to pursue your job search are available for free (although you may choose to copy materials on a machine instead of taking notes by hand). The categories of information detailed here are not hard to find and are yours for the browsing.

Numerous resources described in this section will help you identify actual employers. Use all of them or any others that you identify as available in your geographic area. As you become experienced in this process, you'll quickly figure out which information sources are helpful and which are not. If you live in a rural area, a well-planned day trip to a major city that includes a college career office, a large college or city library, state and federal employment centers, a chamber of commerce office, and a well-stocked bookstore can produce valuable results.

There are many excellent resources available to help you identify actual job sites. They are categorized into employer directories (usually indexed by product lines and geographic location), geographically based directories (designed to highlight particular cities, regions, or states), career-specific directories, periodicals and newspapers, targeted job posting publications, and videos. This is by no means meant to be a complete treatment of resources but rather a starting point for identifying useful resources.

Working from the more general references to highly specific resources, we provide a basic list to help you begin your search. Many of these you'll find easily available. In some cases reference librarians and others will suggest even better materials for your particular situation. Start to create your own customized bibliography of job search references. Use copying services to save time and to allow you to carry away information about organizations' missions, locations, company officers, phone numbers, and addresses.

Geographically Based Directories. The Job Bank series published by Bob Adams, Inc. (aip.com) contains detailed entries on each area's major employers, including business activity, address, phone number, and hiring contact name. Many listings specify educational backgrounds being sought in potential employees. Each volume contains a solid discussion of each city's or state's major employment sectors. Organizations are also indexed by industry. Job Bank volumes are available for the following places: Atlanta, Boston, Chicago, Dallas–Ft. Worth, Denver, Detroit, Florida, Houston, Los Angeles, Minneapolis, New York, Ohio, Philadelphia, San Francisco, Seattle, St. Louis, Washington, D.C., and other cities throughout the Northwest.

National Job Bank (careercity.com) lists employers in every state, along with contact names and commonly hired job categories. Included are many small companies often overlooked by other directories. Companies are also indexed by industry. This publication provides information on educational backgrounds sought and lists company benefits.

Periodicals and Newspapers. Several sources are available to help you locate which journals or magazines carry job advertisements in your field. Other resources help you identify opportunities in other parts of the country.

- *looksmart.com*
  If you want to search the classified sections of newspapers in other cities, a good source is this site. Using the keyword *newspaper classifieds* will lead you to where you can search alphabetically by state.

- *careerpath.com*
  Connects to classified job ads from newspapers around the country. Select the job title and then select the state or region of the state.

Targeted Job Posting Publications. Although the resources that follow are national in scope, they are either targeted to one medium of contact (telephone), focused on specific types of jobs, or less comprehensive than the sources previously listed.

- *Job Hotlines USA* (careers.org/topic/01_002.html)
  Pinpoints more than 1,000 hard-to-find telephone numbers for companies and government agencies that use prerecorded job messages and listings. Very few of the telephone numbers listed are toll-free, and sometimes recordings are long, so—callers, beware!

- *The Job Hunter* (jobhunter.com)
  A national biweekly newspaper listing business, media, government, human services, health, community-related, and student services job openings.

- *Current Jobs for Graduates* (graduatejobs.com)
  A national employment listing for liberal arts professions, including management opportunities, museum work, teaching, and nonprofit work.

- *Environmental Career Opportunities* (ecojobs.com)
  Serves environmental job interests nationwide by listing administrative, marketing, and human resources positions along with

education-related jobs and positions directly related to a degree in an environmental field.

- *Community Jobs*
  An employment newspaper for the nonprofit sector that provides a variety of listings, including project manager, canvas director, government relations specialist, community organizer, and program instructor.

- *College Placement Council Annual: A Guide to Employment Opportunities for College Graduates*
  An annual guide containing solid job-hunting information and, more important, displaying ads from large corporations actively seeking recent college graduates in all majors. Company profiles provide brief descriptions and available employment opportunities. Contact names and addresses are given. Profiles are indexed by organization name, geographic location, and occupation.

- *National Association of Colleges and Employers* (naceweb.org) Job Choices series includes four books: *Planning Job Choices, Job Choices: Diversity Edition, Job Choices in Business,* and *Job Choices in Science, Engineering, & Technology.* The website provides a listing of other books that can be helpful to a wide variety of the job seekers.

Videos. You may be one of the many job seekers who likes to get information via a medium other than paper. Many career libraries, public libraries, and career centers in libraries carry an assortment of videos that will help you learn new techniques and get information helpful in the job search.

Locating Information Resources

Throughout these introductory chapters, we have continually referred you to various websites for information on everything from job listings to career information. These same resources remain our best advice for your general research on career information. Using the Web gives you a mobility at your computer that you don't enjoy if you rely solely on books or newspapers or printed journals. Moreover, material on the Web, if the site is maintained, can be up-to-date, which may be crucial if you are looking at a cutting-edge career, in which technology changes almost daily. Federal government sites offer the option in some cases of downloading application materials, and many will accept your résumé online.

You'll eventually identify the information resources that work best for you, but make certain you've covered the full range of resources before you begin to rely on a smaller list. Here's a short list of informational sites that many job seekers find helpful:

- Public and college libraries

- College career centers

- Bookstores

- Internet

- Local and state government personnel offices

Each one of these sites offers a collection of resources that will help you get the information you need.

As you meet and talk with service professionals at all these sites, be sure to let them know what you're doing. Inform them of your job search, what you've already accomplished, and what you're looking for. The more people who know you're job seeking, the greater the possibility that someone will have information or know someone who can help you along your way.

Public and College Libraries. Large city libraries, college and university libraries, and even well-supported town library collections contain a variety of resources to help you conduct a job search. It is not uncommon for libraries to have separate "vocational choices" sections with books, tapes, computer terminals, and associated materials relating to job search and selection. Some are now even making résumé-creation software available for use by patrons.

Some of the publications we name throughout this book are expensive reference items that are rarely purchased by individuals. In addition, libraries carry a wide range of newspapers and telephone yellow pages as well as the usual array of books. If resources are not immediately available, many libraries have loan arrangements with other facilities and can make information available to you relatively quickly.

Take advantage not only of the reference collections but also of the skilled and informed staff. Let them know exactly what you are looking for, and they'll have their own suggestions. You'll be visiting the library frequently, and the reference staff will soon come to know who you are and what you're working on. They'll be part of your job search network!

College Career Centers. Career libraries, which are found in career centers at colleges and universities and sometimes within large public libraries, contain a unique blend of the job search resources housed in other settings. In addition, career libraries often purchase a number of job listing publications, each of which targets a specific industry or type of job. You may find job listings specifically for entry-level positions for your major. Ask about job posting newsletters or newspapers focused on careers in the area that most interests you. Each center will be unique, but you are certain to discover some good sources of jobs.

Most college career libraries now hold growing collections of video material on specific industries and on aspects of your job search process, including dress and appearance, how to manage the luncheon or dinner interview, how to be effective at a job fair, and many other titles. Some larger corporations produce handsome video materials detailing the variety of career paths and opportunities available in their organizations.

Some career libraries also house computer-based career planning and information systems. These interactive computer programs help you to clarify your values and interests and will combine them with your education to provide possible job titles and industry locations. Some even contain extensive lists of graduate school programs.

One specific kind of service a career library will be able to direct you to is computerized job search services. These services, of which there are many, are run by private companies, individual colleges, or consortiums of colleges. They attempt to match qualified job candidates with potential employers. The candidate submits a résumé (or an application) to the service. This information (which can be categorized into hundreds of separate fields of data) is entered into a computer database. Your information is then compared with the information from employers about what they desire in a prospective employee. If there is a match between what they want and what you have indicated you can offer, the job search service or the employer will contact you directly to continue the process.

Computerized job search services can complement an otherwise complete job search program. They are *not*, however, a substitute for the kinds of activities described in this book. They are essentially passive operations that are random in nature. If you have not listed skills, abilities, traits, experiences, or education *exactly* as an employer has listed its needs, there is simply no match.

Consult with the staff members at the career libraries you use. These professionals have been specifically trained to meet the unique needs you present. Often you can just drop in and receive help with general questions, or you may want to set up an appointment to speak one-on-one with a career counselor to gain special assistance.

Every career library is different in size and content, but each can provide valuable information for the job search. Some may even provide limited counseling. If you have not visited the career library at your college or alma mater, call and ask if these collections are still available for your use. Be sure to ask about other services that you can use as well.

If you are not near your own college as you work on your job search, call the career office and inquire about reciprocal agreements with other colleges that are closer to where you live. Very often, your own alma mater can arrange for you to use a limited menu of services at another school. This typically would include access to a career library and job posting information and might include limited counseling.

Bookstores. Any well-stocked bookstore will carry some job search books that are worth buying. Some major stores will even have an extensive section devoted to materials, including excellent videos, related to the job search process. You will also find copies of local newspapers and business magazines. The one advantage that is provided by resources purchased at a bookstore is that you can read and work with the information in the comfort of your own home and do not have to conform to the hours of operation of a library, which can present real difficulties if you are working full-time as you seek employment. A few minutes spent browsing in a bookstore might be a beneficial break from your job search activities and turn up valuable resources.

Internet. The World Wide Web has made the search and retrieval of information faster, and in many cases, more efficient. Using search engines such as Netscape, Yahoo, Google, AltaVista, MSN, and so on, it is possible to find great quantities of information about careers in general, about specific employers, and about job openings. The Internet should be an important part of any job search strategy.

Using keywords and/or topics in your specific discipline to search the Web will open numerous opportunities for insight and further exploration. It is important to not only look at "career" websites such as Monster.com, BrassRing.com, or CareerBuilder.com but to also read the websites of particular employers. Go beyond reading only their career or employment page. Make sure that you read their pages for customers or clients. Learn how they are promoting themselves to the people who buy or use their services. Pay particular attention to the "news" pages on an employer website. There is a great deal to be learned about an organization by reading its "News" page!

Learning which Internet sites are most accurate and fruitful for your job search will take time, persistence, and caution. There's no doubt about it, the Web is a job hunter's best friend. But the Web can also be an over-whelmingly abundant source of information—so much information that it becomes difficult to identify what's important and what is not. A simple search under a keyword or phrase can bring up sites that will be very mean-ingful for you and sites whose information is trivial and irrelevant to your job search. You need a strategy to master the Web, just as we advise a strat-egy to master the job search. Here are some suggestions:

1. Thoroughly utilize the websites identified throughout this guide. They've been chosen with you in mind, and many of them will be very helpful to you.

2. Begin to build your own portfolio of websites on your computer. Use the "bookmarking" function on your Web browser to build a series of bookmark folders for individual categories of good websites. You may have a folder for "entry-level job ad" sites and another folder for "professional associations," and so on. Start your folders with the sites in this book that seem most helpful to you.

3. Visit your college career center (or ask for reciprocity consideration at a local college) and your nearby local and/or state and university libraries. All of these places have staff who are skilled researchers and can help you locate and identify more sites that are more closely targeted to your growing sense of job direction.

4. Use the E-mail function or Webmaster address that you'll find on many sites. Some sites encourage questions via E-mail. We have found that the response time to E-mail questions for website mailboxes can vary considerably, but more often than not, replies are quite prompt. Sometimes a website will list the E-mail of the "Webmaster" or "Webguru," and we have contacted those individuals with good success as well. So, if you have a question about a website, use these options to get satisfaction.

Local and State Government Personnel Offices. You'll learn that it's most efficient to establish a routine for checking job postings. Searching for a job is a full-time job (or should be!), and you don't want to waste time or feel that you're going around in circles. So, establish a routine by which each week, on the most appropriate day, you check out that day's resources. For example, if you live in a midsize city with a daily paper, you'll probably give the want ads a once-over every morning so that you can act immediately on any good job opening.

The same strategy applies to your local and state government personnel offices. Find out when and how they post jobs, and put those offices on your weekly checklist, so that you don't miss any reasonable openings. Your local municipality's personnel office may simply use a bulletin board in the town hall or a clipboard on a counter in the office. Make these stops part of your weekly routine, and you'll find that people begin to recognize you and become aware of your job search, which could prove to be very helpful. Most local governmental units are required to post jobs in public places for a stated period before the hiring process begins. It should be easy to find out where and how they do this. Keep a close eye on those sites.

State personnel offices are larger, less casual operations, but the principles are the same. State jobs are advertised, and the office can tell you what advertising mechanisms they use—which newspapers, what websites, and when jobs are posted. The personnel offices themselves are worth a visit, if you are close enough. In addition to all the current job postings, many state personnel offices have "spec sheets," which are detailed job specifications of all the positions they are apt to advertise. You could pick up a spec sheet for every job related to your area of interest and keep them in a file for later reference when such a job is advertised.

Many state personnel offices also publish a weekly or biweekly "open recruitment" listing of career opportunities that have not yet been filled. These listings are categorized by job title as well as by branch of government, and often by whether a test is needed to qualify for the position or not. An increasing number of state personnel or human resources offices are online and offer many services on the Web. A fine general website that can help you locate your state personnel office is piperinfo.com/state/index.cfm. While each state's site is different, you can count on access to the state human resources office and sometimes even the human resources offices of many of the state's larger cities. For example, the State of Connecticut lists an additional twenty-seven city sites that each have human resources departmental listings. So, you could search the State of Connecticut Human Resource Office and then jump to the City of Stamford and review city jobs on its site.

Career/Job Fairs. Career or job fairs are common occurrences on most college campuses. The career services office usually sponsors one or more of these each year. Specific student organizations and academic departments on campus may sponsor them as well. In addition, commercial organizations will sponsor these events in major cities. Watch the employment section of local newspapers and/or the general career Internet sites for announcements of events near you.

It is important to begin to attend these fairs as early in your college career as possible. By introducing yourself to recruiters and learning what they look for and value in their top candidates, you can better plan your personal career development throughout your college years. However, if you are getting ready to graduate and will now begin attending these events for the purpose of finding an entry-level position, it is advisable that you utilize these events to not only promote yourself but to learn more about the hiring organizations that recruit from your school.

In addition to coming prepared to tell the recruiter about yourself and why you are interested in the organization, do some preliminary research on the organizations that will be participating in the career or job fair and be prepared to ask the recruiter questions to find out information such as: the ideal candidates whom they seek, the type of opportunities that they offer to entry-level professionals, and their hiring process. In other words, use the career or job fair to increase your knowledge of the organizations in which you think you may have an interest but do not monopolize the recruiter's time. There are others who will want to talk to the representative as well.

Information Sessions. Many recruiters come to campuses and sponsor "information sessions" either in the school or department or in the student commons/center. Look for these events to be announced in your school paper and on bulletin boards around campus. Often the recruiters will be interested in specific types of majors. However, if you have researched the company in the library or on the Internet and feel that you have unique qualifications that match their needs even if you don't have that specific major, you should attend.

When attending an information session bring a résumé that is specifically tailored to the organization sponsoring the session. Dress professionally, whenever possible, but do not let a lab or athletic practice keep you from attending a session sponsored by an organization in which you have a strong interest. Arrive on time and do not attempt to talk to the presenters before the program begins. Listen to the presentation and make notes. After the presentation, ask questions from the audience that will be of general interest to the entire group, not specifically to you. For example, an appropriate question might be "What are the promotional opportunities within your organization?" An inappropriate question might be "I know you are here in the Business School tonight but do you ever hire my major?"

When the question and answer period concludes, go up to the presenter(s) and introduce yourself. Explain briefly why you are interested in the organization and how you believe that your skills and experiences are a fit with the organization. Then ask a question that is specific to you. Do not monopolize the presenter's time. Follow up with a letter and résumé after this event and thank the presenter for taking time to answer your questions.

4

NETWORKING

*N*etworking is the process of deliberately establishing relationships to get career-related information or to alert potential employers that you are available for work. Networking is critically important to today's job seeker for two reasons: it will help you get the information you need, and it can help you find out about *all* of the available jobs.

GETTING THE INFORMATION YOU NEED

Networkers will review your résumé and give you feedback on its effectiveness. They will talk about the job you are looking for and give you a candid appraisal of how they see your strengths and weaknesses. If they have a good sense of the industry or the employment sector for that job, you'll get their feelings on future trends in the industry as well. Some networkers will be very forthcoming about salaries, job-hunting techniques, and suggestions for your job search strategy. Many have been known to place calls right from the interview desk to friends and associates who might be interested in you. Each networker will make his or her own contribution, and each will be valuable.

Because organizations must evolve to adapt to current global market needs, the information provided by decision makers within various organizations will be critical to your success as a new job market entrant. For example, you might learn about the concept of virtual organizations from a networker. Virtual organizations coordinate economic activity to deliver value to customers by using resources outside the traditional boundaries of the organization. This concept is being discussed and implemented by chief executive officers of many organizations, including Ford Motor, Dell, and IBM. Networking can help you find out about this and other trends currently affecting the industries under your consideration.

FINDING OUT ABOUT ALL OF THE AVAILABLE JOBS

Not every job that is available at this very moment is advertised for potential applicants to see. This is called the *hidden job market*. Only a small percentage of all jobs are formally advertised, which means that most available jobs do not appear in published channels. Networking will help you become more knowledgeable about all the employment opportunities available during your job search period.

Although someone you might talk to today doesn't know of any openings within his or her organization, tomorrow or next week or next month an opening may occur. If you've taken the time to show an interest in and knowledge of their organization, if you've shown the company representative how you can help achieve organizational goals and that you can fit into the organization, you'll be one of the first candidates considered for the position.

NETWORKING: A PROACTIVE APPROACH

Networking is a proactive rather than a reactive approach. You, as a job seeker, are expected to initiate a certain level of activity on your own behalf; you cannot afford to simply respond to jobs listed in the newspaper. Being proactive means building a network of contacts that includes informed and interested decision makers who will provide you with up-to-date knowledge of the current job market and increase your chances of finding out about employment opportunities appropriate for your interests, experience, and level of education.

An old axiom of networking says, "You are only two phone calls away from the information you need." In other words, by talking to enough people, you will quickly come across someone who can offer you help. Start with your professors. Each of them probably has a wide circle of contacts. In their work and travel they might have met someone who can help you or direct you to someone who can.

CONTROL AND THE NETWORKING PROCESS

In deliberately establishing relationships, the process of networking begins with you in control—*you* are contacting specific individuals. As your network expands and you establish a set of professional relationships, your search for information or jobs will begin to move outside of your total control. A part of the networking process involves others assisting you by gathering information for you or recommending you as a possible job candidate. As additional people become a part of your networking system, you will have less knowledge about activities undertaken on your behalf; you will undoubtedly be contacted by individuals whom you did not initially approach. If you want to function effectively in surprise situations, you must be prepared at all times to talk with strangers about the informational or employment needs that motivated you to become involved in the networking process.

PREPARING TO NETWORK

In deliberately establishing relationships, maximize your efforts by organizing your approach. Five specific areas in which you can organize your efforts include reviewing your self-assessment, reviewing your research on job sites and organizations, deciding who it is you want to talk to, keeping track of all your efforts, and creating your self-promotion tools.

Review Your Self-Assessment
Your self-assessment is as important a tool in preparing to network as it has been in other aspects of your job search. You have carefully evaluated your personal traits, personal values, economic needs, longer-term goals, skill base, preferred skills, and underdeveloped skills. During the networking process you will be called upon to communicate what you know about yourself and relate it to the information or job you seek. Be sure to review the exercises that you completed in the self-assessment section of this book in preparation for networking. We've explained that you need to assess what skills you have acquired from your major that are of general value to an employer and to be ready to express those in ways employers can appreciate as useful in their own organizations.

Review Research on Job Sites and Organizations
In addition, individuals assisting you will expect that you'll have at least some background information on the occupation or industry of interest to you. Refer

to the appropriate sections of this book and other relevant publications to acquire the background information necessary for effective networking. They'll explain how to identify not only the job titles that might be of interest to you but also what kinds of organizations employ people to do that job. You will develop some sense of working conditions and expectations about duties and responsibilities—all of which will be of help in your networking interviews.

Decide Who It Is You Want to Talk To

Networking cannot begin until you decide whom it is that you want to talk to and, in general, what type of information you hope to gain from your contacts. Once you know this, it's time to begin developing a list of contacts. Five useful sources for locating contacts are described here.

College Alumni Network. Most colleges and universities have created a formal network of alumni and friends of the institution who are particularly interested in helping currently enrolled students and graduates of their alma mater gain employment-related information.

....

> Because environmental studies has been popular since the 1960s, you'll find a large number of graduates employed in the various careers described throughout this book. Just the diversity of employment evidenced by such an alumni list should be encouraging and informative to the environmental studies graduate. Among such a diversified group there are likely to be scores of people you would enjoy talking with and perhaps even meeting.

....

It is usually a simple process to make use of an alumni network. Visit your college's website and locate the alumni office and/or your career center. Either or both sites will have information about your school's alumni network. You'll be provided with information on shadowing experiences, geographic information, or those alumni offering job referrals. If you don't find what you're looking for, don't hesitate to phone or E-mail your career center and ask what they can do to help you connect with an alum.

Alumni networkers may provide some combination of the following services: day-long shadowing experiences, telephone interviews, in-person interviews, information on relocating to given geographic areas, internship information, suggestions on graduate school study, and job vacancy notices.

. . . .

What a valuable experience! If you are interested in a government position, you may be concerned about your environmental studies degree and its relevance for certain
federal positions. Spending a day with alumni in government service whose academic credentials include the same
degree you are seeking will be time well spent. You can
ask questions about their preparedness for the job and
observe firsthand how they have transferred their academic skills to their career as a Park Ranger/Interpreter.
This experience would be much more valuable than any
reading you could do on this subject.

In addition to your own observations, an alumnus will
have his or her own perspective on the relevance of your
degree to a government career and which settings may utilize more of your skills.

. . . .

Present and Former Supervisors. If you believe you are on good terms with
present or former job supervisors, they may be an excellent resource for providing information or directing you to appropriate resources that would have
information related to your current interests and needs. Additionally, these
supervisors probably belong to professional organizations that they might be
willing to utilize to get information for you.

. . . .

If, for example, you were interested in working as an interpreter at a national or state park, and you are currently
working on the waitstaff of a local restaurant, talk with
your supervisor or the owner. He or she may belong to the
local chamber of commerce, whose director might have
information on members affiliated with parks in the
region. You would probably be able to obtain the names
and telephone numbers of these people, which would allow
you to begin the networking process.

. . . .

Employers in Your Area. Although you may be interested in working in a
geographic location different from the one where you currently reside, don't
overlook the value of the knowledge and contacts those around you are able

to provide. Use the local telephone directory and newspaper to identify the types of organizations you are thinking of working for or professionals who have the kinds of jobs you are interested in. Recently, a call made to a local hospital's financial administrator for information on working in health-care financial administration yielded more pertinent information on training seminars, regional professional organizations, and potential employment sites than a national organization was willing to provide.

Employers in Geographic Areas Where You Hope to Work. If you are thinking about relocating, identifying prospective employers or informational contacts in the new location will be critical to your success. Here are some tips for online searching. First, use a "metasearch" engine to get the most out of your search. Metasearch engines combine several engines into one powerful tool. We frequently use dogpile.com and metasearch.com for this purpose. Try using the city and state as your keywords in a search. Keywords *New Haven, Connecticut* will bring you to the city's website with links to the chamber of commerce, member businesses, and other valuable resources. By using looksmart.com you can locate newspapers in any area, and they, too, can provide valuable insight before you relocate. Of course, both dogpile and metasearch can lead you to yellow and white page directories in areas you are considering.

Professional Associations and Organizations. Professional associations and organizations can provide valuable information in several areas: career paths that you might not have considered, qualifications relating to those career choices, publications that list current job openings, and workshops or seminars that will enhance your professional knowledge and skills. They can also be excellent sources for background information on given industries: their health, current problems, and future challenges.

There are several excellent resources available to help you locate professional associations and organizations that would have information to meet your needs. Two especially useful publications are the *Encyclopedia of Associations* and *National Trade and Professional Associations of the United States.*

Keep Track of All Your Efforts

It can be difficult, almost impossible, to remember all the details related to each contact you make during the networking process, so you will want to develop a record-keeping system that works for you. Formalize this process by using your computer to keep a record of the people and organizations you want to contact. You can simply record the contact's name, address, and telephone number, and what information you hope to gain. Each entry might look something like this:

Contact Name	Address	Phone #	Purpose
Mr. Lee Perkins	13 Muromachi	73-8906	Local market
Osaka Branch	Osaka-shi		information

You could record this as a simple Word document and you could still use the "Find" function if you were trying to locate some data and could only recall the firm's name or the contact's name. If you're comfortable with database management and you have some database software on your computer, then you can put information at your fingertips even if you have only the zip code! The point here is not technological sophistication but good record keeping.

Once you have created this initial list, it will be helpful to keep more detailed information as you begin to actually make the contacts. Using the Network Contact Record form in Exhibit 4.1 will help you keep good information on all your network contacts. They'll appreciate your recall of details of your meetings and conversations, and the information will help you to focus your networking efforts.

Create Your Self-Promotion Tools

There are two types of promotional tools that are used in the networking process. The first is a résumé and cover letter, and the second is a one-minute "infomercial," which may be given over the telephone or in person.

Techniques for writing an effective résumé and cover letter are discussed in Chapter 2. Once you have reviewed that material and prepared these important documents, you will have created one of your self-promotion tools.

The one-minute infomercial will demand that you begin tying your interests, abilities, and skills to the people or organizations you want to network with. Think about your goal for making the contact to help you understand what you should say about yourself. You should be able to express yourself easily and convincingly. If, for example, you are contacting an alumnus of your institution to obtain the names of possible employment sites in a distant city, be prepared to discuss why you are interested in moving to that location, the types of jobs you are interested in, and the skills and abilities you possess that will make you a qualified candidate.

To create a meaningful one-minute infomercial, write it out, practice it as if it will be a spoken presentation, rewrite it, and practice it again if necessary until expressing yourself comes easily and is convincing.

Exhibit 4.1

NETWORK CONTACT RECORD

Name: (Be certain your spelling is correct.)

Title: (Pick up a business card to be certain of the correct title.)

Employing organization: (Note any parent company or subsidiaries.)

Business mailing address: (This is often different from the street address.)

Business E-mail address:

Business telephone number: (Include area code and alternative numbers.)

Business fax number:

Source for this contact: (Who referred you, and what is their relationship to

the contact?)

Date of call or letter: (Use plenty of space here to record multiple phone calls or

visits, other employees you may have met, names of

secretaries/receptionists, and so forth.)

Content of discussion: (Keep enough notes here to remind you of the substance of

your visits and telephone conversations in case some time

elapses between contacts.)

Follow-up necessary to continue working with this contact: (Your contact may request

that you send him or her some materials or direct you to

contact an associate. Note any such instructions or

assignments in this space.)

Name of additional networker: (Here you would record the names and phone numbers of

Address: additional contacts met at this employer's site. Often you will

be introduced to many people, some of whom may indicate

E-mail: a willingness to help in your job search.)

Phone:

Fax:	_____
Name of additional networker:	_____
Address:	_____
E-mail:	_____
Phone:	_____
Fax:	_____
Name of additional networker:	_____
Address:	_____
E-mail:	_____
Phone:	_____
Fax:	_____
Date thank-you note written:	(May help to date your next contact.)
Follow-up action taken:	(Phone calls, visits, additional notes.)
Other miscellaneous notes:	(Record any other additional interaction you think may be
	important to remember in working with this networking client.
	You will want this form in front of you when telephoning or
	just before and after a visit.)

Here's a simplified example of an infomercial for use over the telephone:

••••••••••••••••••••••••••••••••••••••

Hello, Mr. Devos. My name is Joyce Johnson. I am a recent graduate of West Coast College, and I hope to find work as an environmental scientist. I feel confident I have many of the skills that are valued in this field. I have a strong background in chemistry, with some good research and computer skills. What's more, I am thorough and exacting and work well under pressure.

Mr. Devos, I'm calling you because I still need more information about environmental science fields. I'm hoping

> you'll have the time to sit down with me for about half an hour and discuss your perspective on careers in this field. There are so many possible employers to approach that I am seeking some advice on which of those settings might be the best fit given my degree and experience.
>
> Would you be willing to do that for me? I would greatly appreciate it. I am available most mornings, if that's convenient for you.

....

It very well may happen that your employer contact wishes you to communicate by E-mail. The infomercial quoted above could easily be rewritten for an E-mail message. You should "cut and paste" your résumé right into the E-mail text itself.

Other effective self-promotion tools include portfolios for those in the arts, writing professions, or teaching. Portfolios show examples of work, photographs of projects or classroom activities, or certificates and credentials that are job related. There may not be an opportunity to use the portfolio during an interview, and it is not something that should be left with the organization. It is designed to be explained and displayed by the creator. However, during some networking meetings, there may be an opportunity to illustrate a point or strengthen a qualification by exhibiting the portfolio.

BEGINNING THE NETWORKING PROCESS

Set the Tone for Your Communications

It can be useful to establish "tone words" for any communications you embark upon. Before making your first telephone call or writing your first letter, decide what you want the person to think of you. If you are networking to try to obtain a job, your tone words might include descriptors such as *genuine*, *informed*, and *self-knowledgeable*. When you're trying to acquire information, your tone words may have a slightly different focus, such as *courteous*, *organized*, *focused*, and *well-spoken*. Use the tone words you establish for your contacts to guide you through the networking process.

Honestly Express Your Intentions

When contacting individuals, it is important to be honest about your reasons for making the contact. Establish your purpose in your own mind and be able and ready to articulate it concisely. Determine an initial agenda, whether it be informational questioning or self-promotion, present it to your contact, and be ready to respond immediately. If you don't adequately prepare before initiating your overture, you may find yourself at a disadvantage if you're asked to immediately begin your informational interview or self-promotion during the first phone conversation or visit.

Start Networking Within Your Circle of Confidence

Once you have organized your approach—by utilizing specific researching methods, creating a system for keeping track of the people you will contact, and developing effective self-promotion tools—you are ready to begin networking. The best way to begin networking is by talking with a group of people you trust and feel comfortable with. This group is usually made up of your family, friends, and career counselors. No matter who is in this inner circle, they will have a special interest in seeing you succeed in your job search. In addition, because they will be easy to talk to, you should try taking some risks in terms of practicing your information-seeking approach. Gain confidence in talking about the strengths you bring to an organization and the underdeveloped skills you feel hinder your candidacy. Be sure to review the section on self-assessment for tips on approaching each of these areas. Ask for critical but constructive feedback from the people in your circle of confidence on the letters you write and the one-minute infomercial you have developed. Evaluate whether you want to make the changes they suggest, then practice the changes on others within this circle.

Stretch the Boundaries of Your Networking Circle of Confidence

Once you have refined the promotional tools you will use to accomplish your networking goals, you will want to make additional contacts. Because you will not know most of these people, it will be a less comfortable activity to undertake. The practice that you gained with your inner circle of trusted friends should have prepared you to now move outside of that comfort zone.

It is said that any information a person needs is only two phone calls away, but the information cannot be gained until you (1) make a reasonable guess about who might have the information you need and (2) pick up the telephone to make the call. Using your network list that includes alumni, instructors, supervisors, employers, and associations, you can begin preparing your list of questions that will allow you to get the information you need. Review the question list that follows and then develop a list of your own.

Questions You Might Want to Ask

1. In the position you now hold, what do you do on a typical day?

2. What are the most interesting aspects of your job?

3. What part of your work do you consider dull or repetitious?

4. What were the jobs you had that led to your present position?

5. How long does it usually take to move from one step to the next in this career path?

6. What is the top position to which you can aspire in this career path?

7. What is the next step in *your* career path?

8. Are there positions in this field that are similar to your position?

9. What are the required qualifications and training for entry-level positions in this field?

10. Are there specific courses a student should take to be qualified to work in this field?

11. What are the entry-level jobs in this field?

12. What types of training are provided to persons entering this field?

13. What are the salary ranges your organization typically offers to entry-level candidates for positions in this field?

14. What special advice would you give a person entering this field?

15. Do you see this field as a growing one?

16. How do you see the content of the entry-level jobs in this field changing over the next two years?

17. What can I do to prepare myself for these changes?

18. What is the best way to obtain a position that will start me on a career in this field?

19. Do you have any information on job specifications and descriptions that I may have?

20. What related occupational fields would you suggest I explore?

21. How could I improve my résumé for a career in this field?

22. Who else would you suggest I talk to, both in your organization and in other organizations?

Questions You Might Have to Answer

To communicate effectively, you must anticipate questions that will be asked of you by the networkers you contact. Review the following list and see if

you can easily answer each of these questions. If you cannot, it may be time
to revisit the self-assessment process.

1. Where did you get my name, or how did you find out about this
   organization?

2. What are your career goals?

3. What kind of job are you interested in?

4. What do you know about this organization and this industry?

5. How do you know you're prepared to undertake an entry-level
   position in this industry?

6. What course work have you done that is related to your career
   interests?

7. What are your short-term career goals?

8. What are your long-term career goals?

9. Do you plan to obtain additional formal education?

10. What contributions have you made to previous employers?

11. Which of your previous jobs have you enjoyed the most
    and why?

12. What are you particularly good at doing?

13. What shortcomings have you had to face in previous
    employment?

14. What are your three greatest strengths?

15. Describe how comfortable you feel with your communication style.

General Networking Tips

Make Every Contact Count. Setting the tone for each interaction is critical.
Approaches that will help you communicate in an effective way include
politeness, being appreciative of time provided to you, and being prepared
and thorough. Remember, *everyone* within an organization has a circle of
influence, so be prepared to interact effectively with each person you
encounter in the networking process, including secretarial and support staff.
Many information or job seekers have thwarted their own efforts by being
rude to some individuals they encountered as they networked because they
made the incorrect assumption that certain persons were unimportant.

Sometimes your contacts may be surprised at their ability to help you. After meeting and talking with you, they might think they have not offered much in the way of help. A day or two later, however, they may make a contact that would be useful to you and refer you to that person.

With Each Contact, Widen Your Circle of Networkers. Always leave an informational interview with the names of at least two more people who can help you get the information or job that you are seeking. Don't be shy about asking for additional contacts; networking is all about increasing the number of people you can interact with to achieve your goals.

Make Your Own Decisions. As you talk with different people and get answers to the questions you pose, you may hear conflicting information or get conflicting suggestions. Your job is to listen to these "experts" and decide what information and which suggestions will help you achieve *your* goals. Only implement those suggestions that you believe will work for you.

SHUTTING DOWN YOUR NETWORK

As you achieve the goals that motivated your networking activity—getting the information you need or the job you want—the time will come to inactivate all or parts of your network. As you do, be sure to tell your primary supporters about your change in status. Call or write to each one of them and give them as many details about your new status as you feel is necessary to maintain a positive relationship.

Because a network takes on a life of its own, activity undertaken on your behalf will continue even after you cease your efforts. As you get calls or are contacted in some fashion, be sure to inform these networkers about your change in status, and thank them for assistance they have provided.

Information on the latest employment trends indicates that workers will change jobs or careers several times in their lifetime. Networking, then, will be a critical aspect in the span of your professional life. If you carefully and thoughtfully conduct your networking activities during your job search, you will have a solid foundation of experience when you need to network the next time around.

5

INTERVIEWING

*C*ertainly, there can be no one part of the job search process more fraught with anxiety and worry than the interview. Yet seasoned job seekers welcome the interview and will often say, "Just get me an interview and I'm on my way!" They understand that the interview is crucial to the hiring process and equally crucial for them, as job candidates, to have the opportunity of a personal dialogue to add to what the employer may already have learned from the résumé, cover letter, and telephone conversations.

Believe it or not, the interview is to be welcomed, and even enjoyed! It is a perfect opportunity for you, the candidate, to sit down with an employer and express yourself and display who you are and what you want. Of course, it takes thought and planning and a little strategy; after all, it *is* a job interview! But it can be a positive, if not pleasant, experience and one you can look back on and feel confident about your performance and effort.

For many new job seekers, a job, any job, seems a wonderful thing. But seasoned interview veterans know that the job interview is an important step for both sides—the employer and the candidate—to see what each has to offer and whether there is going to be a "fit" of personalities, work styles, and attitudes. And it is this concept of balance in the interview, that both sides have important parts to play, that holds the key to success in mastering this aspect of the job search strategy.

Try to think of the interview as a conversation between two interested and equal partners. You both have important, even vital, information to deliver and to learn. Of course, there's no denying the employer has some leverage, especially in the initial interview for recruitment or any interview scheduled by the candidate and not the recruiter. That should not prevent the interviewee from seeking to play an equal part in what should be a fair exchange of information. Too often the untutored candidate allows the interview to become one-sided. The employer asks all the questions and the candidate simply responds. The ideal would be for two mutually interested parties to sit down and discuss possibilities for each. This is a conversation of significance, and it requires preparation, thought about the tone of the interview, and planning of the nature and details of the information to be exchanged.

PREPARING FOR THE INTERVIEW

The length of most initial interviews is about thirty minutes. Given the brevity, the information that is exchanged ought to be important. The candidate should be delivering material that the employer cannot discover on the résumé, and in turn, the candidate should be learning things about the employer that he or she could not otherwise find out. After all, if you have only thirty minutes, why waste time on information that is already published? The information exchanged is more than just factual, and both sides will learn much from what they see of each other, as well. How the candidate looks, speaks, and acts are important to the employer. The employer's attention to the interview and awareness of the candidate's résumé, the setting, and the quality of information presented are important to the candidate.

Just as the employer has every right to be disappointed when a prospect is late for the interview, looks unkempt, and seems ill-prepared to answer fairly standard questions, the candidate may be disappointed with an interviewer who isn't ready for the meeting, hasn't learned the basic résumé facts, and is constantly interrupted by telephone calls. In either situation there's good reason to feel let down.

There are many elements to a successful interview, and some of them are not easy to describe or prepare for. Sometimes there is just a chemistry between interviewer and interviewee that brings out the best in both, and a good exchange takes place. But there is much the candidate can do to pave the way for success in terms of his or her résumé, personal appearance, goals, and interview strategy—each of which we will discuss. However, none of this preparation is as important as the time and thought the candidate gives to personal self-assessment.

Self-Assessment

Neither a stunning résumé nor an expensive, well-tailored suit can compensate for candidates who do not know what they want, where they are going, or why they are interviewing with a particular employer. Self-assessment, the process by which we begin to know and acknowledge our own particular blend of education, experiences, needs, and goals, is not something that can be sorted out the weekend before a major interview. Of all the elements of interview preparation, this one requires the longest lead time and cannot be faked.

Because the time allotted for most interviews is brief, it is all the more important for job candidates to understand and express succinctly why they are there and what they have to offer. This is not a time for undue modesty (or for braggadocio either); it is a time for a compelling, reasoned statement of why you feel that you and this employer might make a good match. It means you have to have thought about your skills, interests, and attributes; related those to your life experiences and your own history of challenges and opportunities; and determined what that indicates about your strengths, preferences, values, and areas needing further development.

A common complaint of employers is that many candidates didn't take advantage of the interview time; they didn't seem to know why they were there or what they wanted. When candidates are asked to talk about themselves and their work-related skills and attributes, employers don't want to be faced with shyness or embarrassed laughter; they need to know about you so they can make a fair determination of you and your competition. If you don't take advantage of the opportunity to make a case for your employability, you can be certain the person ahead of you has or the person after you will, and it will be on the strength of those impressions that the employer will hire.

If you need some assistance with self-assessment issues, refer to Chapter 1. Included are suggested exercises that can be done as needed, such as making up an experiential diary and extracting obvious strengths and weaknesses from past experiences. These simple assignments will help you look at past activities as collections of tasks with accompanying skills and responsibilities. Don't overlook your high school or college career office. Many offer personal counseling on self-assessment issues and may provide testing instruments such as the *Myers-Briggs Type Indicator* (*MBTI*), the *Harrington-O'Shea Career Decision-Making System* (*CDM*), the *Strong Interest Inventory* (*SII*), or any other of a wide selection of assessment tools that can help you clarify some of these issues prior to the interview stage of your job search.

The Résumé

Résumé preparation has been discussed in detail, and some basic examples of various types were provided. In this section we want to concentrate on how best to use your résumé in the interview. In most cases the employer will have seen the résumé prior to the interview, and, in fact, it may well have been the quality of that résumé that secured the interview opportunity.

An interview is a conversation, however, and not an exercise in reading. So, if the employer hasn't seen your résumé and you have brought it along to the interview, wait until asked or until the end of the interview to offer it. Otherwise, you may find yourself staring at the back of your résumé and simply answering "yes" and "no" to a series of questions drawn from that document.

Sometimes an interviewer is not prepared and does not know or recall the contents of the résumé and may use the résumé to a greater or lesser degree as a "prompt" during the interview. It is for you to judge what that may indicate about the individual performing the interview or the employer. If your interviewer seems surprised by the scheduled meeting, relies on the résumé to an inordinate degree, and seems otherwise unfamiliar with your background, this lack of preparation for the hiring process could well be a symptom of general management disorganization or may simply be the result of poor planning on the part of one individual. It is your responsibility as a potential employee to be aware of these signals and make your decisions accordingly.

....

In any event, it is perfectly acceptable for you to get the conversation back to a more interpersonal style by saying something like, "Mr. Zimmermann, you might be interested in some recent experience I gained in a volunteer position at the public research interest group. It is not detailed on my résumé. May I tell you about it?" This can return the interview to two people talking to each other, not one reading and the other responding.

....

By all means, bring at least one copy of your résumé to the interview. Occasionally, at the close of an interview, an interviewer will express an interest in circulating a résumé to several departments, and you could then offer the copy you brought. Sometimes, an interview appointment provides an opportunity to meet others in the organization who may express an interest in you and your background, and it may be helpful to follow up with a copy of your résumé. Our best advice, however, is to keep it out of sight until needed or requested.

Appearance

Although many of the absolute rules that once dominated the advice offered to job candidates about appearance have now been moderated significantly, conservative is still the watchword unless you are interviewing in a fashion-related industry. For men, conservative translates into a well-cut dark suit with appropriate tie, hosiery, and dress shirt. A wise strategy for the male job seeker looking for a good but not expensive suit would be to try the men's department of a major department store. They usually carry a good range of sizes, fabrics, and prices; offer professional sales help; provide free tailoring; and have associated departments for putting together a professional look.

For women, there is more latitude. Business suits are still popular, but they have become more feminine in color and styling with a variety of jacket and skirt lengths. In addition to suits, better-quality dresses are now worn in many environments and, with the correct accessories, can be most appropriate. Company literature, professional magazines, the business section of major newspapers, and television interviews can all give clues about what is being worn in different employer environments.

Both men and women need to pay attention to issues such as hair, jewelry, and makeup; these are often what separates the candidate in appearance from the professional workforce. It seems particularly difficult for the young job seeker to give up certain hairstyles, eyeglass fashions, and jewelry habits, yet those can be important to the employer who is concerned with your ability to successfully make the transition into the organization. Candidates often find the best strategy is to dress conservatively until they find employment. Once employed and familiar with the norms within your organization, you can begin to determine a look that you enjoy, works for you, and fits your organization.

Choose clothes that suit your body type, fit well, and flatter you. Feel good about the way you look! The interview day is not the best time for a new hairdo, a new pair of shoes, or any other change that will distract you or cause you to be self-conscious. Arrive a bit early to avoid being rushed, and ask the receptionist to direct you to a restroom for any last-minute adjustments of hair and clothes.

Employer Information

Whether your interview is for graduate school admission, an overseas corporate position, or a position with a company, it is important to know something about the employer or the organization. Keeping in mind that the interview is relatively brief and that you will hopefully have other interviews with other organizations, it is important to keep your research in proportion. If secondary interviews are called for, you will have additional time to do further research. For the first interview, it is helpful to know the organization's mission, goals, size, scope of operations, and so forth. Your research may uncover recent areas of challenge or particular successes that may help to fuel the interview. Use the "What Do They Call the Job You Want?"

section of Chapter 3, your library, and your career or guidance office to help you locate this information in the most efficient way possible. Don't be shy in asking advice of these counseling and guidance professionals on how best to spend your preparation time. With some practice, you'll soon learn how much information is enough and which kinds of information are most useful to you.

INTERVIEW CONTENT

We've already discussed how it can help to think of the interview as an important conversation—one that, as with any conversation, you want to find pleasant and interesting and to leave you with a good feeling. But because this conversation is especially important, the information that's exchanged is critical to its success. What do you want them to know about you? What do you need to know about them? What interview technique do you need to particularly pay attention to? How do you want to manage the close of the interview? What steps will follow in the hiring process?

Except for the professional interviewer, most of us find interviewing stressful and anxiety-provoking. Developing a strategy before you begin interviewing will help you relieve some stress and anxiety. One particular strategy that has worked for many and may work for you is interviewing by objective. Before you interview, write down three to five goals you would like to achieve for that interview. They may be technique goals: smile a little more, have a firmer handshake, be sure to ask about the next stage in the interview process before leaving. They may be content-oriented goals: find out about the company's current challenges and opportunities; be sure to speak of your recent research, writing experiences, or foreign travel. Whatever your goals, jot down a few of them as goals for each interview.

Most people find that in trying to achieve these few goals, their interviewing technique becomes more organized and focused. After the interview, the most common question friends and family ask is "How did it go?" With this technique, you have an indication of whether you met *your* goals for the meeting, not just some vague idea of how it went. Chances are, if you accomplished what you wanted to, it improved the quality of the entire interview. As you continue to interview, you will want to revise your goals to continue improving your interview skills.

Now, add to the concept of the significant conversation the idea of a beginning, a middle, and a closing and you will have two thoughts that will give your interview a distinctive character. Be sure to make your introduction warm and cordial. Say your full name (and if it's a difficult-to-pronounce name, help the interviewer to pronounce it) and make certain you know your interviewer's name and how to pronounce it. Most interviews begin with some "soft talk" about the weather, chat about the candidate's trip to the interview site, or national events. This is done as a courtesy to relax both you and the interviewer, to get you talking, and to generally try to defuse the atmosphere of excessive tension. Try to be yourself, engage in the conversation, and don't try to second-guess the interviewer. This is simply what it appears to be—casual conversation.

Once you and the interviewer move on to exchange more serious information in the middle part of the interview, the two most important concerns become your ability to handle challenging questions and your success at asking meaningful ones. Interviewer questions will probably fall into one of three categories: personal assessment and career direction, academic assessment, and knowledge of the employer. The following are some examples of questions in each category:

Personal Assessment and Career Direction

1. How would you describe yourself?

2. What motivates you to put forth your best effort?

3. In what kind of work environment are you most comfortable?

4. What do you consider to be your greatest strengths and weaknesses?

5. How well do you work under pressure?

6. What qualifications do you have that make you think you will be successful in this career?

7. Will you relocate? What do you feel would be the most difficult aspect of relocating?

8. Are you willing to travel?

9. Why should I hire you?

Academic Assessment

1. Why did you select your college or university?

2. What changes would you make at your alma mater?

3. What led you to choose your major?

4. What subjects did you like best and least? Why?

5. If you could, how would you plan your academic study differently? Why?

6. Describe your most rewarding college experience.

7. How has your college experience prepared you for this career?

8. Do you think that your grades are a good indication of your ability to succeed with this organization?

9. Do you have plans for continued study?

Knowledge of the Employer

1. If you were hiring a graduate of your school for this position, what qualities would you look for?

2. What do you think it takes to be successful in an organization like ours?

3. In what ways do you think you can make a contribution to our organization?

4. Why did you choose to seek a position with this organization?

The interviewer wants a response to each question but is also gauging your enthusiasm, preparedness, and willingness to communicate. In each response you should provide some information about yourself that can be related to the employer's needs. A common mistake is to give too much information. Answer each question completely, but be careful not to run on too long with extensive details or examples.

Questions About Underdeveloped Skills

Most employers interview people who have met some minimum criteria of education and experience. They interview candidates to see who they are, to learn what kind of personality they exhibit, and to get some sense of how this person might fit into the existing organization. It may be that you are asked about skills the employer hopes to find and that you have not documented. Maybe it's grant-writing experience, knowledge of environmental law, or a knowledge of educational techniques.

To questions about skills and experiences you don't have, answer honestly and forthrightly and try to offer some additional information about skills you do have. For example, perhaps the employer is disappointed you have no grant-writing experience. An honest answer may be as follows:

> No, unfortunately, I was never in a position to acquire those skills. I do understand something of the complexities of the grant-writing process and feel confident that my attention to detail, careful reading skills, and strong writing would make grants a wonderful challenge in a new job. I think I could get up on the learning curve quickly.

The employer hears an honest admission of lack of experience but is reassured by some specific skill details that do relate to grant writing and a confident manner that suggests enthusiasm and interest in a challenge.

For many students, questions about their possible contribution to an employer's organization can prove challenging. Because your education has probably not included specific training for a job, you need to review your academic record and select capabilities you have developed in your major that an employer can appreciate. For example, perhaps you read well and can analyze and condense what you've read into smaller, more focused pieces. That could be valuable. Or maybe you did some serious research and you know you have valuable investigative skills. Your public speaking might be highly developed and you might use visual aids appropriately and effectively. Or maybe your skill at correspondence, memos, and messages is effective. Whatever it is, you must take it out of the academic context and put it into a new, employer-friendly context so your interviewer can best judge how you could help the organization.

Exhibiting knowledge of the organization will, without a doubt, show the interviewer that you are interested enough in the available position to have done some legwork in preparation for the interview. Remember, it is not necessary to know every detail of the organization's history but rather to have a general knowledge about why it is in business and how the industry is faring.

Sometime during the interview, generally after the midway point, you'll be asked if you have any questions for the interviewer. Your questions will tell the employer much about your attitude and your desire to understand the organization's expectations so you can compare it to your own strengths. The following are some selected questions you might want to ask:

1. What are the main responsibilities of the position?

2. What are the opportunities and challenges associated with this position?

3. Could you outline some possible career paths beginning with this position?

4. How regularly do performance evaluations occur?

5. What is the communication style of the organization? (meetings, memos, and so forth)

6. What would a typical day in this position be like for me?

7. What kinds of opportunities might exist for me to improve my professional skills within the organization?

8. What have been some of the interesting challenges and opportunities your organization has recently faced?

Most interviews draw to a natural closing point, so be careful not to prolong the discussion. At a signal from the interviewer, wind up your presentation, express your appreciation for the opportunity, and be sure to ask what the next stage in the process will be. When can you expect to hear from them? Will they be conducting second-tier interviews? If you are interested and haven't heard, would they mind a phone call? Be sure to collect a business card with the name and phone number of your interviewer. On your way out, you might have an opportunity to pick up organizational literature you haven't seen before.

With the right preparation—a thorough self-assessment, professional clothing, and employer information—you'll be able to set and achieve the goals you have established for the interview process.

6

NETWORKING OR INTERVIEW FOLLOW-UP

Quite often there is a considerable time lag between interviewing for a position and being hired or, in the case of the networker, between your phone call or letter to a possible contact and the opportunity of a meeting. This can be frustrating. "Why aren't they contacting me?" "I thought I'd get another interview, but no one has telephoned." "Am I out of the running?" You don't know what is happening.

CONSIDER THE DIFFERING PERSPECTIVES

Of course, there is another perspective—that of the networker or hiring organization. Organizations are complex, with multiple tasks that need to be accomplished each day. Hiring is a discrete activity that does not occur as frequently as other job assignments. The hiring process might have to take second place to other, more immediate organizational needs. Although it may be very important to you, and it is certainly ultimately significant to the employer, other issues such as fiscal management, planning and product development, employer vacation periods, or financial constraints may prevent an organization or individual within that organization from acting on your employment or your request for information as quickly as you or they would prefer.

USE YOUR COMMUNICATION SKILLS

Good communication is essential here to resolve any anxieties, and the responsibility is on you, the job or information seeker. Too many job seekers and networkers offer as an excuse that they don't want to "bother" the organization by writing letters or calling. Let us assure you here and now, once and for all, that if you are troubling an organization by over-communicating, someone will indicate that situation to you quite clearly. If not, you can only assume you are a worthwhile prospect and the employer appreciates being reminded of your availability and interest. Let's look at follow-up practices in the job interview process and the networking situation separately.

FOLLOWING UP ON THE EMPLOYMENT INTERVIEW

A brief thank-you note following an interview is an excellent and polite way to begin a series of follow-up communications with a potential employer with whom you have interviewed and want to remain in touch. It should be just that—a thank-you for a good meeting. If you failed to mention some fact or experience during your interview that you think might add to your candidacy, you may use this note to do that. However, this should be essentially a note whose overall tone is appreciative and, if appropriate, indicative of a continuing interest in pursuing any opportunity that may exist with that organization. It is one of the few pieces of business correspondence that may be handwritten, but always use plain, good-quality, standard-size paper.

If, however, at this point you are no longer interested in the employer, the thank-you note is an appropriate time to indicate that. You are under no obligation to identify any reason for not continuing to pursue employment with that organization, but if you are so inclined to indicate your professional reasons (pursuing other employers more akin to your interests, looking for greater income production than this employer can provide, a different geographic location), you certainly may. It should not be written with an eye to negotiation, for it will not be interpreted as such.

As part of your interview closing, you should have taken the initiative to establish lines of communication for continuing information about your candidacy. If you asked permission to telephone, wait a week following your thank-you note, then telephone your contact simply to inquire how things are progressing on your employment status. The feedback you receive here should be taken at face value. If your interviewer simply has no information, he or she will tell you so and indicate whether you should call again and when. Don't be discouraged if this should continue over some period of time.

If during this time something occurs that you think improves or changes your candidacy (some new qualification or experience you may have had), including any offers from other organizations, by all means telephone or write to inform the employer about this. In the case of an offer from a competing but less desirable or equally desirable organization, telephone your contact, explain what has happened, express your real interest in the organization, and inquire whether some determination on your employment might be made before you must respond to this other offer. An organization that is truly interested in you may be moved to make a decision about your candidacy. Equally possible is the scenario in which they are not yet ready to make a decision and so advise you to take the offer that has been presented. Again, you have no ethical alternative but to deal with the information presented in a straightforward manner.

When accepting other employment, be sure to contact any employers still actively considering you and inform them of your new job. Thank them graciously for their consideration. There are many other job seekers out there just like you who will benefit from having their candidacy improved when others bow out of the race. Who knows, you might at some future time have occasion to interact professionally with one of the organizations with which you sought employment. How embarrassing it would be to have someone remember you as the candidate who failed to notify them that you were taking a job elsewhere!

In all of your follow-up communications, keep good notes of whom you spoke with, when you called, and any instructions that were given about return communications. This will prevent any misunderstandings and provide you with good records of what has transpired.

FOLLOWING UP ON THE NETWORK CONTACT

Far more common than the forgotten follow-up after an interview is the situation where a good network contact is allowed to lapse. Good communications are the essence of a network, and follow-up is not so much a matter of courtesy here as it is a necessity. In networking for job information and contacts, you are the active network link. Without you, and without continual contact from you, there is no network. You and your need for employment are often the only shared elements among members of the network. Because network contacts were made regardless of the availability of any particular employment, it is incumbent upon the job seeker, if not simple common sense, to stay in regular communication with the network if you want to be considered for any future job opportunities.

This brings up the issue of responsibility, which is likewise very clear. The job seeker initiates network contacts and is responsible for maintaining those contacts; therefore, the entire responsibility for the network belongs with him or her. This becomes patently obvious if the network is left unattended. It very shortly falls out of existence because it cannot survive without careful attention by the networker.

You have many ways to keep the lines of communication open and to attempt to interest the network in you as a possible employee. You are limited only by your own enthusiasm for members of the network and your creativity. However, you as a networker are well advised to keep good records of whom you have met and contacted in each organization. Be sure to send thank-you notes to anyone who has spent any time with you, whether it was an E-mail message containing information or advice, a quick tour of a department, or a sit-down informational interview. All of these thank-you notes should, in addition to their ostensible reason, add some information about you and your particular combination of strengths and attributes.

You can contact your network at any time to convey continued interest, to comment on some recent article you came across concerning an organization, to add information about your training or changes in your qualifications, to ask advice or seek guidance in your job search, or to request referrals to other possible network opportunities. Sometimes just a simple note to network members reminding them of your job search, indicating that you have been using their advice, and noting that you are still actively pursuing leads and hope to continue to interact with them is enough to keep communications alive.

The Internet has opened up the world of networking. You may be able to find networkers who graduated from your high school or from the college you're attending, who live in a geographic region where you hope to work, or who are employed in a given industry. The Internet makes it easy to reach out to many people, but don't let this perceived ease lull you into complacency. Internet networking demands the same level of preparation as the more traditional forms of networking.

Because networks have been abused in the past, it's important that your conduct be above reproach. Networks are exploratory options; they are not backdoor access to employers. The network works best for someone who is exploring a new industry or making a transition into a new area of employment and who needs to find information or to alert people to his or her search activity. Always be candid and direct with contacts in expressing the purpose of your E-mail, call, or letter and your interest in their help or information about their organization. In follow-up contacts keep the tone professional and direct. Your honesty will be appreciated, and people will respond as best they can if your qualifications appear to meet their forthcoming needs. The network does not owe you anything, and that tone should be clear to each person you meet.

FEEDBACK FROM FOLLOW-UPS

A network contact may prove to be miscalculated. Perhaps you were referred to someone and it became clear that your goals and his or her particular needs did not make a good match. Or the network contact may simply not be in a position to provide you with the information you are seeking. Or in some unfortunate situations, the party may become annoyed by being contacted for this purpose. In such a situation, many job seekers simply say "Thank you" and move on.

If the contact is simply not the right connection, but the individual you are speaking with is not annoyed by the call, it might be a better tactic to express regret that the contact was misplaced and then tell the person what you are seeking and ask for his or her advice or possible suggestions as to a next step. The more people who are aware that you are seeking employment, the better your chances of connecting, and that is the purpose of a network. Most people in a profession have excellent knowledge of their field and varying amounts of expertise in areas tangent to their own. Use their expertise and seek some guidance before you dissolve the contact. You may be pleasantly surprised.

Occasionally, networkers will express the feeling that they have done as much as they can or provided all the information that is available to them. This may be a cue that they would like to be released from your network. Be alert to such attempts to terminate, graciously thank the individual by letter, and move on in your network development. A network is always changing, adding, and losing members, and you want the network to be composed only of those who are actively interested in supporting you.

7

JOB OFFER CONSIDERATIONS

For many recent college graduates, the thrill of their first job and, for some, the most substantial regular income they have ever earned seems an excess of good fortune coming at once. To question that first income or to be critical in any way of the conditions of employment at the time of the initial offer seems like looking a gift horse in the mouth. It doesn't seem to occur to many new hires even to attempt to negotiate any aspect of their first job. And, as many employers who deal with entry-level jobs for recent college graduates will readily confirm, the reality is that there simply isn't much movement in salary available to these new college recruits. The entry-level hire generally does not have an employment track record on a professional level to provide any leverage for negotiation. Real negotiations on salary, benefits, retirement provisions, and so forth come to those with significant employment records at higher income levels.

Of course, the job offer is more than just money. It can be composed of geographic assignment, duties and responsibilities, training, benefits, health and medical insurance, educational assistance, car allowance or company vehicle, and a host of other items. All of this is generally detailed in the formal letter that presents the final job offer. In most cases this is a follow-up to a personal phone call from the employer representative who has been principally responsible for your hiring process.

That initial telephone offer is certainly binding as a verbal agreement, but most firms follow up with a detailed letter outlining the most significant parts of your employment contract. You may, of course, choose to respond immediately at the time of the telephone offer (which would be considered a binding oral contract), but you will also be required to formally answer the letter of offer with a letter of acceptance, restating the salient elements of the employer's description of your position, salary, and benefits. This ensures that both parties are clear on the terms and conditions of employment and remuneration and any other outstanding aspects of the job offer.

IS THIS THE JOB YOU WANT?

Most new employees will respond affirmatively in writing, glad to be in the position to accept employment. If you've worked hard to get the offer and the job market is tight, other offers may not be in sight, so you will say, "Yes, I accept!" What is important here is that the job offer you accept be one that does fit your particular needs, values, and interests as you've outlined them in your self-assessment process. Moreover, it should be a job that will not only use your skills and education but also challenge you to develop new skills and talents.

Jobs are sometimes accepted too hastily, for the wrong reasons, and without proper scrutiny by the applicant. For example, an individual might readily accept a sales job only to find the continual rejection by potential clients unendurable. An office worker might realize within weeks the constraints of a desk job and yearn for more activity. Employment is an important part of our lives. It is, for most of our adult lives, our most continuous productive activity. We want to make good choices based on the right criteria.

If you have a low tolerance for risk, a job based on commission will certainly be very anxiety-provoking. If being near your family is important, issues of relocation could present a decision crisis for you. If you're an adventurous person, a job with frequent travel would provide needed excitement and be very desirable. The importance of income, the need to continue your education, your personal health situation—all of these have an impact on whether the job you are considering will ultimately meet your needs. Unless you've spent some time understanding and thinking about these issues, it will be difficult to evaluate offers you do receive.

More important, if you make a decision that you cannot tolerate and feel you must leave that job, you will then have both unemployment and self-esteem issues to contend with. These will combine to make the next job search tough going, indeed. So make your acceptance a carefully considered decision.

NEGOTIATING YOUR OFFER

It may be that there is some aspect of your job offer that is not particularly attractive to you. Perhaps there is no relocation allotment to help you move your possessions, and this presents some financial hardship for you. It may be that the health insurance is less than you had hoped. Your initial assignment may be different from what you expected, either in its location or in the duties and responsibilities that comprise it. Or it may simply be that the salary is less than you anticipated. Other considerations may be your official starting date of employment, vacation time, evening hours, dates of training programs or schools, and other concerns.

If you are considering not accepting the job because of some item or items in the job offer "package" that do not meet your needs, you should know that most employers emphatically wish that you would bring that issue to their attention. It may be that the employer can alter it to make the offer more agreeable for you. In some cases it cannot be changed. In any event the employer would generally like to have the opportunity to try to remedy a difficulty rather than risk losing a good potential employee over an issue that might have been resolved. After all, they have spent time and funds in securing your services, and they certainly deserve an opportunity to resolve any possible differences.

Honesty is the best approach in discussing any objections or uneasiness you might have over the employer's offer. Having received your formal offer in writing, contact your employer representative and indicate your particular dissatisfaction in a straightforward manner. For example, you might explain that while you are very interested in being employed by this organization, the salary (or any other benefit) is less than you have determined you require. State the terms you need, and listen to the response. You may be asked to put this in writing, or you may be asked to hold off until the firm can decide on a response. If you are dealing with a senior representative of the organization, one who has been involved in hiring for some time, you may get an immediate response or a solid indication of possible outcomes.

Perhaps the issue is one of relocation. Your initial assignment is in the Midwest, and because you had indicated a strong West Coast preference, you are surprised at the actual assignment. You might simply indicate that while you understand the need for the company to assign you based on its needs, you are disappointed and had hoped to be placed on the West Coast. You could inquire if that were still possible and, if not, would it be reasonable to expect a West Coast relocation in the future.

If your request is presented in a reasonable way, most employers will not see this as jeopardizing your offer. If they can agree to your proposal, they will. If not, they will simply tell you so, and you may choose to continue your candidacy with them or remove yourself from consideration. The choice will be up to you.

Some firms will adjust benefits within their parameters to meet the candidate's need if at all possible. If a candidate requires a relocation cost allowance, he or she may be asked to forgo tuition benefits for the first year to accomplish this adjustment. An increase in life insurance may be adjusted by some other benefit trade-off; perhaps a family dental plan is not needed. In these decisions you are called upon, sometimes under time pressure, to know how you value these issues and how important each is to you.

Many employers find they are more comfortable negotiating for candidates who have unique qualifications or who bring especially needed expertise to the organization. Employers hiring large numbers of entry-level college graduates may be far more reluctant to accommodate any changes in offer conditions. They are well supplied with candidates with similar education and experience so that if rejected by one candidate, they can draw new candidates from an ample labor pool.

COMPARING OFFERS

The condition of the economy, the job seekers' academic major and particular geographic job market, and individual needs and demands for certain employment conditions may not provide more than one job offer at a time. Some job seekers may feel that no reasonable offer should go unaccepted for the simple fear there won't be another.

In a tough job market, or if the job you seek is not widely available, or when your job search goes on too long and becomes difficult to sustain financially and emotionally, it may be necessary to accept an inferior offer. The alternative is continued unemployment. Even here, when you feel you don't have a choice, you can at least understand that in accepting this particular offer, there may be limitations and conditions you don't appreciate. At the time of acceptance, there were no other alternatives, but you can begin to use that position to gain the experience and talent to move toward a more attractive position.

Sometimes, however, more than one offer is received, and the candidate has the luxury of choice. If the job seeker knows what he or she wants and has done the necessary self-assessment honestly and thoroughly, it may be clear that one of the offers conforms more closely to those expressed wants and needs.

However, if, as so often happens, the offers are similar in terms of conditions and salary, the question then becomes which organization might provide the necessary climate, opportunities, and advantages for your professional development and growth. This is the time when solid employer research and astute questioning during the interviews really pays off. How much did you learn about the employer through your own research and skillful questioning? When the interviewer asked during the interview "Do you have any questions?" did you ask the kinds of questions that would help resolve a choice between one organization and another? Just as an employer must decide among numerous applicants, so must the applicant learn to assess the potential employer. Both are partners in the job search.

RENEGING ON AN OFFER

An especially disturbing occurrence for employers and career counseling professionals is when a job seeker formally (either orally or by written contract) accepts employment with one organization and later reneges on the agreement and goes with another employer.

There are all kinds of rationalizations offered for this unethical behavior. None of them satisfies. The sad irony is that what the job seeker is willing to do to the employer—make a promise and then break it—he or she would be outraged to have done to him- or herself: have the job offer pulled. It is a very bad way to begin a career. It suggests the individual has not taken the time to do the necessary self-assessment and self-awareness exercises to think and judge critically. The new offer taken may, in fact, be no better or worse than the one refused. You should be aware that there have been incidents of legal action following job candidates' reneging on an offer. This adds a very sour note to what should be a harmonious beginning of a lifelong adventure.

8

THE GRADUATE SCHOOL CHOICE

T he reasons for furthering one's education in graduate school can be as varied and unique as the individuals electing this course of action. Many continue their studies at an advanced level because they simply find it difficult to end the educational process. They love what they are learning and want to learn more and broaden their academic exploration.

....

Continuing to work with a particular subject, such as the cultural, social, and political foundations of modern environmental policy can provide excitement, challenge, and serious work. Some environmental planning majors have loved this aspect of their academic work and want to continue that activity.

Others go to graduate school for purely practical reasons. They have examined employment prospects in their field of study and all indications are that a graduate degree is required. For example, you have a B.S. in environmental planning and the jobs you're most interested in seem to demand a law degree. You sense your opportunities to be directly involved in environmental policy will be very limited without this advanced degree.

Alumni who are working in the fields you are considering can be a good source of information about the degree level required. Ask your college career office for some alumni names and give them a call or E-mail them. Talk to them about degree requirements and whether an advanced degree is needed for the work you are interested in.

CONSIDER YOUR MOTIVES

The answer to the question of "Why graduate school?" is a personal one for each applicant. Nevertheless, it is important to consider your motives carefully. Graduate school involves additional time out of the employment market, a high level of critical evaluation, significant autonomy as you pursue your studies, and considerable financial expenditure. For some students in doctoral programs, there may be additional life choice issues, such as relationships, marriage, and parenthood, that may present real challenges while in a program of study. You would be well advised to consider the following questions as you think about your decision to continue your studies.

Are You Postponing Some Tough Decisions by Going to School?

Graduate school is not a place to go to avoid life's problems. There is intense competition for graduate school slots and for the fellowships, scholarships, and financial aid available. This competition means extensive interviewing, résumé submission, and essay writing that rivals corporate recruitment. Likewise, the graduate school process is a mentored one in which faculty stay aware of and involved in the academic progress of their students and continually challenge the quality of their work. Many graduate students are called upon to participate in teaching and professional writing and research as well.

In other words, this is no place to hide from the spotlight. Graduate students work very hard and much is demanded of them individually. If you elect to go to graduate school to avoid the stresses and strains of the "real world," you will find no safe place in higher academics. Vivid accounts, both fictional and nonfictional, have depicted quite accurately the personal and professional demands of graduate school work.

The selection of graduate studies as a career option should be a positive choice—something you *want* to do. It shouldn't be selected as an escape from other, less attractive or more challenging options, nor should it be selected as the option of last resort (i.e., "I can't do anything else; I'd better just stay in school."). If you're in some doubt about the strength of your reasoning about continuing in school, discuss the issues with a career counselor or a faculty member at your school. Together you can clarify your reasoning, and you'll get some sound feedback on what you're about to undertake.

On the other hand, staying on in graduate school because of a particularly poor employment market and a lack of jobs at entry-level positions has proven to be an effective "stalling" strategy. If you can afford it, pursuing a graduate degree immediately after your undergraduate education gives you a year or two to "wait out" a difficult economic climate, while at the same time acquiring a potentially valuable credential.

Have You Done Some "Hands-On" Reality Testing?

There are experiential options available to give some reality to your decision-making process about graduate school. Internships or work in the field can give you a good idea about employment demands, conditions, and atmosphere.

· ·

Perhaps as a geography major you're considering a graduate program in environmental studies so that you can teach at the community college level. A summer position teaching environmental programs at an adult day camp will bring home some of the reality of a teaching career. You will struggle with explaining concepts and planning effective lessons. After a short time, you will have a stronger concept of the pace of the job, one's interaction with colleagues, and opportunities for personal development. Talking with these colleagues is invaluable in helping you better understand the objective of your graduate study.

· ·

Have You Compared Your Expectations of What Graduate School Will Do for You with What It Has Done for Alumni of the Program You're Considering?

Most colleges and universities perform some kind of postgraduate survey of their students to ascertain where they are employed, what additional education they have received, and what levels of salary they are enjoying. Ask to see this information either from the university you are considering applying to or from your own alma mater, especially if it has a similar graduate program. Such surveys often reveal surprises about occupational decisions, salaries, and work satisfaction. This information may affect your decision.

The value of self-assessment (the process of examining and making decisions about your own hierarchy of values and goals) is especially important in analyzing the desirability of possible career paths involving graduate education. Sometimes a job requiring advanced education seems to hold real promise but is disappointing in salary potential or number of opportunities available. Certainly it is better to research this information before embarking on a program of graduate studies. It may not change your mind about your decision, but by becoming better informed about your choice, you become better prepared for your future.

Have You Talked with People in Your Field to Explore What You Might Be Doing After Graduate School?

In pursuing your undergraduate degree, you will have come into contact with many individuals trained in the field you are considering. You might also have the opportunity to attend professional conferences, workshops, seminars, and job fairs where you can expand your network of contacts. Talk to them all! Find out about their individual career paths, discuss your own plans and hopes, get their feedback on the reality of your expectations, and heed their advice about your prospects. Each will have a unique tale to tell, and each will bring a different perspective on the current marketplace for the credentials you are seeking. Talking to enough people will make you an expert on what's out there.

Are You Excited by the Idea of Studying the Particular Field You Have in Mind?

This question may be the most important one of all. If you are going to spend several years in advanced study, perhaps engendering some debt or postponing some lifestyle decisions for an advanced degree, you simply ought to enjoy what you're doing. Examine your work in the discipline so far. Has it been fun? Have you found yourself exploring various paths of thought? Do you read in your area for fun? Do you enjoy talking about it, thinking about it, and sharing it with others? Advanced degrees often are the beginning of a lifetime's involvement with a particular subject. Choose carefully a field that will hold your interest and your enthusiasm.

If nothing else, do the following:

■ Talk and question (remember to listen!)

■ Reality test

■ Soul-search by yourself or with a person you trust

FINDING THE RIGHT PROGRAM FOR YOU: SOME CONSIDERATIONS

There are several important factors in coming to a sound decision about the right graduate program for you. You'll want to begin by locating institutions that offer appropriate programs, examining each of these programs and their requirements, undertaking the application process by reviewing catalogs and obtaining application materials, visiting campuses if possible, arranging for letters of recommendation, writing your application statement, and, finally, following up on your applications.

Locate Institutions with Appropriate Programs

Once you decide on a particular advanced degree, it's important to develop a list of schools offering such a degree program. Perhaps the best source of graduate program information is Peterson's. The website (petersons.com) and the printed *Guides to Graduate Study* allow you to search for information by institution name, location, or academic area. The website also allows you to do a keyword search. Use the website and guides to build your list. In addition, you may want to consult the College Board's *Index of Majors and Graduate Degrees*, which will help you find graduate programs offering the degree you seek. It is indexed by academic major and then categorized by state.

Now, this may be a considerable list. You may want to narrow the choices down further by a number of criteria: tuition, availability of financial aid, public versus private institutions, United States versus international institutions, size of student body, size of faculty, application fee, and geographic location. This is only a partial list; you will have your own important considerations. Perhaps you are an avid scuba diver and you find it unrealistic to think you could pursue graduate study for a number of years without being able to ocean dive from time to time. Good! That's a decision and it's honest. Now, how far from the ocean is too far, and what schools meet your other needs? In any case, and according to your own criteria, begin to put together a reasonable list of graduate schools that you are willing to spend time investigating.

Examine the Degree Programs and Their Requirements

Once you've determined the criteria by which you want to develop a list of graduate schools, you can begin to examine the degree program requirements, faculty composition, and institutional research orientation. Again, using resources such as Peterson's website or guides can reveal an amazingly rich level of material by which to judge your possible selections.

In addition to degree programs and degree requirements, entries will include information about application fees, entrance test requirements, tuition, percentage of applicants accepted, numbers of applicants receiving financial aid, gender breakdown of students, numbers of full- and part-time faculty, and often gender breakdown of faculty as well. Numbers graduating in each program and research orientations of departments are also included in some entries. There is information on graduate housing; student services; and library, research, and computer facilities. A contact person, phone number, and address are also standard information in these listings.

It can be helpful to draw up a chart and enter relevant information about each school you are considering in order to have a ready reference on points of information that are important to you.

Undertake the Application Process

Program Information. Once you've decided on a selection of schools, obtain program information and applications. Nearly every school has a website that contains most of the detailed information you need to narrow your choices. In addition, applications can be printed from the site. If, however, you don't want to print out lots of information, you can request that a copy of the catalog and application materials be sent to you.

When you have your information in hand, give it all a careful reading and make notes of issues you might want to discuss via E-mail, on the telephone, or in a personal interview.

· ·

If you are interested in graduate work in chemistry, for example, consider colloquiums, directed research opportunities, and specialized seminars that focus on environmental topics and issues.

· ·

What is the ratio of faculty to the required number of courses for your degree? How often will you encounter the same faculty member as an instructor?

If the program offers a practicum or off-campus experience, who arranges this? Does the graduate school select a site and place you there, or is it your responsibility? What are the professional affiliations of the faculty? Does the program merit any outside professional endorsement or accreditation?

Critically evaluate the catalogs of each of the programs you are considering. List any questions you have and ask current or former teachers and colleagues for their impressions as well.

The Application. Preview each application thoroughly to determine what you need to provide in the way of letters of recommendation, transcripts from undergraduate schools or any previous graduate work, and personal essays. Make a notation for each application of what you will need to complete that document.

Additionally, you'll want to determine entrance testing requirements for each institution and immediately arrange to register for appropriate tests. Information can be obtained from associated websites, including ets.org (GRE, GMAT, TOEFL, PRAXIS, SLS, Higher Education Assessment), lsat.org (LSAT), and tpcweb.com/mat (MAT). Your college career office should also be able to provide you with advice and additional information.

Visit the Campus if Possible

If time and finances allow, a visit, interview, and tour can help make your decision easier. You can develop a sense of the student body, meet some of the faculty, and hear up-to-date information on resources and the curriculum. You will have a brief opportunity to "try out" the surroundings to see if they fit your needs. After all, it will be home for a while. If a visit is not possible but you have questions, don't hesitate to call and speak with the dean of the graduate school. Most are more than happy to talk to candidates and want them to have the answers they seek. Graduate school admission is a very personal and individual process.

Arrange for Letters of Recommendation

This is also the time to begin to assemble a group of individuals who will support your candidacy as a graduate student by writing letters of recommendation or completing recommendation forms. Some schools will ask you to provide letters of recommendation to be included with your application or sent directly to the school by the recommender. Other graduate programs will provide a recommendation form that must be completed by the recommender. These graduate school forms vary greatly in the amount of space provided for a written recommendation. So that you can use letters as you need to, ask your recommenders to address their letters "To Whom It May Concern," unless one of your recommenders has a particular connection to one of your graduate schools or knows an official at the school.

Choose recommenders who can speak authoritatively about the criteria important to selection officials at your graduate school. In other words, choose recommenders who can write about your grasp of the literature in your field of study, your ability to write and speak effectively, your class performance, and your demonstrated interest in the field outside of class. Other characteristics that graduate schools are interested in assessing include your emotional maturity, leadership ability, breadth of general knowledge, intellectual ability, motivation, perseverance, and ability to engage in independent inquiry.

When requesting recommendations, it's especially helpful to put the request in writing. Explain your graduate school intentions and express some of your thoughts about graduate school and your appreciation for their support. Don't be shy about "prompting" your recommenders with some suggestions of what you would appreciate being included in their comments. Most recommenders will find this direction helpful and will want to produce a statement of support that you can both stand behind. Consequently, if your interaction with one recommender was especially focused on research projects, he or she might be best able to speak of those skills and your critical thinking ability. Another recommender may have good comments to make about your public presentation skills.

Give your recommenders plenty of lead time in which to complete your recommendation, and set a date by which they should respond. If they fail to meet your deadline, be prepared to make a polite call or visit to inquire if they need more information or if there is anything you can do to move the process along.

Whether or not you are providing a graduate school form or asking for an original letter to be mailed, be sure to provide an envelope and postage if the recommender must mail the form or letter directly to the graduate school.

Each recommendation you request should provide a different piece of information about you for the selection committee. It might be pleasant for letters of recommendation to say that you are a fine, upstanding individual, but a selection committee for graduate school will require specific information. Each recommender has had a unique relationship with you, and his or her letter should reflect that. Think of each letter as helping to build a more complete portrait of you as a potential graduate student.

Write Your Application Statement

· ·

Many graduate applications require a personal statement. For anyone interested in the environment, this should be an exciting and challenging assignment and one that you should be able to complete successfully. It is an opportunity for you to talk about the factors and circumstances that led to your interest in this field. Certainly, any required essay on a graduate application will weigh heavily in the decision process of the graduate school admissions committee.

....

An excellent source to help in writing this essay is *How to Write a Winning Personal Statement for Graduate and Professional School,* by Richard J. Stelzer. It has been written from the perspective of what graduate school selection committees are looking for when they read these essays. It provides helpful tips to keep your essay targeted on the kinds of issues and criteria that are important to selection committees and that provide them with the kind of information they can best utilize in making their decision.

Follow Up on Your Applications

After you have finished each application and mailed it along with your transcript requests and letters of recommendation, be sure to follow up on the progress of your file. For example, call the graduate school administrative staff to see whether your transcripts have arrived. If the school required your recommenders to fill out a specific recommendation form that had to be mailed directly to the school, you will want to ensure that they have all arrived in good time for the processing of your application. It is your responsibility to make certain that all required information is received by the institution.

RESEARCHING FINANCIAL AID SOURCES, SCHOLARSHIPS, AND FELLOWSHIPS

Financial aid information is available from the academic department to which you apply and from the university's graduate school. Some disciplines provide full tuition and a monthly stipend for graduate students. These decisions are made in the specific academic department. It is important that you ask about the availability of this type of financial support. If it is not available, you may be eligible for federal, state, and/or institutional support. There are lengthy forms to complete, and some of these will vary by school, type of school (public versus private), and state. Be sure to note the deadline dates on each form.

There are many excellent resources available to help you explore all of your financial aid options. Visit your college career office or local public library to find out about the range of materials available. Two excellent resources are Peterson's website (petersons.com) and its book *Peterson's Grants for Graduate and Post Doctoral Study*. Another good reference is the Foundation Center's *Foundation Grants to Individuals*. These types of resources generally contain information that can be accessed by indexes including field of study, specific eligibility requirements, administering agency, and geographic focus.

EVALUATING ACCEPTANCES

If you apply to and are accepted at more than one school, it is time to return to your initial research and self-assessment to evaluate your options and select the program that will best help you achieve the goals you set for pursuing graduate study. You'll want to choose a program that will allow you to complete your studies in a timely and cost-effective way. This may be a good time to get additional feedback from professors and career professionals who are familiar with your interests and plans. Ultimately, the decision is yours, so be sure you get answers to all the questions you can think of.

SOME NOTES ABOUT REJECTION

Each graduate school is searching for applicants who appear to have the qualifications necessary to succeed in its program. Applications are evaluated on a combination of undergraduate grade point average, strength of letters of recommendation, standardized test scores, and personal statements written for the application.

A carelessly completed application is one reason many applicants are denied admission to a graduate program. To avoid this type of needless rejection, be sure to carefully and completely answer all appropriate questions on the application form, focus your personal statement given the instructions provided, and submit your materials well in advance of the deadline. Remember that your test scores and recommendations are considered a part of your application, so they must also be received by the deadline.

If you are rejected by a school that especially interests you, you may want to contact the dean of graduate studies to discuss the strengths and weaknesses of your application. Information provided by the dean will be useful in reapplying to the program later or applying to other, similar programs.

PART TWO

THE CAREER PATHS

9

INTRODUCTION TO THE ENVIRONMENTAL STUDIES CAREER PATHS

W ith the publication of the now classic book, *Silent Spring* (1962), Rachel Carson drew the attention of college students to a pervasive and deadly environmental problem, dichlorodiphenyltrichloroethane. Commonly known as DDT, it is an effective pesticide that was first isolated in 1873, but used extensively worldwide after World War II. It is suggested that its application saved millions of human lives by killing lice that spread typhus and mosquitoes responsible for malaria. However, beginning in the postwar period, it became obvious that its use was causing reproductive failure in birds such as eagles and hawks. Stored in fatty tissues in animals that these birds fed upon, the chemical then affected eggshell formation, rendering them fragile and easily crushed during incubation. Unchecked, this reproductive failure would ultimately lead to extinction of the affected species. Students and other activists knew this was a critically important issue to address and thus the modern environmental movement began. One of the earliest successes of this movement was the ban on DDT use in the United States in 1973. Eagles and hawks are once again plentiful in their natural habitats.

A NEW ACADEMIC DISCIPLINE EMERGES

During this time of activism, colleges and universities began to give attention to environmental problems. As a consequence, many courses with environmental or ecological themes were developed and majors and minors soon followed. This field of study remains popular today as evidenced by the number of colleges and universities that continue to offer degree programs focusing on the environment. A search of *Peterson's Guide* reveals that more than two hundred colleges and universities in the United States and Canada offer course work in various environmental studies fields.

Environmental studies, most academics would agree, is interdisciplinary. Many subjects are drawn upon to form the basis of the field. Zoology, biology, botany, engineering, chemistry, geography, geology, soils, chemistry, health, economics, education, natural resources, technology, and hydrology are just some of the subjects that may be included in environmental studies that are offered.

In environmental studies, the natural and social sciences meet. Training in field and laboratory procedures, along with an appreciation for ethics and societal issues, are important in this field. Within this discipline, though, the education or training emphasis can range from a heavy focus on social science to a heavy emphasis on natural science, or somewhere in between. Environmental studies is both theoretical and practical. People with these degrees are prepared for the world of work; they are occupationally ready, with marketable skills; and they can fill the human resources needs of local, state, and federal government as well as private industry. An education in environmental studies is also good preparation for an advanced professional degree, especially in environmental law, or in business when coupled with an MBA.

WHAT SKILLS WILL YOU OFFER AN EMPLOYER?

Some environmental studies programs help their students develop technical skills, including laboratory, field data gathering, sampling, and instrumentation. For this group, it is now assumed that they are well versed in employing numerous types of computer software, such as those for computation, statistics, and spreadsheet development and word processing. If you are interested in a technically oriented job and you have not yet picked up these skills, make a strong effort to remedy that situation before graduation. Or, if you have completed college, consider some extra training at a nearby college or technical school.

Some students have majored in a field or have developed specialized skills that are valued in environmental fields. The ability to use aerial photography and satellite images, for instance, to identify patterns and solve problems of the natural landscape, locate sites of toxic spills or storage of hazardous materials, inventory land use, and monitor habitat change over time are all extremely useful. Digital image processing, which is designed to improve the utility of aerial imagery, is becoming a commonly used technique even among relatively small environmental consulting firms. Expertise in geographic information systems (GIS) and computer cartography are valuable and very employable skills. GIS involves the utilization of databases to create maps of various landscape elements such as streets and roads, utility lines, streams, and soils, as well as land use patterns. Global positioning systems (GPS) provide the ability to precisely locate features of the landscape. Portable receivers that link with orbiting satellites are being used more and more in environmental studies disciplines to facilitate and improve mapping accuracy. If you haven't been trained in some mix of these techniques, and you are still in school, be sure to enroll in classes where these topics are covered. If you are out of school and missed course work in these areas, consider enrolling in classes so that you can develop these sought-after skills.

However, these technical skills do not represent the full range of training needed in environmental studies. Research design skills essential for problem solving or technical writing, which facilitate the ability to communicate, are critically important in certain jobs. You may have covered the development of environmental impact statements in one or more of your classes, and you have undoubtedly been required to write numerous reports of one type or another. All of these are valuable training, as the world of work requires you to call upon such expertise on a daily basis. The importance of being able to communicate effectively in writing cannot be overemphasized.

Additionally, your general education classes enabled you to sharpen your critical thinking skills, allowing you to separate fact from misinformation, causing you to question, and helping you learn how to probe into an issue or problem more deeply. You were probably assigned to work in groups in some classes. As a member of a working team you learned to identify the elements of an assignment, break the task into manageable units, undertake subtasks, and come together as a unit to deliver a presentation or to produce a written report. Working in teams is an essential skill for the workplace of the twenty-first century.

Hopefully you have become comfortable, at least a little more comfortable, in front of audiences, facilitating meetings, and leading discussions. Many jobs in each of the five paths require you to undertake these tasks. No employer will expect you to be an accomplished presenter, but they may look to you to build these skills over time.

THE ENVIRONMENTAL STUDIES CAREER PATHS

Five career paths have been developed for environmental studies:

- Environmental education

- Environmental policy, planning, and management

- Environmental sciences

- Environmental technology

- Environmental engineering

Each path involves different preparation, training, skills, orientation, goals, and level of technical expertise. Your degree program has most likely prepared you for more than one of these paths. Read on to find out which might be the best career fit for you.

Environmental Education

Environmental education is not just classroom teaching, but it can be. The environmental education career path includes working as a docent, naturalist, recreation program leader, interpreter, or teacher. Employing organizations might include the Peace Corps; nature centers or museums; local, state, or federal parks and monuments; camps; outdoor and adventure education centers; and environmental advocacy groups such as the Audubon Society, as well as schools.

Environmental Policy, Planning, and Management

The environmental policy, planning, and management career path involves natural resource policy, planning, and management, including conservation. Jobs in this area focus upon interrelationships between soil, water, flora, and fauna. Graduates commonly secure positions with a variety of employers including environmental consulting firms, federal resource management agencies like the Bureau of Land management and the U.S. Forest Service, the Environmental Protection Agency, U.S. Fish and Wildlife Service, or any number of state agencies that focus upon resource development or preservation.

Environmental Sciences

Environmental sciences graduates are equipped for careers in environmental consulting, environmental monitoring for private industry, water resources, pollution regulation, environmental advocacy groups, and planning agencies.

This career path is more technically oriented than either environmental education or environmental policy, planning, and management paths, but less so than environmental technology or environmental engineering paths.

Environmental Technology

The environmental technology career path is technically oriented with an emphasis upon both field and laboratory data sampling, collection, classification, storage, analysis, and retrieval. Statistics, computer skills, laboratory techniques, and field procedures are utilized on a daily basis for entry-level positions within this career path. Graduates with training for this path might seek employment as environmental technicians at water treatment plants; as hydrologic technicians; in private industry in quality assurance labs as lab scientists; or in the occupational and health safety department with environmental consulting firms or with companies that seek to remediate toxic spills.

Environmental Engineering

Environmental engineers work to provide safe drinking water; design waste disposal systems; design clean-up procedures for contaminated sites; and develop methods, procedures, and equipment for maintaining air and water quality. They design solid and hazardous waste disposal and recycling systems. Additionally, they assist in the development of environmental protection plans and in the administration of environmental regulations. Graduates may be employed by municipalities where they maintain and operate water treatment and waste disposal facilities; environmental consulting firms; the Environmental Protection Agency; law firms specializing in environmental law; and local, state, and federal agencies.

The next five chapters will explain each path in detail. As you decide which path or paths you will pursue, draw upon what you learned as you undertook your self-assessment, developed a résumé and cover letter, researched careers, and prepared to network and interview to achieve success in your job search. And do so knowing that your work will be important to all of us.

10

PATH 1: ENVIRONMENTAL EDUCATION

Mountains colored with the spectacular oranges, yellows, and maroons of fall foliage. Crystal-clear gurgling streams laughingly running down their riverbeds. Your senses are delighted as you travel through rural Virginia on a brilliantly sunny weekend day. You glance down and notice that fuel is running low so you pull into a gas station that sits between the road and the nearby stream. While there, you run into the restroom, and notice a warning above the sink that advises against drinking the water from the tap, as it is fouled by petroleum. Your delight with the day and your surroundings is shattered. What has happened here?

Gasoline storage tanks were formerly constructed of steel and manufactured with welds. Many such tanks are in use today. After a time, these tanks begin to weaken along welds and also where in contact with moist soil and groundwater. The result is, of course, rust and eventual petroleum leakage. To remediate such sites, the tanks must be removed and the soil excavated, removed, and replaced—and the petroleum could have migrated great distances during the lifetime of the storage tanks before leakage was discovered or before there was concern.

THE NEED FOR ENVIRONMENTAL EDUCATORS

The earth's natural environment is a complex web that some nonscientists may find difficult to comprehend. The scenario described above demonstrates the relationships among the geology, hydrology, and land use of an area. For lay people to understand the workings of natural systems and their responses to human interaction, they must be educated. Environmental educators can provide solid information, organized in such a way as to be easily understood. This translates to a need for individuals prepared to educate the public about environmental problems, increase their awareness and understanding of issues, and teach the techniques that can prevent environmental degradation as well as methods to clean up decades of abuse and neglect. Although the emphasis placed upon environment protection in the United States and abroad waxes and wanes with changes in public interest and political leadership, there is and will continue to be a need for workers trained in the disciplines related to environmental studies.

THE REWARDS OF WORKING IN ENVIRONMENTAL EDUCATION

Lots of rewards stem from a career in environmental education. First and perhaps foremost is the reward of working in an area of interest that has a wide appeal. You'll also remain abreast of environmental issues. You'll work with people who hold interests similar to yours, and you'll experience student growth. Finally, you'll develop a sense that your life's work is filled with success stories as you have a positive impact on students' lives.

Continue Learning About the Environment

One obvious reward of working as an environmental educator is the opportunity to stay abreast of developments that focus upon your first academic love, the environment. Good teachers continually participate in professional development. K–12 and college and university educators alike need to be retrained and to update their knowledge and skills. New technologies may help resolve environmental crises. Unless you make an ongoing effort, your knowledge will not be up to date and you'll quickly become a dinosaur. There are lots of ways to keep up with your subject, and among the easiest is to read science journals such as *Science News, Discover* magazine, *National Wildlife,* or *National Geographic* magazine.

Use Your Creative Energies

Another advantage of a career teaching environmental studies is the freedom in the workplace. This will vary from school to school, between levels of education (middle school, high school, college), and by employment setting. But regardless of the level, there is considerable flexibility with respect to the type of material, content, teaching style, evaluation methods, and scheduling. Teaching is in large measure a self-directed activity that involves creativity. There are state guidelines, syllabi, learning goals, and assessments, but there are still lots of aspects that the educator designs and builds alone. This freedom to create is one of the most attractive aspects of the profession.

Work with People Who Hold Similar Interests

The coterie of people that you spend your day with is often rewarding. You'll be around folks who share your interests, who can counsel you and help with development of activities, who can provide guidance and advice, and with whom you can have fun. There is a certain fellowship among teachers, a bond that develops as they share stories about the things that happened that day, funny stories about what "Johnny" said that day, their successes, and sometimes failures, too. We learn from the good and the bad, from personal experience, and vicariously as well.

Watch Your Students Mature

Another reward is the realization that you contributed to the academic growth and maturation of an individual. You'll be pleasantly surprised that, by the time students become college seniors, they have learned to give an organized presentation, write an effective report, think critically on their feet, and do independent research, despite many shortcomings observed while they were freshmen. Sometimes, in class, I'll direct a question to the group or the individual, and am at first disappointed that no one is able to cobble together a reply to the query, that no one is on the same wavelength. But often, if I persist, I'll find that one student, perhaps a quiet one, one that you'd least expect a sophisticated answer from, has thought the process through and reveals an astonishing level of understanding. That is truly a tiny reward for that day.

Know You've Made a Difference in Someone's Life

Finally, perhaps one of the best rewards are those little "thanks" from a student at the end of a course, at the end of the year, or upon graduation at the end of their middle, high school, or college careers. Sometimes alumni return with special greetings and thanks, too. There is no reward more fulfilling than knowing your efforts have had a positive impact on a student's life.

CLASSROOM TEACHING AND BEYOND

If you're interested in teaching, subject matter relating to the environment is taught at the middle, high school, and college levels. Few middle and high school systems will offer an environmental studies course in their curriculum, however. But many will require that environmental issues be addressed in the curriculum as a part of another course. Colleges and universities offer a variety of majors that focus on environmental issues, and those people who are interested in pursuing a Ph.D. can fill their days teaching courses directly related to the environment.

Environmental education is not restricted, however, to teaching in the traditional classroom setting. In this chapter we will also discuss somewhat nontraditional delivery of information in settings outside the classroom—such as parks, museums, camps, outdoor leadership schools, science centers, nature parks, and zoos—and with employers such as Trout Unlimited, the National Wildlife Federation, the National Park Service, United States Forest Service, or the World Wildlife Fund.

DEFINITION OF THE CAREER PATH

Before we begin defining teaching in both the traditional classroom setting and in other nontraditional settings, let's look at some recent job listings.

Science Teacher, Grades 5–8. Must be certified. Position to start immediately. New graduates or little teaching experience OK. Send résumé to . . .

High School Science Teacher. Teach science to 9–12 grade students, including biology, chemistry, physics, and environmental science. Class size is 15 or less. Bachelor's degree in science ed required. Apply to . . .

Environmental Teaching Associate. (Private) College is now accepting applications for this new position in the Program in Environmental Studies. Full time, 3-yr staff position will work with faculty who teach required senior seminar focusing on local & regional issues. Responsibilities include planning the courses, including field site visits, interviews, class visits, information gathering; assisting students during the courses with gathering information, arranging meetings, facilitating access to equipment; and when the courses are completed, working to disseminate information to local regional communities through presentations, publications, and Web-based media. Bachelor's degree in environmental studies or related field required. Excellent verbal and written communication skills; excellent computer skills. Strong interpersonal and organizational skills a must. Ability to work well with both faculty and students, as well as independently. Working knowledge of GIS a plus. The Program in Environmental Studies is an interdisciplinary major. Send letter & résumé to . . .

Assistant Professor, Environmental Science & Policy. The Environmental Science & Policy Program within the College of Arts & Sciences at (state) University seeks half-time, non-tenure track, one-year faculty replacement. Teach 4 courses & service to the Program: 1 lab section for undergrad Fundamentals of Environmental Science, 1 undergrad environmental communications course, upper level wetlands ecology course. Qualifications: Ph.D. with some relevant teaching experience preferred, but ABD considered. Submit cover letter, recent curriculum vitae, transcripts, & 3 references to . . .

Park Ranger–Interpretation (National Park Service). This position will be working in the Division of Interpretation in (a national recreation area). Duties: work as a member of a team of park staff, volunteers, students, and teachers to develop, prepare, evaluate, and present curriculum-based education programs on a variety of topics including Native American Culture, biodiversity, ecology, fire, U.S. and (state) history; conduct interpretive and education programs both at the park and at schools; develop and prepare education materials, publications, and temporary exhibits; represent the park at fairs, workshops, and conferences; work with schools on scheduling and transportation; and coach and lead volunteers and assist with the planning of work group operations. Bachelor's degree in natural resource management, natural sciences, earth sciences, history, archaeology, anthropology, parks and recreation management, law enforcement/police science, social sciences, museum sciences, business administration, public administration, behavioral sciences, or sociology. Send application materials to . . .

Environmental Education Instruction (local arm of national nonprofit environmental education organization). Educator leading and teaching approximately 12 youth in a variety of coastal habitats, including nearby barrier islands and Okefenokee Swamp; complete training; some animal care is required, as is some office and administrative work; opportunity to help develop curriculum. Qualifications: Bachelor's degree (Biology, Environmental Science, or a related field is a plus); strong work ethic; leadership qualities; experience working with children is a plus; and love of working outdoors.

Program Leader (community nonprofit environmental education organization). The Program Leader drives to schools, youth groups, and adult groups and gives environmental presentations on recycling, ocean pollution, energy conservation, and more. The program leader also hosts environmental education booths at special events around the community. 75% of the work is out of the office and the other

25% is in the office. When not doing presentations, program leader assists with other environmental projects within the organization. Qualifications: minimum of a bachelor's degree in environmental studies, outdoor recreation, education, or related field. Send cover letter and résumé to . . .

What are the common threads that run through all of these jobs? If you reread the descriptions, you will find that each position, as well as all other positions in environmental education, demands that you:

- Love to teach

- Respect the natural environment

- Operate as an effective team member

- Develop and prepare educational materials

- Present educational programs

- Attend to administrative duties

- Undertake other, setting-specific duties

Build on Your Love of Teaching

Opting to follow teaching environmental studies as a career path must be carefully pursued because, as with any teaching position, the subject matter becomes subordinate to its delivery. In other words, your sheer love for the environment will not ensure success in teaching. An environmental educator must not only love his or her subject, but also experience satisfaction from working with the clientele, that is, students. Environmental educators, like all educators, are just that, they are teachers *first,* and environmentalists *second.* In order to be a successful educator, it must be apparent to your students that you are both enthusiastic about being in the classroom and about your subject! Not everyone is prepared to elect education as a career path. For those who do, there are considerable rewards and some drawbacks, too.

Respect the Natural Environment

No matter where you may find yourself employed as an environmental educator, your respect for the natural environment was a driving force in your career choice. Whether it was your disgust at seeing dead birds, mammals, and fish lying on an oil-covered beach in Prince William Sound, Alaska, or simply an overgrown, trash-strewn lot in your neighborhood that you passed on the way to school, this interest in the environment has led you to want to teach others to prevent problems or mitigate them once they have occurred. Somewhere, somehow, you acquired an extraordinary appreciation for the natural world, and you derive a sense of accomplishment from teaching others.

Operate as an Effective Team Member

Educators work with overseers, administrators, peers who are specialists in their own fields, and, often, volunteers. You will be called on to interact effectively with the group of professionals you'll work with. Whether it is in a middle school with a counselor, in a high school with a curriculum coordinator, in a college with your department chair, in a government organization with a group of volunteer workers, or in a nonprofit agency with the chair of the board of directors, you'll need to be able to operate successfully in a team environment.

Develop and Prepare Audience-Specific Educational Materials

Knowing your audience is critical to your success as a teacher. In the following section we discuss some working conditions that affect the materials you prepare to use in your teaching. A presentation to a group of fourth graders will be different from one that focuses upon the same subject matter but is directed to an eighth-grade class. A field trip with high school students must emphasize hands-on instruction, because if you just talk at the students, you will quickly lose many of them. You'll find a few listening, a few more looking around, and a cluster at the back of your group whispering about what they will be doing over the weekend. Not only do you have to plan to tailor the presentation to the group, but also to the setting. Environmental educators have to devote lots of time to planning projects and to field preparation in order to develop real-world examples, both good and bad, of prevention practices, the results of environmental decisions, and remediation and mitigation strategies.

Present Audience-Specific Educational Programs

There may be great variability in your class's receptiveness to learning, depending on whether they are required to be in attendance or not. And the age of your class will play a major role in how you go about presenting your material. Working with high school sophomores who are in a required science class will be very different from educating adults who have signed up to learn more about the local habitat that supports a colony of loons.

Attend to Administrative Duties

Teachers at the middle and high school levels must deal with lots of meetings, both with staff and parents. Additionally, they must attend to lots of record keeping, grading of papers, development of assignments and presentations, and a myriad other duties. College teachers have similar duties, though dealing with parents is not usually among them. At this level, fewer assignments are required, so the amount of record keeping is reduced. But effective presentations and assignments are required, and grading is also essential. Students learn more effectively if they receive written feedback from an assignment soon after it has been turned in. If a great deal of time passes between the due date and the return of assignments, students tend to pay less heed to suggestions for improving their work. They often forget the context of the assignment and have moved on to other priorities.

Undertake Other Setting-Specific Duties

The range of other duties you will be responsible for undertaking varies with the work setting. While the middle school teacher who is called upon to teach general science might also be charged with teaching earth science, a high school science teacher offering a class in biology may be responsible for serving as the advisor to one of the school's clubs. College professors who have their doctoral degree in environmental biology may be expected to undertake a community outreach effort, such as developing a plan to create a local natural area that has been deeded to the community, and an environmental interpreter working for a nonprofit organization may be responsible for feeding animals housed at the center. The point is that you must be sure that you understand the full range of duties your environmental educator position will require. The job descriptions shown throughout this chapter provide a sense for the range of tasks that fall within a given type of job.

WORKING CONDITIONS: TRADITIONAL SETTINGS

The term *traditional setting* as used in this chapter refers to schools that offer formal classroom training via individual courses or programs of study. In this section we will address the three traditional settings where an educator can expect to teach courses in environmental studies. Those settings include middle schools, high schools, and colleges and universities.

Let's begin by examining tasks and duties that environmental educators share, regardless of the level at which they teach.

Developing a Teaching Plan

A teaching plan, whether it be for a two-week unit, thirteen-week marking period, the semester, or an entire academic year can be a formidable task for a beginning teacher, no matter what the school level. It is best to start with an overall, broad list of the objectives of the course or unit and break the task down into manageable parts. Then it is relatively easy to carve out day-to-day lectures, presentations, activities, assignments, and discussions. Try for variety in your presentations. You can sometimes have a lecture-oriented class but sprinkle in educational video clips, in-class readings, group work, and discussion. Or try the Socratic approach where you draw the information from the students instead of lecturing at them.

Developing Meaningful Assignments

Another skill that teachers learn is the development of meaningful assignments. Students, with too much frequency, speak of assignments in other classes where their instructor said, "Give me a thirty-page term paper on _____, and it is due on the last day of class." You fill in the topic, any topic. Such general assignments lack direction and purpose. Assignments should improve students' research, organizational, writing, and critical thinking skills. They shouldn't be assigned just for the purpose of giving students something to do. Reading a thirty-page paper for content, clarity, mechanics, and grammar is a daunting task, let alone reading, perhaps thirty of them! In order for a paper to help the student learn, there must be timely and effective feedback. You cannot simply read the paper and slap a C+ on it. There must be commentary, suggestions for improvement, and encouragement. The assignment of thirty-page papers will likely prevent you from making effective comments. A ten-page (or shorter) paper, when returned quickly, with solid criticism, where the student has the opportunity to improve their work is often superior to a "mini-book" of thirty pages. In addition, having the paper due at the end of the semester will prevent the student from reviewing the paper and making improvements. There may not even be an opportunity for the student to receive any feedback at all!

Evaluating Student Progress

Perhaps one of the most difficult skills that a new educator must acquire is the ability to evaluate a student's progress. This skill does not come automatically or even easily. It requires effort, practice, experimentation, and trial and error. Fair, objective, and timely grading policies are essential. Sometimes assignments reinforce the notion that the students did not distill the amount of knowledge that you had planned or that they'd missed the point of the presentation or demonstration. You thought it was clear; maybe it wasn't. Yet grading assignments, essays, and exams can also be rewarding. When you read a clearly expressed thought that shows the student has synthesized information, you are filled with a sense that you have successfully imparted knowledge. Those are the exciting moments that make teaching so worthwhile!

Accommodating Different Learning Styles

One of the skills that an educator must develop is that of accommodating different learning styles. Most people would likely teach in the way that they learn best. Some people learn from a lecture very easily while others need to be able to see flow diagrams, photographs, schematics, and maps, and rely on connections to examples and concrete materials. Still other students must have a participatory experience in order to fully grasp concepts. Educators develop techniques that are aimed toward a variety of these learning styles so that all students can benefit from a presentation. Perhaps you will incorporate a number of teaching styles in a single class meeting, or perhaps over the course of a few weeks, you will present in different ways.

Now let's compare and contrast several factors as they relate to the two settings we've been discussing, middle and high school versus college.

Typical Workday Responsibilities

Comparing the middle and high school work environment to that of the college setting is difficult because, even though all three are classified as educators, their duties, responsibilities, and schedules are quite different. For example, many college professors don't take attendance in their classes and some don't even require it. The middle and high school teacher, on the other hand, must be careful to account for each and every student, each and every hour. Middle and high school teachers meet frequently with parents to discuss student progress or other issues. College professors seldom, if ever, have such meetings.

College professors have significant freedom to teach what they believe to be the truth; sometimes such issues are controversial, but owing to the maturity of the audience, subjects can be covered that could not be broached with younger students. The teaching schedule for the middle and high school teacher is often quite rigid with little ability for flex, while at the college level, there is sometimes the opportunity to cancel a class, reschedule for another hour, or hold a meeting outside the prescribed time frame for the course. Teachers at the middle and high school levels frequently have five to seven class meetings per day. They often have a free period where they can regroup, work on assignments, grade papers, prepare for the next class, or have a peaceful lunch. College professors, on the other hand, have classes that meet with much less frequency. Typically, professors at institutions where the primary focus is upon teaching might be assigned three to four classes per semester that each meet two to three times per week for a total of nine to twelve hours. At large research institutions, professors are often responsible for one to two classes per semester. Of course, there are lots of other duties and expectations for the college professor outside the classroom, including committee work, writing, and office hours.

Student Behavior

Another significant difference between the middle and high school setting and the college setting has to do with student behavior. Discipline is not a problem for the majority of college and university professors. Most college-age students do not disrupt classes. They have chosen to pay a sum of money to be in attendance. College students want to learn. There are exceptional cases where a student behaves inappropriately, but these are few and far between. At the middle and high school levels, however, dealing with student behavioral problems is a daily part of the teacher's job. Additionally, most colleges and universities don't enforce a dress code, while very strict dress codes are in place at many middle and high schools.

Managing Your Classroom

If you have prepared for a teaching career in the middle or high school classroom setting, you most likely have taken a number of education courses where you first observed a classroom, then learned how to develop lesson plans, and finally learned to manage a classroom. You likely became aware very quickly that classroom management can be very challenging. Students in the middle and high schools are not there necessarily because they wish to be. There often is lots of resistance to learning, and many adolescents try to impress their friends and classmates, often with disruptive behavior. Classroom management is a skill that can be learned. Over time most teachers develop a very good set of techniques to handle various situations, and you will too.

College and university professors, surprisingly enough, usually have had no formal training in this area. As mentioned earlier, this is not often a problem at this level. But, classroom management is not confined merely to disciplinary matters. Timing and pace are critical. Did I deliver this material effectively? Did the students follow the material? Was my presentation well organized? Did I allow enough time for questions? Was the pace too slow or did I dwell on a single point too long? All of these are management issues that you will learn to deal with as your experience grows.

Supervision

College and university professors receive must less direct supervision compared to middle and high school teachers. For example, college professors may go weeks without hearing from their department chair outside of department meetings, while principals are much more attentive to supervisory responsibilities.

Scope and Depth of Environmentally Related Courses

Middle school and high school teachers will primarily teach individual courses that include environmentally related subjects, while college and university teachers focus their attention on specific kinds of environmental subjects. A note is appropriate here on environmental education at the middle and high school levels. Few public schools have distinct courses that focus upon the environment. A new teacher would most likely be able to include units in an earth science, chemistry, or biology class that emphasize the environment, but it is less likely that the teacher would be given the opportunity to deliver a course with a primary focus on environmental issues. Higher education has many more opportunities to focus solely on environmental issues. The remaining four paths, environmental policy, planning, and management; environmental sciences; environmental technology; and environmental engineering, are all areas in which the college or university environmental studies professor might specialize.

Academic Freedom

Creativity and content at the middle and high school levels are limited by local and state standards. There are certain topics that must be carefully addressed. You have some input into the material covered, but you are governed by external forces such as local school boards and state boards of education. It is likely that course textbooks will be selected by someone other than yourself. They may not be the latest editions, and the material could be out of date. It is your job to use the best material from these texts and add in more current information of your own from other sources. There are ways, then, that you can be creative even when you find yourself in a restrictive environment.

The college or university setting is very different from middle or high school. The level of freedom and creativity is not remotely comparable. A committee of the discipline responsible for the course usually governs course content for introductory classes. But the development of upper level classes is usually at the discretion of the faculty member offering the course. This is where creativity enters the profession, because the topics covered are those that you regard as important or interesting. Not a committee, not a school board, nor a state or federal mandate.

Other Duties

You can expect lots of other duties aside from teaching science classes, too. Often, middle and high school teachers are expected to monitor study halls, take a turn at lunchroom duty, and act as chaperones for various activities. There are department and school wide meetings to attend and parent-teacher conferences to prepare for. Some teachers are asked by their students to act as advisors for clubs or the yearbook. Some serve as a coach for an athletic team or a club sport. None of these activities are to be regarded as exceptional; they are merely part of a typical day. Attendance records; evaluations; grading of quizzes, exams, and essays; and preparation of report cards will consume your time. Most of this work is accomplished outside of school hours. Planning for classroom presentations, creating meaningful activities, designing assignments, and preparing lectures demand a great deal of time and energy. But, preparation of these sorts of materials and activities is fun!

Teaching in Traditional Settings

Here are some final notes to consider.

All That Time Off! You might have noticed that we didn't mention the amount of time away from the responsibilities of the classroom. Sure, educators at all levels do enjoy long breaks. But those breaks are simply from classroom meeting time. Most educators will spend much of their break time working. There is an endless parade of meetings, planning sessions, curriculum development workshops, reading, lecture writing, course revision, professional development, research, travel to professional meetings, and committee meetings. But, even with all of these demands there is still considerable flexibility during your time off. You have a large measure of control over when, where, and how you focus your time and effort.

The Reality of Teaching. Some aspects of a teaching career in the middle and high schools are not all positive, and you are likely already aware of many of these. Student behavioral problems are principal among these. Lack of support from both parents and administrators is often cited by veteran teachers as an issue. Declining budgets resulting in a lack of resources have been suggested as problems for decades. And dealings with uncooperative school boards is a difficulty encountered by teachers in some districts.

Those interested in teaching in higher education also need to be aware of several kinds of situations. It can be very difficult to get tenure, and some candidates do not get a decision until well into their service period at the school. And some schools face the budget challenges often found at the middle and high school levels. This can result in facility degradation, old equipment, and inadequate library holdings.

WORKING CONDITIONS: NONTRADITIONAL SETTINGS

Oftentimes in the traditional classroom setting the learner is there only because it is required. Educators working in nontraditional settings have the pleasure of working with learners who want to be there! Members of the general public who are interested in the mission of your organization, teachers who want to learn more, schoolchildren escaping their school-day routine, or campers heading off for a day or more away from home all make for a lively audience and hence a fun and challenging workday.

Environmental educators work in a variety of nontraditional classroom settings. The settings we will focus on here include: national, regional, and local nonprofit organizations and federal, state, and local governments.

Typical Workday Responsibilities

A variety of workday responsibilities await educators working in nontraditional settings. Work schedules may be nonstandard and working out-of-doors may be a regular part of the job. You'll need to prepare to educate a variety of audiences and create appropriate resources to do so. In the following sections, read about each of these factors that affect individuals working in nontraditional environmental education.

Nonstandard Work Schedules

Imagine if you will, an environmental educator working for a science center as an interpreter. The bulk of the work may take place in the summer months when the hours of the center are extended into the evening. Expectations for weekend work are also high as such institutions are open every day of the week to accommodate vacationers. Summer is when families can travel, when teachers have free time to take advantage of development activities, and when students are out of school and ready for opportunities like summer camps.

Working Outside

In a nontraditional setting there may be lots of outdoor work involved. Educators might be expected to construct outdoor displays, build trails and paths, lead interpretive hikes or canoe excursions on a pond or lake, or walk along the seashore at low tide to identify specimens.

Your Audiences Will Vary

Environmental educators working in nontraditional settings must be prepared for audiences with very different backgrounds, degrees of preparation, and highly varying ages and abilities. As an example, your assignment might be to develop a field experience that focuses on a local pond. If the audience is composed of fifth graders, you will have to be prepared to take a nontechnical approach with lots of hands-on examples, allowing the students to participate in the gathering of specimens. If the group is from Elder Hostel, you can accommodate people who are less needful of tactile examples and are much more willing and able to listen and learn effectively by simple observation. You must also be flexible because the ages of your audience may vary widely. A group of visiting biologists will require yet another very different approach. You must be prepared for technical discussions, probing questions, and people who might disagree with your interpretation. You'll need to know scientific names of specimens and be generally prepared at a much more technical level.

The General Public. In many positions, you'll be expected to cover a variety of subjects. You'll have to become an expert on a wide range of topics. Often the full range of natural history will become your world, from aquatic biology to landscape evolution, and from mammalian ecology to rock identification. For example, at the Science Center of New Hampshire, educators design and deliver programs aimed at the general public that focus upon the northern forest, flowering plants, watershed ecology, and geology of the Lakes Region of New Hampshire. They also design, build, and supervise the maintenance of displays of various types. The tasks are varied; you'll learn to be an environmental jack-of-all-trades.

A Destination for Class Field Trips. You might also be given an assignment to create opportunities for classroom teachers to bring their students to your nature center for field trips where the youngsters receive hands-on experiences with wildlife, earth science, and wetlands ecology. Environmental educators at such sites plan and lead field trips, identify areas suitable for river walks, and develop plant identification trails and interest points with significant elements of earth history. Again, the tasks and duties are highly variable.

Summer Learning Opportunities for School-Age Children. Many organizations generate summer programs for children of all ages, for families, and even for teachers. The Audubon Society holds such camps. Program leaders have created programs that focus upon the North Woods of Minnesota and Wisconsin, coastal kayaking along the rocky Maine coast, and trips that are directed toward bird-watchers. All of these programs require individuals trained in the environment but also prepared to educate at many levels, from small children to teenagers and adult learners. Four former employees of the National Wildlife Federation cooperated to establish the Wilderness Education Institute whose goal is to deliver quality outdoor programs to young people. This organization staffs its summer programs with environmental educators.

Professional Development Opportunities for Educators. Certain organizations provide opportunities for classroom teachers to enhance their knowledge of the environment. Summer institutes, where teachers can gain expertise in wetlands ecology, conservation and recycling, plant and wildlife identification, and earth science, for example, provide exciting settings for professional development.

Creating Effective Displays

Quite a number of organizations require staff to develop and maintain displays at museums and exhibits. Part of this is assessment of audience needs. Educators can contribute to this end. A display does little to educate the public if it is poorly designed, too static, aimed at a level that is over the head of the intended audience, or too elementary. Educators can help produce interactive and hands-on experiences that both attract and educate students of all ages.

There is such breadth to this category, it would be impossible to discuss all of the various settings in this type of book. You should be cautioned, if you are concerned about a nontraditional work schedule and/or responsibilities that require you to be exposed to the outdoors, do ask questions about job expectations during your interview. It is better to find out about these things up front than to have to deal with them after you've accepted the job.

TRAINING AND QUALIFICATIONS

Traditional environmental educators teach at various levels, including middle school, high school, and colleges and universities. The level that you choose will dictate the amount of required education needed for you to secure the proper credentials. Teaching at the middle and high school level requires a bachelor's degree in education while college and university educators must have at least a master's degree, and preferably a doctorate.

Those individuals teaching in nontraditional settings can bring quite a variety of degrees to any given job. Listings may state an education requirement in the following way, "Biology, Environmental Science, or a related field." And the key here is the notion of a related field. If you can fulfill the basic position requirements, the actual degree itself becomes less relevant.

Show That You Can Teach

Teaching is a skill, and like any other skill, it can be learned. No matter which environment you plan to teach in, you'll need to prove that you can teach.

Middle and High Schools. Middle and high school environmental science teachers usually prepare for their careers by completing a science education degree program. Such programs deliver content area, such as biology, geology, chemistry, meteorology, resource issues, conservation, and geography in addition to courses that enable students to develop the skills necessary to handle a classroom, prepare lesson plans, and develop meaningful demonstrations, discussions, and other activities. The capstone for many of these courses of study includes a semester where the student teacher leaves campus and actually teaches a course under the guidance of an experienced teacher. State certification often requires participation in the National Teachers Exam (NTE).

Teacher certification requirements vary from state to state. Some states have reciprocal certification agreements with a number of other states. You can check certification requirements at academploy.com/resources.cfm. At the time of this writing, approximately forty-three states had certification requirements posted here.

Colleges. College and university teaching requires a terminal degree. This usually means completion of a doctorate. Some schools will, however, hire those who have completed all course work for the degree and lack only the dissertation. Junior and community colleges will sometimes hire full-time faculty with master's degrees, but are more often looking for those with a completed doctorate.

College and university teachers usually have not participated in formal education classes. Most often, college professors are thrown into the classroom with little or no instruction on such topics as developing a syllabus, preparing for and delivering a lecture, or engaging students in classroom dialogue. Instead, they often model the style of their favorite professors, the ones who most inspired them, the teachers who most made them want to learn.

Nontraditional Settings. If your interest lies in working in nontraditional educational settings and you don't have a degree in education, you'll need to explain with concrete examples how your educational and work experiences have provided an opportunity for you to learn the teaching "tools of the trade." This may be the time to do some extracurricular reading to learn more about educational theory and how to educate populations of various ages. In any event, you will need to demonstrate very strong organizational and communication skills.

EARNINGS

Earnings for environmental educators will vary by the sector of the economy in which they are employed. Read on to learn more about starting wages in education (middle and high school, higher education), nonprofit, and government (federal, state, and local).

Middle and High Schools

Information about middle and high school teacher salaries at public schools is readily available through the school advertising the position. If a job advertisement does not include salary information, don't hesitate to contact the school directly. General information about teacher salaries is published by the American Federation of Teachers and is available on their website (aft.com). Look for a table titled "Actual Average Beginning Teacher Salaries." At the time of publication, the beginning salary range went from a high of $33,676 in Alaska to a low of $20,422 in North Dakota. The average beginning teacher salary in the United States was $27,989.

Higher Education

Several factors affect the salary of environmental educators working in higher education. A few of these include the region in which the institution is located, whether the campus is in an urban versus rural setting, and the type of institution. For example, you will find variation among the average salaries paid at a community college versus a four-year university versus a comprehensive, doctoral-degree-granting institution. *The Chronicle of Higher Education* regularly publishes articles about salaries. Copies of this publication are widely available on most college campuses or you can visit their website (chronicle.com). Or talk to your current or former advisor about starting salaries.

Nonprofit Organizations

Earnings for educators working in the nonprofit sector most often are lower than what is offered to teachers who are employed in traditional classroom settings. Salary survey information for nonprofit environmental educators is not available as such. Starting salary information available at the time this book went to press indicated that pay ranged from $11,700 plus room and board at an environmental camp to $35,000 at a national nonprofit organization.

Federal Government

New college graduates with a bachelor's degree, no matter what the job title, can expect to obtain jobs at the General Schedule (GS) 5–7 level depending on academic achievement. Starting pay for these levels in the year 2001 was $21,947–$27,185, although GS pay is adjusted geographically and the majority of jobs pay a higher salary. If you would like to find out more about federal government salaries, visit the Office of Personnel Management's home page at usajobs.opm.gov.

State Government

Job titles relating to environmental education will vary by state. And there will be multiple types of jobs within a state that require this kind of work. So you will also find a wider range of salaries than at the federal government level. Your best bet is to find some sample job titles and descriptions that interest you, then check with the state employment office to find out the starting salary levels for those jobs. Information is available online, but each state arranges its employment information differently, so it may require patience on your part. Don't hesitate to call the state employment office to obtain starting salary information once you have a job title or two that interest you. Appendix A lists the employment site for nearly every state's Web page.

Local Government

As with state government environmental education jobs, the titles will vary as will the salaries paid. Contact the local governments where you think you may like to work and talk with the human resources manager about job titles and related salaries.

CAREER OUTLOOK

Employment of environmental educators varies by employment setting. Traditional educational opportunities are expected to grow, while government employment is expected to decline. Review each of the sections below to learn more about the career outlook for the various sectors of the economy in which you may be interested.

Middle and Secondary Schools

The *Occupational Outlook Handbook* (http://stats.bls.gov/ocohome.htm) indicates than middle school teaching positions are expected to grow as fast as the average (10 to 20 percent) through the year 2008, while employment for secondary school teachers will grow faster than the average (21 to 35 percent) for all occupations.

Higher Education

Employment for college and university educators is supposed to grow faster than the average through 2008 according to the *Occupational Outlook Handbook*. Please be aware that competition for tenure-track jobs will be keen. Almost one-third of this group of teachers works part-time in education. Some do so by choice, but an increasing number are forced into this category by a variety of changes taking place in colleges and universities.

Nonprofit Organizations

Official statistics for environmental education jobs in the nonprofit sector are just not available. What we can tell you, though, is that we found thousands of job listings as we researched this book. Many were entry level and looked like reasonable places to begin a career in environmental education in a nontraditional setting. Use the information in this chapter to explore the reality of finding employment in this sector.

Government

According to the U.S. Department of Labor's Career Guide to Industries (http://stats.bls.gov/oco/cg), federal employment is projected to decline slightly due to budgetary constraints, the growing use of private contractors, and the transfer of some functions to state and local governments.

POSSIBLE EMPLOYERS

A range of potential employers is described in this section. Whether you are interested in working in a traditional educational setting (middle or high school, higher education), a nonprofit organization (national, regional, local), for a government agency (federal, state, local), or camps, information is provided that will help you in your job search. Read those sections that interest you and follow up on the information provided.

Middle and High Schools

There are some different settings to consider at the middle and high school levels. Public schools, private schools, and Department of Defense schools are three of the primary options.

Help in Locating These Employers. Public middle and high school jobs are usually well advertised, so be sure to check classified ads appearing in newspapers that serve the geographic area where you hope to work. If you are thinking about relocating, many of these classifieds can be found online. If there are specific schools where you'd like to work, contact them directly. In addition, specialized services, such as the American Association for Employment in Education's *Project Connect* (ub-careers.buffalo.edu/aaee), offer job listings. A username and password are required for this website and can be obtained through your college's career office. Other websites, including k12jobs.com or http://altavistacareers.careercast.com, list teacher job openings.

Private school positions are not as easy to find. Work with personnel at your college career office to find out more about the job fairs that are held and to obtain sources that list the schools and their contact information.

Department of Defense schools educate the children of military and civilian personnel who are in service both stateside and abroad. You can find out more about job opportunities and how to apply for them by visiting odedodea.edu.

Higher Education

Institutions of higher education include community colleges, technical colleges, and public and private colleges and universities. Some community colleges in metropolitan areas can be as large as many private schools. Programs or departments looking for environmental educators might include: natural resources, comparative ecology, oceanography, marine biology, environmental science and policy, and environmental studies, just to name a few.

Help in Locating These Employers. Many jobs available in higher education are advertised in *The Chronicle of Higher Education* (chronicle.com). Paper copies of this publication are widely available in college departmental offices and in the library. You can view older job listings via their website. Institutional Web pages usually contain a link to current job listings. And environmentally related websites, such as Environmental Career Opportunities Jobs in Higher Education (ecojobs.com/higher-ed.htm), will often include job advertisements for higher education.

Federal, State, and Local Governments

Park rangers and naturalists, docents, and field interpreters work as environmental educators for local, state, and national parks. The National Park Service, for example, employs environmental educators as interpreters at its various exhibits at national battlefield sites, national parks, and national monuments. Aside from leading interpretive walks and tours, educators also make presentations, help to create indoor and outdoor displays, and develop educational and supportive materials.

Help in Locating These Employers. Your best bet for locating federal jobs is the U.S. Office of Personnel Management's website (usajobs.opm.gov) or check the websites of the various federal departments that are of interest to you. The Nonprofit Career Network's website (nonprofitcareer.com) also lists government jobs. State jobs are listed at state employment offices, in regional newspapers, and on websites. Appendix A shows the Internet addresses for personnel offices for most of the states. Local government jobs are often listed in local newspapers. Don't hesitate to place a call to the personnel department to find out how they advertise their job openings.

National Nonprofit Organizations

Several very large national organizations are dedicated to the protection of the environment. Included in this group are The National Wildlife Federation (nwf.org), National Audubon Society (audubon.org), the Sierra Club (sierraclub.org), Student Conservation Association (sca-inc.org), Greenpeace (greenpeacecanada.org; greenpeaceusa.org), and the World Wildlife Fund (worldwildlife.org).

Many of these groups have developed strong programs for the schools. Resource packets of education materials, with lesson plans, visuals and graphics, worksheets, ideas for projects, such as the installation of a pond on school property, and plans to make equipment to use in gathering and displaying specimens are presented. These activity programs are developed by environmental educators who work in settings other than the traditional classroom.

Help in Locating These Employers. Be sure to check the websites of each of the organizations listed above for national job listings and also for links to regional and local chapters that will have their own job listings posted. Also check the Nonprofit Career Center's site (nonprofitcareer.com), *The NonProfit Times* site (nptimes.com), and a site that is dedicated to nonprofit job listings (nonprofitjobs.org).

Regional or Local Nonprofit Organizations

Charlotte (NC) Women for Environmental Justice, the Society for Protection of New Hampshire Forests, and many other similar organizations employ staff naturalists whose charge is to create interpretive programs, analyze the value of land tracts proposed as donations to the trust, and perform the more mundane tasks of plant and animal identifications. They also serve as program leaders and nature interpreters. Creativity and perseverance will be the key to finding regional and local nontraditional environmental education jobs.

Help in Locating These Employers. Nonprofit organizations like Action Without Borders (idealist.org) seek to find solutions to environmental problems and they use the Web to advertise jobs for member organizations. ACCESS: Networking in the Public Interest, a nonprofit employment clearinghouse (accessjobs.org) includes some job listings for environmental educators. A good "umbrella" website that you might want to visit is the Foundation Center's Researching Philanthropy page (http://fdncenter.org/research). It has links to nonprofit websites, some of which include job listings. AssociationCentral.com (associationcentral.com/jobs) works in conjunction with Headhunter.net and the American Society of Association Executives to offer job listings. Another umbrella organization is GuideStar (guidestar.org). Their website can link you to hundreds of thousands of nonprofit organizations. Keywords *environmental education* bring up more than 900 organizations. You can then link to these organizations and any jobs they have posted. And finally, the following umbrella site: (http://dir.hotbot.lycos.com/society/issues/environment/) links you with sites related to environmental education, jobs, and organizations.

Camps

Camps are no longer just for children and operated just in the summer. There is a wide range of camps in operation all year long and they serve every age group. Many are focused on helping people learn about the environment.

Help in Locating These Employers. The American Camping Association (acacamps.org) website contains valuable information about careers in camping, including job descriptions, qualifications, professional development core areas, salary information, career potential, and how to prepare for a career in camping. There were almost 300 matches on their website when looking for camps with environmental programs. Many such jobs are posted at various Internet sites and can be accessed by searching with the keywords: *environmental education jobs*. For example, camppage.com lists summer camping

jobs for boys' camps, girls' camps, coed camps, Canadian camps, and expe-
dition programs. The Camp & Conference home page links to a variety of
camping associations and organizations. Be sure to review the sites associated with the organizations listed at the end of the chapter. And you may
also want to review the publication, *Opportunities in Summer Camp Careers.*

STRATEGY FOR FINDING THE JOB

Those graduates seeking traditional classroom environmental education jobs
will use a different strategy than those seeking nontraditional education jobs.
Strategies are outlined for middle and high school educators, college and university educators, and nontraditional educators.

Middle and High Schools

If your employment goal is to teach middle and high school students and
you want to include environmental issues in some of your classes, the road
to a successful job hunt includes several steps. You'll want to establish a credentials file at your college or university, utilize the network your professors
and advisors have established, review job advertisements, attend job fairs, and
contact schools where you'd like to work.

Establish a Credentials File. Some college and university education departments or career offices administer credential files for their education majors.
Files can include résumés, letters of recommendation, transcripts, writing
samples, and limited portfolios. The use of these files reduces demands on
professors in terms of having to write multiple letters of recommendation
for their students and demands on the college's transcript office. Generally
all a student needs to do is complete paperwork that details where the file
should be mailed and pay a fee to cover processing and mailing costs. Be
sure to find out whether your institution offers this service.

Use Established Networks. Often your professors and career office professionals are well established at the institution and they have developed a wide
network of contacts in the community, the region, and throughout the state.
If you have earned the respect of your professors and have taken the time
to work with the career professionals at your school, you will find that they
are more than willing to provide contact names and insights into the schools
that have posted job advertisements.

Review Job Advertisements. Jobs at the middle and high school level are widely advertised so you shouldn't have any problem identifying current openings. Check local and regional newspapers. Don't forget, many of these openings can be accessed via the Internet by entering as keywords the names of newspapers published in the area where you'd like to work.

Attend Job Fairs. Your college or university may organize job fairs for education majors. These events bring together potential employers and the students who are looking for teaching jobs. Every school hiring official tries to identify candidates who will be a "good fit" for their school. Job fairs offer these officials an opportunity to informally meet with potential interviewees and develop lists of people who they'd like to know more about. Check with your career office and don't overlook the importance of attending this kind of event.

Contact Schools Directly. As you finish your degree program you'll have heard about various schools and school districts in your region and state and you may have made some decisions about where you'd like to work. Don't hesitate to contact these districts and schools directly to find out how you should go about applying for current and future positions.

Higher Education

The primary audience for the Great Jobs series includes those people who are going to or who have recently attained a bachelor's degree. Nearly every teaching job in higher education requires a doctorate, so we won't go into great detail here on the strategy for finding collegiate-level teaching positions. Note that three important tasks include networking at regional and national professional meetings held for your specific environmental discipline, utilizing contacts your advisor and committee may refer you to, and reviewing job listings in appropriate publications, including *The Chronicle of Higher Education.*

Government

As you might expect, a well-defined process is in place for federal, state, and local government employment. The Internet can be a valuable tool for helping you gain employment in the public sector. But don't overlook the importance of networking. Review Chapter 4 as you think about seeking employment in the public sector.

Understand How the System Works. The federal government and each state and local government has a system in place that guides how new employees are evaluated and hired. Be sure you understand the system for the governmental unit where you'd like to work.

Complete All Necessary Paperwork with Care. Part of the system mentioned above involves paperwork. Be sure to carefully read all instructions and follow them to a "T" otherwise your application may be discarded.

Gather All the Required Supporting Documents. Be sure that transcripts and letters of support have been mailed, and check that others who must provide information needed to complete your application have done so.

Follow Up. Government employers are just like any other employer. They are interested in hiring people who want to work for them. So follow up on your government applications the same way you would if applying in the private sector.

Nonprofit Organizations

If you are interested in working in the nonprofit world, there are three essential activities to undertake. They include customizing your résumé for each job, highlighting relevant specialized skills you possess, and personalizing your interest in the organization's mission. The following three sections describe the needed efforts.

Customize Your Résumé for Each Job. Employers want to know that you read the job description that they crafted and paid to advertise. Don't let your résumé look like it could have been written for any old job. Customize your objective statement, craft your work history to highlight the relevant experience you have obtained, and list course work that is directly linked to the job you will be performing.

Highlight Relevant Specialized Skills. In either your cover letter or your résumé be sure to describe any special skills you bring to the table. You might be able to talk about your ability to use spreadsheets and databases, or your knowledge of GIS, or your weekend use of a GPS as you hiked local trails. Don't miss the opportunity to highlight your skills.

Personalize Your Interest in the Organization's Mission. Many people choose to work in the nonprofit sector because they deeply believe in a cause and want to spend their life's work furthering it. Your cover letter presents a good opportunity to express the feelings you have about helping others learn about the environment. Craft your letters carefully and see what a positive impact it will have on your job search.

POSSIBLE JOB TITLES

As you can see from the list of job titles shown here, environmental educators are not just called teachers. Add to this list as you review job advertisements.

Camp director	Park naturalist
Camp staffer	Park ranger
Director of education	Professor (assistant, associate, full)
Education naturalist	Program coordinator
Educator	Program director
Environmental education instructor	Program instructor
Environmental educator	Program leader
Instructor	Program staffer
Lecturer	Senior naturalist
Naturalist	Teacher
Nature interpreter	Trip leader
Outdoor environmental instructor	Workshop manager

RELATED OCCUPATIONS

As we've discussed, the environmental educator uses a variety of skills and many are transferable to other settings. Your respect for the natural environment, your ability to operate as an effective team member, and your strong communication skills would all be useful in the jobs shown below. If any of these job titles strike your interest, be sure to explore them using the strategies discussed earlier in this book.

Conference coordinator	Not-for-profit administrator
Counselor: career; financial aid	Public relations specialist
Educational administrator	Researcher
Employment interviewer	Sales representative
Librarian	Training specialist
Lobbyist	Writer

PROFESSIONAL ASSOCIATIONS

American Association of University Professors
1012 Fourteenth St. NW, Ste. 500
Washington, DC 20005-3465
Members/Purpose: College and university faculty members, administrators, graduate students, and the general public. Advances academic freedom and shared governance, defines fundamental professional values and standards for higher education, and ensures higher education's contribution to the common good.
Training: Conducts training, meetings, and conferences
Journals/Publications: *Academe; AAUP Today; Faculty Salary Report; Footnotes; ASC Newsletter; CBC Newsletter*
Job Listings: None
Website/E-mail: aaup.org; aaup@aaup.org

American Camping Association
5000 State Rd. 67 N
Martinsville, IN 46151-7902
Members/Purpose: Camp owners, directors, counselors, camps, businesses, and students interested in resident and day camp programs for youth and adults. Conducts camp standards and camp director certification programs. Offers information services in several areas including educational programs.
Journals/Publications: *Guide to Accredited Camps; Camping Magazine; Facilities for Conferences, Retreats and Outdoor Education*
Job Listings: Sponsors placement service
Website: acacamps.org

American Park and Recreation Society
1800 Silas Deane Hwy., No. 1
Rocky Hill, CT 06067
Members/Purpose: Professional park and recreation directors who provide cultural, physical, and intellectual opportunities in recreational settings throughout the country.
Training: Conducts educational sessions and research symposia at annual congressional meetings
Journals/Publications: *APRS National Resource Directory; Keeping You Current* (newsletter); *Programmer's Information Network*
Job Listings: Must join NRPA to access the job bulletin board on the site.
Website: nrpa.org

Greenpeace Canada
250 Dundas St. W, Ste. 605
Toronto, ON M5T 2Z5
Canada

Greenpeace USA
702 H St. NW
Washington, DC 20001
Members/Purpose: An independent campaigning organization that uses nonviolent direct action and creative communication to expose global environmental problems and to promote solutions that are essential to a green and peaceful future.
Training: Available to members and employees
Journals/Publications: Variety of fact sheets, reports, brochures available online
Job Listings: Jobs and internships posted on website
Website: greenpeacecanada.org; greenpeaceusa.org

National Association for Interpretation
P.O. Box 2246
Ft. Collins, CO 80522
Members/Purpose: Specialists who prepare exhibits and conduct programs at information centers maintained by public and private institutions; persons engaged in education programs at museums, zoos, parks, arboretums, botanical gardens, historical sites, schools, and camps. Seeks to advance education and develop skills in interpreting the natural, historical, and cultural environment.
Training: Provides national training opportunities; conducts regional training workshops
Journals/Publications: Directory of members; *Legacy; Journal of Interpretation*
Job Listings: Provides information on job opportunities through employment hotlines and listings
Website: interpnet.com

National Audubon Society
700 Broadway
New York, NY 10003
Members/Purpose: Persons interested in ecology, energy, and the conservation and restoration of natural resources, with emphasis on wildlife, wildlife habitats, soil, water, and forests.

Training: Local chapters sponsor education programs
Journals/Publications: *American Birds; Audubon; Audubon Activist; Audubon Adventures; Wildlife Report*
Job Listings: Available on their website
Website/E-mail: audubon.org; join@audubon.org

National Wildlife Federation

11100 Wildlife Center Dr.
Reston, VA 20190-5362
Members/Purpose: To educate, inspire, and assist individuals and organizations of diverse cultures to conserve wildlife and other natural resources and to protect the earth's environment in order to achieve a peaceful, equitable, and sustainable future.
Training: Offers a range of education programs including: Backyard Wildlife Habitat, NatureLink, Family Summits, Animal Tracks, National Wildlife Week, Campus Ecology, Earth Tomorrow
Journals/Publications: *National Wildlife; International Wildlife; Conservation Directory*
Job Listings: Provides information on job opportunities through website listings
Website: nwf.org

National Wildlife Refuge Association

10824 Fox Hunt Ln.
Potomac, MD 20854
Members/Purpose: Conservation clubs, National Audubon Society chapters, birding groups, NWR employees and retirees, and interested individuals. Seeks to protect the integrity of the National Wildlife Refuge System and to increase public understanding and appreciation of it.
Training: Conducts education and information programs
Journals/Publications: *Blue Goose Flyer*
Job Listings: None
Website/E-mail: refugenet.com; nwra@refugenet.org

North American Association for Environmental Education

NAAEE, 8th Fl.
1825 Connecticut Ave. NW
Washington, DC 20009-5708
Members/Purpose: Individuals associated with colleges, public schools, nature centers, government agencies, and environmental organizations;

associates include students in environmental education and environmental studies.

Training: Annual conferences

Journals/Publications: *The Environmental Communicator;* newsletter; conference proceedings

Job Listings: Jobs and internships listed on website

Website: naaee.org

Sierra Club

85 Second St., Second Fl.

San Francisco, CA 94105-3441

Members/Purpose: Protect the wild places of the earth, practice and promote the responsible use of the earth's ecosystems and resources, and educate and enlist humanity to protect and restore the quality of the natural and human environment.

Training: Arranges outings

Journals/Publications: *Sierra* magazine

Job Listings: Internships and jobs listed on main and chapter websites

Website: sierraclub.org

Student Conservation Association

P.O. Box 550

Charlestown, NH 03603

Members/Purpose: Provider of national and community conservation service opportunities, outdoor education and career training for youth

Training: Provides on-the-job training through volunteer and internship opportunities it facilitates

Journals/Publications: *e-Volunteer* (monthly electronic newsletter)

Job Listings: Volunteer, internship, and employment opportunities listed on website

Website: sca-inc.org

Wilderness Education Association

P.O. Box 158897

Nashville, TN 37215

Members/Purpose: To promote the professionalization of outdoor leadership and to thereby improve the safety and quality of outdoor trips and enhance the conservation of the wild outdoors. Trains and certifies outdoor leaders; operates in affiliation with thirty colleges, universities, and

outdoor programs. Conducts National Standard Program for Outdoor Leadership Certification.
Training: Offers training to employers, administrative agencies, insurance companies, and the public. Sponsors special courses for experienced professionals.
Journals/Publications: *WEA Legend; Wilderness Education Association Affiliate* handbook
Job Listings: Job referral service for members
Website/E-mail: wildernesseducation.org; wea@edge.net

Wilderness Education Institute
(No address information available)
Members/Purpose: To empower youth and their families to create positive change in their lives and for the earth's environment by simplifying lifestyles, exploring nature, experiencing personal growth, and building communities.
Training: None
Journals/Publications: None
Job Listings: Summer employment opportunities listed on website
Website: weiprograms.org

World Wildlife Fund
1250 Twenty-Fourth St. NW
P.O. Box 97180
Washington, DC 20090-7180
Members/Purpose: Preserves wild places, saves endangered species, and addresses global threats.
Training: Website contains education links
Journals/Publications: *Living Planet* magazine
Job Listings: Job opportunities listed on the website
Website: worldwildlife.org

11

PATH 2: ENVIRONMENTAL POLICY, PLANNING, AND MANAGEMENT

That slippery substance, petroleum, moves our world. Without a sustained flow of processed petroleum, what we call gasoline, people and economies literally come to a grinding halt. The use of petroleum-processing by-products, including plastics, shapes the quality of life for residents of nearly every nation, including the United States and Canada. When the world's petroleum reserves are depleted—and some scientists estimate that date to be approximately 2040—life on earth will drastically change.

RESOURCES DEFINED

Resources, as used in this book, are materials that humans draw upon to meet their needs and wants for living. This is a purposefully very broad definition. As we explore the topic of resources, we must examine several factors, including availability, distribution, renewability, and strategic value in order to gain a reasonable understanding of the situation.

Availability and Distribution

Some resources such as water, air, soil, and plant life are, generally speaking, readily available across the surface of the earth. Most other resources are found below the surface of the earth, so availability is affected by the distribution that has been created by natural processes. Geology, rather than political boundaries, governs the occurrence of minerals. For example, gold, silver, antimony, and copper have small raw supplies because they occur in association with relatively scarce igneous and metamorphic rocks. However, limestone, which is used in fertilizers and steelmaking, is in relatively large supply. It is is associated with deposition in vast ocean basins.

Renewability

Some resources are renewable, while others are not. Much of the world's timber supply is grown on tree farms and most of the shrimp and salmon that we consume are "farm" raised, and thus, renewable. Resources such as coal, natural gas, and petroleum are nonrenewable because current supplies can and will be exhausted.

Strategic Value

A resource having strategic value is one that is necessary to our modern economy. A number of resources that are classified as "strategic" by the U.S. government do not naturally occur within its political boundaries. Cobalt, chromium, manganese, and platinum, which are essential in the U.S. metallurgical and electronics industries, are distributed irregularly across the earth and tend to be concentrated in what are now politically unstable nations. Others, like iron, petroleum, and coal, are available within the United States, but they require considerable effort to extract and process.

THE COMPLEXITY OF
ENVIRONMENTAL POLICY, PLANNING, AND MANAGEMENT

In 1971, Barry Commoner, who has been advocating, researching, and publishing about the environment for more than three decades, wrote *Laws of Ecology*. He described three tenets in this publication. First, he suggested that an intrusion into nature will have multiple effects, many of which will be unpredictable. Let's use the example of clear-cutting a mountain slope in the Pacific Northwest. Some of the effects might be increased and more rapid runoff, which will lead to accelerated erosion. Eroded sediments then make their way into stream courses, negatively impacting trout and salmon food supplies and leading to reproductive failure. Fewer fish, in turn, leads to fewer opportunities for fishermen. Fewer fishermen translates to an economic impact upon a community as motel reservations decrease, fewer meals are consumed in restaurants, and the need for guide services declines. All together, these impacts adversely affect tax revenues.

Professionals in the field of environmental policy, planning, and management have to be able to plan for, detect, and mitigate the effects of all kinds of environmental intrusions. Many of the implications of activities, such as logging and mining, are well known to scientists. But other issues, like global warming, are just beginning to be understood.

Commoner's second tenet is that people and nature are tightly bound. Changes in the natural environment impact society and society, in turn, impacts nature. Humans and nature are inextricably linked. There is no better example of this link than global warming. Beginning in the latter half of the nineteenth century, human activity set a temperature increase in motion. Enormous quantities of fossil fuels started being burned to support industrialized society. Earth mean temperatures are expected to continue to rise, as are greenhouse gas concentrations, including carbon dioxide. Now we must deal with the changes this temperature increase has wrought in the earth's terrestrial, atmospheric, biotic, and hydrologic subsystems.

Finally, by-products of human activities must be monitored to assure that negative impacts are minimized. Nearly everything that we do results in waste. A quick road trip to the mini-mart leads to carbon dioxide and carbon monoxide emissions. The car we drive requires the extraction of petroleum for the fuel and lubricants. This petroleum refining has its own associated wastes. Additionally, iron and limestone are mined to create steel to build the car. The resulting mines leave deep scars on the face of the earth and create areas that have no further use. We must be very careful to be as efficient as possible in using natural resources.

It is important that we undertake a full complement of actions given the strategic importance of and competition among all of the world economies for nonrenewable resources. Trained professionals are needed to develop policies, implement plans, and carefully manage current supplies of resources. Still more professionals are needed to undertake similar activities as a viable range of sustainable alternate resources and strategies are identified and put in place.

DEFINITION OF THE CAREER PATH

This career path involves the development and interpretation of natural resource policy, planning, and management (including development, conservation, and preservation) of the materials that humans need and want to sustain life. There is a focus on the interrelationships of people with earth systems, such as air, water, biota, soil, and landforms. This work is centered in the social sciences, but it demands a working knowledge of some combination of biology, chemistry, geography, geology, and other subjects. Without a foundation in the sciences, it is impossible to understand human impacts upon the environment and environmental impacts on humans.

Environmental policy, planning, and management are highly integrative subfields of environmental studies. People trained to work in this career path deal with the interface of the natural and social sciences. They, therefore, must understand and accommodate various perspectives on an issue, including science, policy development and interpretation, and management.

Environmental Policy

Environmental policy work involves the formulation of rules by which organizations must operate. The Environmental Protection Agency website (epa.gov) suggests that you might be interested in a policy development career if you have a background in the social sciences with negotiation skills and risk assessment. You would also, by necessity, possess a solid foundation in the natural sciences so that you can understand the complexity of the scientific matters addressed in the policies. Although you have to understand the science behind the issues and problems, you are not involved with field data gathering, lab analyses, and interpretation.

Environmental Planning

Environmental planning is the interpretation of policies and the formulation of plans that adhere to the policies. Environmental planners consider the allocation and use of resources in a manner that is consistent with fundamentally sound environmental practice. It is the planner's job to work with the landscape in light of the "rules" established by policy developers. Environmental planning involves a wide variety of issues, including land use and development, wetlands preservation, watershed protection, environmental quality, and toxic waste disposal, just to name a few.

Environmental Management

Environmental management is the ongoing execution of environmental plans. It stresses stewardship of the landscape and its resources, emphasizing ecology and social issues. It involves control over the processes of development with sustainability as a principal goal. Environmental managers seek to attain a balance between natural resource use and preservation. They identify goals for resource development and balance those with conservation, and then initiate and implement the means to achieve these goals. These activities can be intertwined, and sometimes all three of these tasks are completed by individuals working at planning agencies, in environmental law firms, or at nonprofit advocacy organizations.

Let's examine some actual recent job postings that fit within this career path. Then we'll summarize the common threads that run throughout jobs in this career path. The first position description is an excellent example of the environmental policy and planning subset of environmental studies where human skills play a more important role than field data gathering and analyses.

The (State) Center for Land Recycling. Requires background in urban policy and familiarity with landfills. Demonstrate the ability to do research, write proposals, and interact with community and volunteer groups. Candidate responsible for creating policy briefs, facilitating workshops, and identifying funding sources. Must also be able to work in groups and speak publicly. Bachelor's degree required.

Water Treatment and Wastewater Disposal Specialist. (Consulting firm) in San Francisco seeking person to fill a junior level position. Successful candidate expected to analyze and interpret data, and to prepare written reports that focus on various water projects. Requires degree in Environmental Policy with excellent writing skills.

Policy, planning, and management also deal with legislation that will ensure protection against over-exploitation of the natural environment. The development of new legislation requires research by technically oriented professionals who understand the impacts of such regulations and who can determine cost benefits and risks. Training in statistics, economics, land-use law, and risk analysis is important in dealing with legislative matters.

State Public Interest Research Groups (PIRG) advocate for consumer welfare and the environment in a number of ways. One is by educating the public about related issues. The education process might include sponsoring forums, organizing rallies, distribution of literature, and lobbying public officials.

(State) PIRG Legislative Advocate. Hiring person with a strong commitment to the environment who would be responsible for identifying, documenting, and developing solutions to environmental issues. The person selected would develop campaign strategies, lobby, broaden the support base, and help to draft legislation. Related degree required.

Watershed Leadership Program Coordinator. The (state) Rivers Alliance, in the (state capitol). Requires strong leadership and organizational skills working with nonprofits, an aptitude for public policy analysis, and an understanding of watershed science. Duties include: organizing public interest meetings to involve the public in watershed planning, constructing a grassroots volunteers organization, establishing a watershed guardian network, planning conferences, delivering presentations, conducting outreach, advocating for the organization, and fund-raising. Qualifications include: good written and oral communications skills, commitment to river conservation, basic understanding of aquatic ecosystems and hydrology, basic understanding of environmental laws, and public policy training. Degree in environmental policy preferred.

Restoration Coordinator, (national nonprofit), California. Organizational goals are to protect, restore, and manage lands along the river and the natural processes that sustain them. The position is responsible for planning, designing, coordinating, and monitoring programs to ensure scientific restoration of river corridor lands. This position involves the understanding of natural systems, data collection techniques, mapping, using GIS software, utilization of a number of different software types in order to produce reports, writing and editing of conservation plans, and goal setting and assessment. Planning degree preferred.

Conservation Coordinator II, The Lower (major) River Authority. Position involves development and implementation of water conservation programs for customers of municipal water authority. Duties include planning, implementation, and evaluation of established programs, including plumbing retrofit, clothes washer rebate programs, and a public school water conservation education agenda. Looking for someone who can communicate effectively in writing and verbally, make public presentations, and create educational materials. Environmental degree required.

Program Manager. The Tidelands of the (major) River is seeking to fill leadership position in an effort to address threats to critical natural systems in the Lower (state) River area. Duties include working with property owners, development of community partnerships, conservation planning, and fund-raising. Bachelor's degree in related field required.

NEPA Environmental Regulatory Analyst (UT). Develop NEPA expertise while supporting client contracts for EIS and Natural Resources Management Planning. Work with Department of Interior, with BLM, or for federal sites within Utah,

Nevada, Wyoming, Colorado, or Arizona. Must have excellent verbal & written communication skills. Must be able to handle multiple projects. Qualifications: B.S. degree in Natural Resources Management, Land Use Planning, Land Use Law, Public Administration, Public or Environmental Policy, Chemistry, or related field.

To summarize the commonalities in these positions, a range of skills is called for and many of these positions combine duties associated with each of the three major categories of policy, planning, and management—and sometimes more. It is extremely important that job-seekers be prepared by developing a solid understanding of scientific principles, knowing how to analyze and integrate sometimes apparently conflicting data, learning how to negotiate, gaining experience working on a team, being able to write clearly, and feeling comfortable speaking in public settings.

WORKING CONDITIONS

Many of the positions that fall under environmental policy, planning, and management are, by nature, office jobs that involve working with similarly trained individuals. The importance of teamwork and effective communication cannot be overemphasized. Positions often require at least some travel—a bit of field work or at least field visits, but most of the tasks will be completed indoors.

You might work for a government agency, a nonprofit, a planning agency, or an environmental consulting firm. Sometimes environmental policy analysts, planners, and managers are required to attend public hearings or meetings that take place during evening hours or on weekends. Deadlines are often associated with the documentation required of this work, so you may feel the pressure of either having to work overtime to prepare paperwork or, if you're working on the regulatory side, facing piles of paperwork immediately following the passage of a deadline. And interest groups often place pressure on individuals working in this field as efforts that are in conflict with their missions move through the planning process.

If you are excited about the prospect of advocating for the environment, doing research, developing planning and assessment documents, and managing projects and personnel, then this career path is just right for you.

TRAINING AND QUALIFICATIONS

The environmental policy, planning, and management career path encompasses a variety of jobs, and there is a corresponding variety in the training and qualifications required for these three activities. A minimum of a bachelor's degree is required. Review the job postings presented throughout this chapter and you'll find that quite a variety of degrees are acceptable. Your training should have included classes in effective communication, both written and verbal presentation. Courses in business negotiation, risk analysis, urban planning, business management, and policy analysis and development are all skills that will prove valuable as you advance in your career.

Environmental Policy

More specifically, classes that might prove especially valuable for someone interested in the policy analysis and development aspects of environmental studies include a substantial mix of regional, community, environmental, and urban planning; economics; public administration; public policy analysis; land use law; argumentation and debate; and philosophy courses, such as logic and ethics. Some combination of these classes will provide a solid foundation for careers in environmental policy. The two job descriptions shown below highlight this.

Environmental Policy Analyst. Apply environmental knowledge of land use tracking and work on a dynamic project. Qualifications: B.S. degree in environmental field. Experience in science and environmental policy a plus. Ability to provide support in organizing training sessions, conferences, and workshops. Knowledge of MS Office. Ability to create reports and presentations.

Environmental Analyst, Junior (MA). Support data quality and data assurance efforts for a large environmental project. Produce data reports using Infomaker or Access. Work in a team-oriented, challenging environment. Qualifications: B.A. or B.S. degree in environmental studies or a related field required. Knowledge of database programs, including Access, Excel, FoxPro, and InfoMaker. Knowledge of GIS. Possession of solid verbal communication skills. Knowledge of report writing, data gathering, and researching. Possession of excellent detail-oriented and analytical skills required. Knowledge of environmental processes a plus.

Environmental Planning

Specialists in environmental planning should also develop a foundation of courses in the sciences, then build onto that a selection of courses such as urban, regional, community, and environmental planning; resource conservation; environmental biology; freshwater ecology; hydrology; conservation economics; Geographic Information Systems; aerial photograph interpretation; remote sensing; landscape architecture; horticulture; soil science; natural hazards; and environmental geology. It is obvious that if you were to take classes in all of these areas of study, it would require about seven years to obtain a bachelor's degree. Instead, highlight the core of relevant courses you have completed and indicate a willingness to continue learning whatever is needed. The following job postings show that you can bring a core of basic skills to the employment arena and build new skills on the job.

Research Associate/Transportation Planner (nonprofit), Washington, DC. Seeking a creative and motivated individual to advance economic and environmental goals through research, policy development, and planning. Will have considerable responsibility for carrying out national-level research and advocacy projects in the program area. Areas of focus will include travel demand management, improving energy-efficiency of goods movement, and marketing of fuel-efficient vehicles. Conduct studies and author reports. Work with representatives of other organizations in coordinated efforts to achieve policy outcomes. Obtain and analyze data and prepare technical summaries. Represent organization in public forums and meetings with public officials. Minimum of a bachelor's degree in relevant academic area. Strong verbal & written communication skills. Ability to work independently. Any of the following would be advantageous: familiarity with travel demand and land use models; knowledge of freight movement issues; and interest in social marketing.

Environmental Planner (national consulting firm), MD. Undertake natural and socioeconomic analyses in support of environmental impact statement development, environmental assessments, & categorical exclusion evaluations. B.S. in related field required.

Environmental Management

Environmental management involves the implementation of plans that are based on policies. Therefore, it is imperative for people working in this area to have the usual scientific foundation, but added to that would be a strong layer of business classes that might include organizational communications and behavior, management science, business law, land use law, and public relations. Planning, conservation, and public policy are also valuable courses that will prepare you for this endeavor.

Environmental Project Manager. Facilitate environmental projects by assisting client government agency. Candidate should possess understanding of CEQA and will help prepare an EIR from start to finish. Candidate should also have the ability to review technical documents related to CEQA. Ideal Candidate: Looking for someone who is presentable and able to effectively communicate. B.S. degree required.

Environmental Protection Program Manager (federal agency research center), CA. Entry-level position. Looking for detail-oriented team player willing to support diverse environmental program responsibilities. Ability to understand environmental issues affecting research center. Knowledge of EPA analytical methods. Ability to work on multiple projects. Knowledge of environmental laws, regulations, and standards. Bachelor's degree in a science or environmental program or science education acceptable.

EARNINGS

Current salary offerings for positions in environmental policy, planning, and management represent quite a range. Public Interest Research Group jobs showed starting salaries in the $20,000–$23,000 range. Other nonprofit environmental research groups started their workers in the $27,500–$30,000 range. Those workers earning the highest salaries were employed in private industry. Some entry-level positions in the energy industry started at $35,750. As with nearly every type of job, there will be some salary variation by region. Be sure to undertake the activities outlined in Chapter 1, Self-Assessment, to determine the salary you want to earn as you enter the job market and then begin exploring salaries for the specific kinds of positions that interest you.

CAREER OUTLOOK

Most of the various types of positions described in this chapter are expected to grow as fast as the average, according to the *Occupational Outlook Handbook,* although individuals working for consulting firms are expected to have more opportunities open to them. Competition will be keen for all positions given the current interest in environmental issues. Many job listings indicated that a master's degree would be preferred, so if you are interested in attending graduate school know that you will be more attractive as an employee and able to command a higher salary.

STRATEGY FOR FINDING THE JOB

There are four specific activities you can undertake to be in the running for the jobs that are of interest to you. They include developing a solid understanding of environmental programs, laws, and issues; gaining writing and public presentation experience; knowing how to use word-processing and database software to create reports; honing your analytical skills; and learning basics about fund-raising. Here are specific tips on developing and improving these skills.

Develop a Solid Understanding of Environmental Programs, Laws, and Issues

Throughout your years of study you undertook class readings that informed you about environmental issues directly related to the topics you studied. You'll want to expand your knowledge of the range of current environmental issues, the laws and regulations associated with those issues, and environmental programs that have been developed to address them. The association list at the end of this chapter highlights some publications that may be held by your college library. Some are available online. From the *Journal of the American Planning Association* to the National Association of Environmental Professionals' *Environmental Practice,* begin a reading program now and draw upon your expanded knowledge as you write cover letters, create an effective résumé, and interview for environmental policy, planning, and management positions.

Another option is to gain experience by volunteering. AmeriCorps will take volunteers with no experience and assign them to relevant work situations. Some of these assignments are in the environmental sciences. One position recently advertised was with their Watershed Stewards Project. It is a comprehensive, community-based watershed education and restoration program whose mission is to conserve and restore anadromous watersheds. The salaries are low but credit is given toward tuition; awards will vary depending upon the length of service. The educational awards could be applied to tuition for graduate school or even for completion of a bachelor's degree if the volunteer program were completed prior to graduation. This is a great way to apply skills that you developed in school and gain on-the-job experience at the same time.

Gain Writing and Public Presentation Experience

Each of the job descriptions shown in this chapter lists either writing or presentation duties, or some combination of the two. One job calls for writing proposals, creating policy briefs, interacting with the community, and facilitating workshops. Another wants a professional who can utilize excellent writing skills to prepare reports. Yet another position needs someone to document environmental issues and undertake lobbying efforts. During your college career you will be offered the opportunity, both in and outside of the classroom, to build these skills. Don't pass them up! Participate in extracurricular activities like campus clubs and organizations, and offer to be the person who drafts requests for club funding from the student government finance committee. Or, offer to be the spokesperson for a work group in a class and be the one to present the group's findings. All of these activities help you build skills that will make a favorable impression on potential employers.

Know How to Use Word-Processing and Database Software to Create Reports

Professionals working in environmental policy, planning, and management rely on reports and the data analyses they contain. In order to create a report in today's world of work, you must be proficient with word-processing and database software. You will need to know how to enter data, store it, extract and manipulate it, and import it into your report. Take courses that will provide you with both database and word-processing experience, and also take advantage of your campus's computer labs and their staffs' knowledge to learn more as you practice using those computing skills.

Hone Your Analytical Skills

Whether you have innate analytical skills or you have been able to develop them through your education and experience, they will be important in your work. As you undertake policy analysis, data analysis, or any other kind of analysis, you'll be looking for causes, precursors, connections, and results. As you write the final papers of your college career, meet with your professors to get specific feedback on how clearly your analyses are presented and how well they stand up under questioning. Use this feedback to continually make improvements in your writing. Prospective employers may want to see writing samples, so be sure to show them your best work.

Learn Some Basics About Fund-Raising

The smaller the organization, the wider the range of duties each professional is expected to undertake. Many of the hundreds of job postings we reviewed mentioned fund-raising in some form. So learn some of the basic concepts associated with this kind of activity, whether it be grant writing, annual fund activities, or major donor relations. Each is very different, so you'll want to ask intelligent questions during the interview process to better understand what the organization expects of you. You can get direct experience by working as a student volunteer fund-raiser on your campus. Or, there are some excellent books available on the subject, so be sure to check with the campus library. A third activity you might undertake is an informational interview with a representative of a local nonprofit. Use the tips discussed in Chapter 5 to develop an interview agenda that will allow you to find out about the nonprofit's fund-raising activities.

POSSIBLE EMPLOYERS

As with the other four career paths, new graduates interested in environmental policy, planning, and management work for federal, state, and local governments, private industry including consulting firms, and nonprofit organizations.

Federal Government

Agencies such as the U.S. Fish and Wildlife Service, U.S. Forest Service, Bureau of Land Management, Department of Defense, and Environmental Protection Agency hire professionals with job titles like program manager, research assistant, or natural resource specialist. Use the information that follows to begin exploring all the possible positions available with the federal government.

Help in Locating These Employers. Visit the U.S. Office of Personnel Management's website (usajobs.opm.gov) to kick off your search for federal jobs. Select the Entry Level Professional option. In the menu of job types, the first item you will see is "all." Simply highlight this job type; enter one of the following keywords: *policy, planning,* or *management*; and then submit your request. Generally, many jobs were available for review.

State Govermnent

State departments including environmental quality, wildlife management, land management, natural resources, and transportation all require the skills of environmental policy, planning, and management professionals.

Help in Locating These Employers. If you have access to the Internet, use the information contained in Appendix A and visit the official state websites for the state(s) where you may want to work. Explore the site to determine the names of the various related agencies and then connect to each agency to read about its mission. Then use the information on each state's human resources Web pages to review current state job openings. If you don't have access to the Internet, review your local telephone directory. It should contain listings under (state name)–State of (e.g., Illinois, State of), for the various agencies that hire environmental policy, planning, and management professionals.

Local Government

Local government jobs are often listed in both regional and local newspapers. And you can call the human resources department of those local governments where you'd like to work to find out about their policies and procedures for advertising positions.

Industry

Coal mining companies, companies that create and provide electricity, crude petroleum and natural gas exploration companies, and environmental consulting firms (one company mentioned their utilities group) are just a few of the kinds of companies in industry that call upon environmental policy, planning, and management professionals to help them accomplish their goals.

Help in Locating These Employers. Many websites can link you to hundreds of job listings. One way to start is to access the *Wall Street Journal's* site (wsj.com) and use their career section. Keywords such as *environmental policy, environmental planning,* and *environmental management* reveal lots of entry level jobs all over the country. Other good sites include the Environmental Career Opportunities site (ecojobs.com), Earthworks (earthworks -jobs.com), Environment Career Center (environmentalcareer.com), and Environmental Career Bulletin Online (ecbonline.com).

Nonprofit Organizations

Nonprofit organizations undertake critically important environmental policy, planning, and management efforts. The Rainforest Alliance works to improve the effectiveness of certification as a tool protecting biodiversity, promoting sustainable communities, and enhancing the economic performance of forest operations managed by small forest enterprises. The Conservation Association hires people to work as part of a collaborative effort to protect major rivers. Research associates work for a nonprofit institute that conducts environmental research and provides consulting services. Some institutions of higher education have policy/research centers that hire professionals to help public officials develop environmental policies.

Help in Locating These Employers. Many of the websites that we have listed elsewhere in this book also list position openings in environmental policy, planning, and management with nonprofit organizations. They include: Environmental Career Center (environmentalcareer.com/policy.htm) and Environmental Career Opportunities (ecojobs.com). Additional sites to look at are River Network (rivernetwork.org) and Colorado Guide (http://colorado guide.com/careers/). PIRG jobs can be found at tomah.com/jobseeker/.

POSSIBLE JOB TITLES

As you look for job announcements for environmental policy, planning, and management, keep your eyes open for jobs with the titles listed below.

Conservation analyst	Policy analyst
Conservation coordinator	Program manager
Conservation manager	Recycling policy analyst
Conservation specialist	Research assistant
Consultant	Research associate
Environmental advocate	Resource manager
Environmental analyst	Restoration coordinator
Environmental health specialist	Water treatment and wastewater
Environmental planner	disposal specialist
Land stewardship director	Watershed ecologist
Legislative advocate	Watershed leadership program coordinator
Natural resources specialist	Watershed steward
Planning analyst	Wildlife habitat manager

RELATED OCCUPATIONS

Many companies support the work of environmental policy, planning, and management activities. For example, there are technology companies that create artificial intelligence software that allows professionals to model, predict, control, and optimize nonlinear processes. Planning activities often involve the use of Geographic Information Systems (GIS software). There are salespeople representing both types of companies interacting with the environmental professionals.

Other occupations draw upon some of the same skills used in environmental policy, planning and management. Be sure to consider these job titles:

City manager	Environmental editor/researcher
Computer programmer	Financial analyst
Computer scientist	GIS sales associate
Computer systems analyst	Management analyst
Director of community development	Mathematician
Director of economic development	Operations research analyst
Economist	Reporter
Environmental sales account manager	Statistician

PROFESSIONAL ASSOCIATIONS

Review the professional association listings shown here and explore the associated websites to review job listings; gain information about environmental policy, planning, and management issues; and review publications.

American Planning Association
122 South Michigan Ave., Ste. 1600
Chicago, IL 60603
Members/Purpose: Citizens, academics, practicing planners, state and local planning agencies. Purpose is to contribute to the public good by encouraging wise planning.
Training: Books available from online bookstore; annual meeting with workshops; workshops; training videos; and audiotapes. Links to continuing education resources
Journals/Publications: Proceedings of annual meeting; *Journal of the American Planning Association,* plus numerous other periodicals, including newsletters
Job Listings: None
Website/E-mail: planning.org; see home page for specific addresses to various departments.

Canadian Society of Environmental Biologists
CSEB National Offices
P.O. Box 962
Station F
Toronto, ON M4Y 2N9
Canada
Members/Purpose: Biology professionals and students working to improve resource management through ecology.
Training: Annual meeting
Journals/Publications: Symposia proceedings
Job Listings: None
Website/E-mail: freenet.edmonton.ab.ca/cseb/; cseb@freenet.ed.ab.ca

International Association for Impact Assessment
1330 23rd St. S, Ste. C
Fargo, ND 58103
Members/Purpose: Community groups, individuals, educational institutions, academics, government officials. Purpose is scientifically based and ecologically sound sustainable development.
Training: Annual meeting with workshops and training course; also, training course database available online
Journals/Publications: *IAIA Journal; IAIA Newsletter;* online publications focusing upon impact assessment
Job Listings: None
Website/E-mail: iaia.org; info@iaia.org

National Association of Environmental Professionals
P.O. Box 2086
Bowie, MD 20718
Members/Purpose: Planning agencies, governmental officials, individuals, academics, and students. Promotes education and certification of environmental professionals, emphasizing the balance of economic growth and environmental excellence.
Training: Annual conference with workshops and short courses, including HAZWOPER refresher
Journals/Publications: *Environmental Practice;* conference proceeding; online links to other resources
Job Listings: Online links cataloged by date of receipt
Website/E-mail: NAEP.org; office@naep.org

National Association of Local Government Environmental Professionals
1350 New York Ave. NW, Ste. 1100
Washington, DC 20005
Members/Purpose: Local governments. Encourages communication among local environmental officials, and promotes education and training.
Training: Conducts research and produces reports that focus on environmental problems of importance to local government officials
Journals/Publications: *Newsflash,* newsletter
Job Listings: None
Website/E-mail: nalgep.org; nalgep@spiegelmcd.com

National Registry of Environmental Professionals
P.O. Box 2068
Glenview, IL 60025
Members/Purpose: Accrediting agency for environmental professionals, including environmental managers, scientists, technologists, technicians, and engineers.
Training: Workshops
Journals/Publications: Study guides
Job Listings: Dozens of online links
Website/E-mail: nrep.org; nrep@nrep.org

National Society of Consulting Soil Scientists, Inc.
325 Pennsylvania Ave. SE, Ste. 700
Washington, DC 20003
Members/Purpose: Academics and practicing soil scientists. Advances the practice of soil science and promotes interaction among soil scientists.
Training: Annual meeting; links to many educational soil science sites with online tutorials and resources
Journals/Publications: None
Job Listings: Many links to soil and environmental sites with job postings
Website/E-mail: nscss.org; info@nscss.org

Society for Conservation Biology
University of Washington
Box #351800
Seattle, WA 98915
Members/Purpose: Resource managers, educators, students, government officials, conservation groups. Promotes study affecting the maintenance, loss, and restoration of biological diversity.
Training: Annual meeting

Journals/Publications: *Conservation Biology; Conservation Biology in Practice; Neotropical Conservation,* newsletter
Job Listings: Dozens of links online
Website/E-mail: http://conbio.net/scb/; conbio@u.washington.edu

Society of Wetlands Scientists
810 E. Tenth St.
P.O. Box 1897
Lawrence, KS 66044-8897
Members/Purpose: Educators, students, and conservation officials. Fosters conservation and understanding of the ecological importance of wetlands.
Training: Annual meeting; links to many wetlands conservation courses, professional certification
Journals/Publications: *Wetlands,* journal; regional chapter newsletters
Job Listings: Dozens of online links
Website/E-mail: sws.org; sws@allenpress.com

Soil Science Society of America
677 South Segoe Rd.
Madison, WI 53711
Members/Purpose: Academics, students, and practicing soil scientists. To advance discipline and the practice of soils science through disseminating information about the science of soils, ecosystems management, bioremediation, waste management, recycling, and wise land use.
Training: Annual meeting with workshops, continuing education opportunities
Journals/Publications: *Soil Science Society of America Journal; Journal of Environmental Quality; Journal of Natural Resources and Life Sciences Education;* lots of books and materials available from online bookstore
Job Listings: Lots of job links online
Website/E-mail: soils.org; heaquarters@soils.org

Soil and Water Conservation Society
7515 N.E. Ankeny Rd.
Ankeny, LA 50021
Members/Purpose: Conservation professionals. Fosters the science and art of soil, water, and related resource management to achieve sustainability.
Training: Online resources available
Journals/Publications: *Journal of Soil and Water Conservation; Conservation Voices: Listening to the Land; Conservogram,* newsletter
Job Listings: None
Website/E-mail: swcssss.org; swcs@swcs.org

12

PATH 3: ENVIRONMENTAL SCIENCES

You have just been hired at a large environmental consulting firm in a medium-sized midwestern city. On the second day of the job, after you've filled out all of the paperwork for the human resources department, and after you have been introduced to various individuals in many, many departments and labs, you are assigned to a field team. With all of the new people, all of the new acronyms, and all of the new responsibilities, you are at once nervous, excited, anxious, and challenged.

A team meeting reveals that the company has landed a contract to remediate petroleum pollution reaching a municipal water treatment plant that has resulted in intermittent closures due to sporadic high levels of toxins reaching the water intakes. At that meeting you find that by Thursday, you will be whisked off to a field site in Oregon where you will reside in a motel. You have to get everything in your life in order and be ready to go in two days. While in Oregon you will be part of a survey team whose mission is to delimit the extent of the pollution problem and begin to develop a strategy for its mitigation. Your team will be responsible for gathering samples of water and soil to return to the lab—the beginning stages of the site remediation process. This is what you spent four (or more) years training for. This was your goal: participating in projects that will improve our environment. You've hit the wall; there will be no party this Thursday night. You are out of school and ready to begin an exciting career!

DEFINITION OF THE CAREER PATH

In this book we treat the environmental sciences career path, in terms of technical components, as intermediate between the environmental education and environmental policy, planning, and management paths at one end of the spectrum, and environmental technology and environmental engineering at the other. Elements of the other four paths converge in environmental sciences. That is, environmental issues are important but there is a strong technical side of this path, too. Not only is someone following a career covered in this path expected to be knowledgeable of environmental problems, to be able to write, to be able to communicate effectively, but also to collect and analyze field data and solve problems. Environmental Sciences has perhaps the greatest variety of job duties and the broadest expectations in terms of education and training.

Environmental scientists are employed in a variety of settings. Local, state, and federal governments regulate activities that help ensure that certain elements of the environment are not further degraded, for example, air and water quality. Additionally, governments set the rules for environmental cleanup and remediation. Larger industrial firms have in-house scientists who insure compliance with regulations and undertake steps to prevent industrial accidents. Some companies are not sufficiently large to justify the employment of a staff of environmental scientists. Instead, they utilize environmental consulting firms on a contract basis to complete this work for them. And nonprofit organizations undertake environmental cleanup and protection activities that are not being addressed to their satisfaction by current regulations. They identify gaps in current laws, lobby for improvements to them, and serve as watchdogs to make sure that government, industry, and consultants are all adhering to the current set of rules and regulations.

Before we continue the formal definition of this path, let's examine a few job descriptions that fit within our vision of careers that reside beneath the umbrella of environmental sciences. These recent postings are excellent examples.

Hydrogeologists/Geophysicists, (international water resources consulting firm). Junior management positions in (Texas) office. Candidates should have a B.S. in hydrogeology or geophysics. Knowledge of geophysical exploration tools and groundwater modeling packages incorporating MODFLOW is also preferred. Must be excellent communicator and work well in a team environment.

Land Steward. 70-year-old historic landscape garden and nature preserve (in FL) seeks a full-time Land Steward. Position oversees ecological management of the natural areas of the foundation for the conservation and enhancement of plant, mammal, reptile, and bird habitat. Qualifications: Bachelor's degree in natural science, knowledge of FL native ecosystems, and willingness to obtain Florida Certified Burner certificate and pesticide applicator's license. Additional requirements: ability to work under physically demanding conditions; operate a tractor, chainsaw, and backpack sprayer (other like equipment); and work well alone or with a variety of people; good written/verbal communication skills. Salary + full benefits.

As you can see, the second job requires a great deal of field work. The candidate must also be able to perform some physically challenging tasks. But interestingly, effective communication skills are specifically identified as a requirement.

The following description is similar to the previous one in that field work is expected, but writing, speaking, and environmental advocacy, too, are very important job elements.

Environmental Associate. (regional) Environmental Resource Center seeks enthusiastic applicants with a degree in biology, natural resources, or a related field, who want to work on the "frontlines" in forest, river, wildlife, and land planning issues. Applicants should be prepared to do every imaginable task from writing newsletters to setting up wildlife photo-detection stations, from speaking at intense public meetings to measuring livestock grazing impacts in remote, high wilderness meadows. Dedication to protecting nature and the ability to be respectful of all points of view are essential requirements for applicants. Candidates should also be physically capable of hiking within the beautiful, but rugged, terrain of the Sierra Nevada. Salary dependent upon degree and experience. Send résumé, cover letter, and contact information to . . .

The next job description seeks someone with a wide array of technical skills, including statistics, GIS, database design, field biology skills, and natural resource inventory experience, in addition to budgeting and report-writing duties.

Southeast Regional Ecologist. The Trustees of (land trust), the world's oldest land trust, seeks an individual to help develop and implement policies, plans, and programs to protect the ecological resources of properties within the region. Identify and develop strategies and implement management plans to protect ecological resources; provide baseline ecological descriptions for all properties within the region; coordinate and/or conduct applied research; review, approve, supervise, and report on all ecological research; write an annual report that describes activities and research; maintain communications with federal and state agencies and other conservation groups; prepare an annual budget; research, apply for, and administer grants. Requirements: B.S. degree in the environmental sciences plus two years' experience; strong field biology skills; working knowledge of natural resource inventory and assessment techniques; familiarity with plant ecology, wildlife biology, rare species management, wetlands ecology, and land conservation management planning; working knowledge of Windows-based operating system and related software. Experience with database design and statistical software package, ArcView (or other GIS software products), is desirable.

Environmental Scientist (national environmental consulting firm). Candidate must have knowledge of wastewater discharge & stormwater permitting, hazardous waste program administration, & other compliance assistance issues. OSHA & DOT familiarity a plus. B.S. in environmental science required. Excellent communication skills (verbal & written) & ability to handle multiple priorities in fast-paced, service-oriented setting essential.

Environmental Geologist. Full-time position for geologist with a B.S. and strong communication skills to perform geologic investigations, site remediation & assessments, and UST closures. Knowledge of CERCLA and RCRA regulations a plus.

Wetland Scientist. Must have B.S. degree in biology or related field. Perform wetland delineations, assessments, mitigation design, and monitoring.

An environmental scientist might be employed in one of five broad settings: (1) government agency, (2) private industry, (3) environmental consulting, (4) nonprofit/advocacy group, or (5) higher education. A group of common issues are addressed in each setting. They would, however, be handled differently depending on the point of view they are organized to address. Governments regulate; industry and consulting firms implement based on regulations; nonprofits and advocacy groups serve as caretakers and watch-dogs; and higher education researches and educates.

ENVIRONMENTAL ACTIVITIES AND SERVICES

A variety of activities and services require the expertise of environmental scientists. And many of these may be viewed differently by an environmental scientist depending on the work setting. For example, environmental scientists working for a government agency develop remediation plans. Others are employed by consulting firms to implement the resulting cleanup operations. Still other environmental scientists work for nonprofits that advocate for improved and more complete methods of remediation. So as you review each of the environmental activities and services listed, keep in mind that multiple perspectives exist.

Brownfield Investigations, Remediation, Redevelopment, and Voluntary Cleanups

The U.S. Environmental Protection Agency defines *brownfields* as "abandoned, idled, or under-used industrial and commercial facilities where expansion or redevelopment is complicated by real or perceived environmental contamination." Such environmentally compromised sites are huge problems for the real estate industry, government regulating bodies, industrial corporations, and all of society. The federal government advocates for such sites to be cleaned up and reused so that fewer industrial sites need to be developed further reducing human exposure to environmental problems.

Soil and Groundwater Investigations

Hydrologists, geologists, and soil scientists are often required to perform the sampling, data gathering, and instrumentation required to identify the type and extent of problems associated with soil and groundwater contamination. Sources of contamination might include agricultural runoff, petroleum spills, leaking chemical tanks, and highway and rail accidents in which toxic substances are being transported.

Remediation Engineering, Design, Construction, Operation, and Maintenance

Another series of tasks that environmental scientists must deal with includes remedial action, planning, design, project implementation, monitoring, and project oversight. It is fairly easy to see how environmental scientists working in several of the five settings described earlier might be involved in this work. Governmental regulating bodies must develop rules and guidelines and be able to enforce them; industry and consulting firms have to determine methods to employ that will allow for successful compliance; and advocacy groups need to watch out for noncompliance. This includes demolition and removal of chemical or petroleum storage facilities, both above and below ground, and asbestos removal from dwellings, factories, and commercial buildings, and a whole host of other situations. Some of these tasks will require the expertise of an engineer, but often the engineer must work in conjunction with a trained environmental scientist.

For example, a private company realized that environmental integrity has been compromised at one of their plants and they wished to make amends. A consulting firm was called upon to design, implement, and manage a means to remove or reduce the effects of the improper disposal of toxic materials on plant property. More specifically, diesel fuel and gasoline contaminated groundwater that was moving in the subsurface and polluting a large body of surface water. The horizontal and vertical extent of the contamination was determined with test wells. A corrective action plan was designed and approved; this plan involved a soil washing technique and the introduction of air to the subsurface to allow for bioremediation of the hydrocarbons. A team, including an environmental engineer and an environmental scientist trained in groundwater hydrology and environmental chemistry, was needed to remediate this problem.

Emissions Reduction

Regulating agencies, industry, and consulting firms also design and implement strategies that reduce point source emissions into the air, surface water, or groundwater. In one example, a firm evaluated airborne air pollution from an industrial plant by using a method to directly assess stack emissions. It then designed an air handling system to remove or reduce particulates and/or gases, oversaw its installation, and finally, continued to monitor emissions. Environmental scientists with field data gathering training and laboratory procedures were valuable in this situation.

Cleanup or Demolition of Contaminated Structures

Construction engineers play an important role in a project involving the destruction of a building, but again a team approach is required. Environmental scientists trained in hazardous materials handling also contribute on a project of this type. The Environmental Protection Agency HAZWOPER

Training courses (see explanation in Chapter 13) would be essential for workers in this field.

Contaminant Fate, Transport, and Modeling

Many of the tasks that a typical environmental consulting firm, private firm, regulating agency, or advocacy group handle require personnel who possess multidisciplinary backgrounds. Usually the training and experience needed to design regulations and bring a site into compliance exceeds that of a single individual. In this instance people with experience and training in transportation engineering, mathematical modeling, environmental chemistry, environmental law, and environmental science would be required to complete a job as multifaceted and complex as moving hazardous materials to an appropriate site for proper disposal.

Risk Assessment/Toxicology

Another category of service is environmental risk assessment. An old factory site, sometimes termed a "brownfield," might be suitable to the needs of a new industry. The Environmental Protection Agency encourages industry to clean up and redevelop these sites. A team of environmental scientists provides the knowledge that underlies the development of manageable solutions. They are able to understand old surveys that will enable them to pinpoint the location of toxic sites that are now long gone, perform field sampling, assist in the laboratory analysis of samples, interpret and analyze the results of various tests, and document the procedures and outcomes of the investigation. In this way, a company could determine the cost of remediating a site and, if too expensive, that locale could be rejected in favor of one with less risk.

Strategy Development and Negotiating with Federal and State Agencies

Oftentimes legal departments of large environmental consulting firms and environmental advocacy groups require people who are skilled not only in written and verbal communications, but who are also extremely knowledgeable about scientific topics. Broadly trained environmental scientists are suited for this type of work. They have had training in basic chemistry, geology, hydrology, and biology and can be very effective communicators.

Hazardous Waste Management

Society today depends upon a vast array of chemicals from chlorine bleach, chemical fertilizers, acids of various types, petroleum and its by-products, mercury, and radionuclides to support the lifestyle that has evolved. These materials are often used as part of a manufacturing process. Many of these substances are transported in bulk by truck and rail. After such substances are used, processing residuals must be disposed. A huge industry has evolved over the past three decades or so to manage the removal, transport, and safe disposal of these materials. Governmental regulations help ensure that proper steps are taken to dispose of these materials, and watchdog groups must be ever vigilant to make sure that industry and government remain accountable.

RCRA Closure/Corrective Action/Permits

The Resource Conservation and Recovery Act (RCRA) and its associated regulations establish a strict and comprehensive regulatory program applicable to hazardous waste. EPA regulations under RCRA for new and existing treatment, storage, and disposal facilities include incinerators, storage and treatment tanks, storage containers, storage and treatment surface impoundments, waste piles, and landfills. Every facility that treats, stores, or disposes of hazardous waste must obtain an RCRA permit. Environmental scientists work with clients and government representatives to facilitate the permitting process.

Superfund RI/FS

The EPA established a pool of funds to remediate sites designated as those most in need of immediate remediation. Remedial Investigations (RI) and Feasibility Studies (FS) are conducted by consulting firms to assist their clients in meeting EPA guidelines at minimum cost. Tasks are varied and complex. First, an assessment of the nature and extent of the chemicals of concern in the soil or groundwater from on-site or off-site sources is made. Existing and potential chemical migration pathways and rates are identified. The magnitude and probability of actual or potential harm to public health, safety, or welfare, or to the environment, posed by the release of chemicals at the site is assessed. And, finally, appropriate remedial measures are identified to prevent migration of future releases and mitigation of any releases that have already occurred. Data are collected and analyzed in order to prepare a Remedial Action Plan (RAP) in accordance with established regulatory guidelines.

Environmental Analysis

Even small environmental consulting firms are able to offer services where a general environmental analysis or an Environmental Impact Statement is needed. Many governmental agencies will not approve a building permit until an environmental survey has been completed for that site. The analysis or survey will determine if endangered species are present, if the site will impact a wetland, if a flood hazard is present, or if archeological resources are present. Environmental scientists with training in botany, zoology, hydrology, and archaeology are needed for these investigations.

Petroleum Contamination

Environmental consulting firms work with clients to quickly contain spills or to remediate those of the past. Hydrologists, engineers, and environmental scientists compose teams that work to remove contaminated soils to handling facilities and to abate spills that affect groundwater and surface water.

Investigation and Remediation

EPA environmental scientists are teamed with engineers and technicians to identify sites that have been compromised by toxic spills. Environmental consulting firms are often contracted to determine the nature and extent of pollution at compromised sites. Interdisciplinary teams are dispatched to the location in question where numerous tests are completed in order to identify the hazard, its concentration, and the extent of travel, either overland or in groundwater. After these properties and characteristics have been determined, a remediation strategy is developed and implemented.

UST Closure and Management

Underground storage tanks (USTs) can become a major problem when they are left in the ground longer then their engineered life expectancy. Environmental consulting firms are contracted to remove them, and often they must also clean up the compromised site after the tank has been safely relocated to a hazardous waste disposal site. This process typically involves a hydrological study to determine if the soil moisture zone and groundwater table have been impacted. Large consulting firms utilize interdisciplinary teams for projects such as this. And governmental agencies responsible for the regulation of these activities need scientists with the knowledge of soil and groundwater behavior to insure that appropriate actions are undertaken.

Compliance Monitoring and Risk Management Plans

Environmental consulting firms, governmental agencies, and advocacy groups employ individuals with lots of experience with environmental legislation. Consulting firms want to be sure that their clients are able to comply with air and water quality laws and to take steps to minimize their exposure to risks associated with the handling of dangerous materials. Governmental agencies require scientists with expertise to ensure that risk management plans take into account a broad spectrum of potential problems, that regulations are sufficiently rigorous, and that monitoring procedures are carefully followed.

Compliance Audits and Assistance

Government regulating agencies often require proof that an industrial operation is complying with regulations. Environmental scientists can be employed as auditors and to provide assistance with reaching environmental goals. Environmental consulting firms often assist clients by helping them to comply with environmental laws and negotiations. Support staff for such departments may include environmental scientists who would act in an advisory capacity.

Modeling

Environmental scientists with strong backgrounds in mathematics, engineering, and statistics are called upon to build theoretical models, such as flow models, for groundwater movements and air quality problem situations in large factories or other institutions. A great deal of expertise in computer science and mathematics is required for positions of this sort.

Title V and Air Construction Permits

Businesses need licenses or permits for all sorts of activities, such as land development or manufacturing. EPA regulations require manufacturers to seek permits to discharge air and water back into the environment from factory processing. In effect, these emissions are also pollution sources, but they can be monitored and regulated. Governmental agencies use environmental scientists to design strong regulations while nonprofits need these specialists to develop strategies to strengthen them. Environmental consulting firms advise manufacturers on how to secure permits and to comply with various regulations.

Stack Testing, Air Emission Inventories, and Technology Assessments (BACT, MACT)

Manufacturers must continually monitor their atmospheric discharges for sulfur dioxide, gases, dust, and other particulates. Often, individuals trained in chemistry work for large firms or with independent labs and some work freelance or subcontract with consulting firms. The acronyms BACT and MACT refer to Best Available and Maximum Available Control Technologies.

Certified Visible Emissions Inspections

Some large environmental consulting firms offer certified inspections, which are required periodically by the EPA. These individuals are specialists with backgrounds in environmental chemistry.

Database Development

The very large consulting firms employ environmental scientists to work in database development. There is a huge amount of data and information to manage, and workers trained in science and computers combine knowledge of these two fields to create powerful and efficient database systems.

Coke Oven Inspections

Coke oven batteries (a group of ovens connected by common walls) are used to convert coal into coke, which is then used in blast furnaces to convert iron ore to iron. Coke oven emissions contain benzene (a known carcinogen) and other chemicals that can cause cancer of the respiratory tract, kidney, and prostate. EPA scientists and attorneys set emissions limits for existing sources and even tighter limits for new sources. Freelance consultants and large firms help their clients keep within the emissions limits.

Indoor and Ambient Air Monitoring

Environmental scientists trained in industrial hygiene are often employed to sample, analyze, and determine solutions to problems of indoor air quality at hospitals, manufacturing plants, and other large facilities.

Due Diligence

Due diligence is the level of judgment, care, prudence, determination, and activity that a person would reasonably be expected to do under particular circumstances. Applied to environmental science, due diligence means that institutions shall take all reasonable precautions, under the particular circumstances, to protect the public from harm. This translates to an effort to prevent public exposure to harmful substances in the environment. To exercise due diligence, an institution must implement a plan to identify possible hazards and to implement measures to mitigate their impact. Some firms perform such studies in order to determine any negative environmental impacts or hazards, then produce a plan to mitigate any effects. Environmental scientists are often teamed with other specialists in these investigations.

Phase I and II Site Assessments and Remediation

Beginning in the 1980s, environmental consulting firms began performing property evaluations primarily for major banks, law firms, and insurance companies. A Phase I Environmental Site Assessment, or ESA, is designed to identify (1) existing or potential environmental hazards, and (2) resources with natural, cultural, recreational, or scientific value of special significance. Information on potential environmental hazards is typically presented for use in the evaluation of legal and financial liabilities for transactions related to the purchase, sale, or lease of a particular property. Identification of "special resources" aids in the evaluation of the property's overall development potential and associated market value. Prior to financing a property, lenders usually require a Phase I ESA to identify any potential environmental liabilities associated with the property. This site assessment is usually paid for by the potential buyer, since the seller may harbor a natural bias. A Phase I investigation involves historical research of the site, interviews with persons knowledgeable about the site and surrounding land, and a visual inspection of a property; it does not include testing and analysis of potentially hazardous materials.

A Phase II investigation achieves the testing and analyses of soils or other materials, if such testing was recommended in the Phase I report. It is common for the seller to be asked to participate in the cost of this testing. Examples are: testing of soils where solvents or oils may have leaked, testing of building materials for asbestos and/or lead-based paints, sampling of potentially hazardous materials such as abandoned drums, and testing for PCBs in transformers and ballasts. Teams of environmental specialists would conduct such site assessments.

Industrial Compliance Audits

Industrial environmental compliance audits are complex reviews of the environmental procedures and manufacturing processes in use at a given facility. Usually plant personnel, environmental consultants, and attorneys work together to perform these functions.

Asbestos and Lead Inspections and Abatement Management

Asbestos and lead-based paint management and abatement is a complex field with a number of state and federal agencies regulating the actions performed by consultants. Many state and local laws require owners to disclose the presence of asbestos-containing building materials (ACBMs) and lead-based paint (LBP) to facility occupants and to take steps to decrease exposure risks. In addition to training in an environmental science field, workers may also need Hazard Emergency Response Act (HERA) training.

Water Resources and Marine Studies

Watershed management issues have become exceedingly important as demand grows for water supplies to both residences and commercial establishments, and for industry. Both water quality and quantity are at stake. Environmental scientists with strong backgrounds in hydrology, geohydrology, and modeling are hired by municipalities, regional planning authorities, regulating agencies, and consulting firms.

NPDES Permitting and Water Quality Standards Applications

The National Pollutant Discharge Elimination System (NPDES) permit program controls water pollution by regulating the disposal of point source pollutants into waters of the United States. Individual homes that are connected to a municipal system, use a septic system, or do not have a surface discharge do not need an NPDES permit; however, industrial, municipal, and other facilities must obtain permits if their discharges go directly to surface waters. Hydrologists and geohydrologists with experience in and knowledge of water-related regulations are needed to fill such positions.

Pretreatment

Publicly owned treatment works (POTWs) collect wastewater from homes, commercial buildings, and industrial facilities and transport it via a series of pipes to treatment plants. Here, the POTWs remove harmful organisms and other contaminants from sewage so it can be discharged safely into the receiving stream. Generally, POTWs are designed to treat domestic sewage only, but POTWs also receive wastewater from industrial (nondomestic) users. The General Pretreatment Regulations establish responsibilities of federal, state, and local governments, industry, and the public to implement pretreatment standards to control pollutants from the industrial users that may pass through or interfere with POTW treatment processes or that may contaminate sewage sludge. Environmental scientists who specialize in regulations that govern the operations of these facilities play a role in their success.

Wetlands Delineation and Construction

Within the last two decades it has been found that wetlands are made up of a complex web of life and that they can cleanse many pollutants from a watershed. But wetlands must be protected from overdevelopment. Advocacy groups monitor the activities of both government agencies and commercial establishments to ensure that these resources are not misused or destroyed. Governmental agencies develop regulations to ensure their protection. Environmental consulting firms help clients by assisting them in the identification of wetlands and procedures that mitigate the impact of construction projects in areas that bound or otherwise impact wetlands. Environmental scientists trained in ecology and hydrology are valuable to firms that provide these services.

Waste Management Evaluations

Managing waste is becoming increasingly difficult as existing disposal facilities approach capacity and available land resources diminish. Environmental engineers and scientists address waste disposal issues by incorporating emerging technologies with established practices to maximize site efficiency and minimize waste generation. A manufacturer, for example, may need to reduce by-products of its processing techniques. A waste management evaluation would be conducted by a team to determine a strategy for the most cost-efficient removal of these materials, potential recycling, and possible resale within another industry needing the by-product as a raw material.

Landfill Siting and Design

A well-sited, carefully designed landfill is integral to most solid waste management programs. Engineers and environmental scientists use GIS mapping, Global Positioning Systems, and computer design software for all phases from designing, siting, and permitting a new landfill to expanding or closing existing sites to landfill operations.

Landfill Monitoring, Operation, and Maintenance

Environmental consulting firms can provide assistance to municipalities and private corporations involved in landfill operation and maintenance. A number of issues are associated with the operation and closure of landfills; some of these problems involve gas emissions, migration of leachate, and odors. Different types of scientists and engineers are required to address these very different types of problems that stem from the disposal of residential, commercial, and industrial materials. Work includes development of regulations, monitoring and oversight, and implementation.

Litigation Support

Some consulting firms provide expert witnesses for a variety of cases that involve environmental issues. In one case, a chain reaction collision involving more than 100 cars occurred on a fog-obscured freeway in Tennessee. To mitigate the responsibility of the company that owned the truck found responsible for the accident, a meteorologist was brought in as an expert witness to testify that indeed, on the day and time of the accident, visibility on that section of highway was significantly impaired.

WATCH OUT FOR WOLVES IN SHEEP'S CLOTHING

A cautionary note is due at this point. The field called "environmental consulting" has a number of connotations, or is subject to a number of interpretations. Environmental consulting can be interpreted as environmental advocacy, cleanup, remediation, pollution prevention, or reduction. As a matter of fact, one firm suggests in its mission statement that their goal is to "provide . . . services that emphasize integrity, creativity, professionalism, and commitment . . . not only for the environment's sake, but for God's green Earth as well."

But for other people, environmental consulting can mean something different, something dark. Some consulting firms enable organizations that have been found to be in noncompliance with environmental regulations to duck their responsibilities to society. In other words, their job is to reduce the financial obligation of a polluter to clean up a contaminated site. The following quote found on the website of a consulting firm describes this philosophy. They "help reduce our clients' environmental liabilities." If you are indeed an advocate of the environment and this type of approach offends you, then you will want to be aware of the organizational philosophy *before* you accept a job offer. Research on your part can steer you away from this type of firm.

WORKING CONDITIONS

As an inexperienced environmental scientist, you will initially be expected to perform a number of tasks that you may not find challenging. Keep in mind that you are initially being trained to follow institutional procedures and to learn the "ropes." This is called on-the-job training. You should expect a substantial training period; don't be discouraged by this. We saw many examples where an entry-level scientist was being sought and the organizations indicated they would work closely with the hiree in the acquisition of skills in methods, specific equipment, and techniques needed for success within the organization.

You should also expect a great deal of close supervision in the field. Most employers will want to be sure that you are knowledgeable of and confident with procedures, methods, instruments, and proper data-gathering techniques before they allow you to work on your own. There are also considerable safety considerations, especially when working with toxic substances.

New employees can also expect to be assigned the tasks that more experienced personnel would rather avoid. One recent graduate returned for a visit.

He was hired by a hydrologic consulting firm that had been contracted to find water for a municipality. He joined a team whose job was to use ground-penetrating radar to locate potential aquifers. That data would be later analyzed in the lab to identify the best sites to drill for water. First, however, before the ground-penetrating radar sled could be dragged across the ground surface, weeds, shrubs, and saplings had to be removed to make way for the equipment. It was mid-summer and it was in Virginia. Guess whose job it was to ready the site with a machete? Did he do it? Yes, indeed. Did he perform the job well? Absolutely. Did he learn a great deal from other tasks associated with greater responsibility? Of course! After the firm became more confident in his abilities and assured of his skills, he was given more complex assignments. He was also asked to work independently on projects, and even participate in the analysis of data, report writing, and the preparation of a paper to be given at an international meeting of geologists.

Report writing and summaries must also be checked before release. You will receive reports back from your immediate supervisor for revision, corrections, and, sometimes, complete rewrites. Incorrect or poorly completed work will not be allowed, as it would be a bad reflection on the organization. If your writing skills are not up to snuff, you may be reminded of a college experience when a professor handed you a paper that looked as if it had red ink spilled on it. If you find yourself in this situation, don't be discouraged. Show your employer in future written duties that you used the feedback to improve your writing.

TRAINING AND QUALIFICATIONS

A reasonably large number of specific academic majors will qualify you for many of these jobs. Examples include geology, physical geography, soil science, meteorology, atmospheric science, botany, or chemistry. Since the skills needed for environmental science jobs are reasonably diverse, so too is the training and experience required. If you lack specific qualifications, it is often useful to alert the potential employer that you are adaptable, learn quickly, and have the motivation to pick up skills that you might lack. Be enthusiastic!

A number of employers are searching for broadly trained environmental scientists. They are seeking people with strong backgrounds in the sciences and with experience in basic laboratory procedures, including lab safety, research design skills, and sampling techniques.

Know Something About Field Procedures

Knowledge of field procedures may be essential. Some employers wish to hire applicants who are comfortable working outside under physically demanding situations and who are able to use chainsaws, backpack sprayers, and other types of mechanical equipment, such as an all-terrain vehicle (ATV). All those hours spent in the gravel pit on your dirt bike might actually pay off here! Some employers identify other skills that would be helpful in securing a position, such as first aid and CPR. Other jobs require the ability to hike long distances over rough terrain. You must ask yourself if that is what you are prepared to do. Some would see such a job as a perfect match while others would declare that using a chainsaw or administering CPR is not what they had envisioned doing in their career.

Transferable Skills Are Important

Some employers seek applicants with fairly specific training in subjects such as wildlife biology, ecology, plant identification, or natural resource inventorying. You may have had a botany or forestry class where you learned how to key out plants and forest trees. If you did not have the opportunity to learn all of the trees in the eastern forests, for example, and a job description suggests that that skill is essential, tell the employer that you know how to approach this requirement. You learned to identify some trees, and now you can quickly learn those species you've never seen.

Basic Lab Skills Are Required

Some employers have a need for lab scientists who know their way around the equipment and instrumentation that they use to perform routine analyses. You acquired skills in this area in biology courses, chemistry, fisheries and wildlife, or soil science classes. If you did not have the opportunity to learn specific instrumentation, don't worry; you at least learned the basic procedures and how to operate safely in a laboratory environment. Employers realize that not every new employee can be turned loose on a project and will have someone looking after you and "showing you the ropes."

Computers Are Everywhere You Want to Be

Virtually every employer, from various U.S. government agencies to the smallest consulting firms, depends very heavily on the use of computers. You will be asked to use spreadsheets, word-processing packages, and aerial image interpretation software, and to feel comfortable using instrumentation that depends upon associated software for analysis. Again, you may not have been trained on specific software packages, but you can easily pick up and move around in any packaged program if you've had some training and experience.

EARNINGS

Environmental scientist salaries vary widely, starting at $23,500. If you are interested in the Land Steward position with the local nonprofit, expect to start at $23,700. Remember that there was a lot of field work associated with this job. They were looking for brawn and brain, with a heavier emphasis on brawn. Entry-level salaries for state environmental scientist jobs, such as an environmental specialist in a Division of Natural Heritage or a waterfowl project leader, range from $25,000 to $32,000. Environmental consulting firms offer starting salaries of $25,000. One job for a wetland scientist offered a starting salary of $28,000. Regional nonprofit environmental groups pay up to $29,000 for environmental associates. If you have some specialized skills, like knowledge of GIS, mapping software, and databases, you can expect to earn more at consulting firms and larger nonprofit organizations. Positions requiring specialized skills have starting salaries in the $30,000 range.

CAREER OUTLOOK

The career outlook for environmental scientists is a stable one. The *Occupational Outlook Handbook* indicates that the range of positions that we describe as environmental scientists will grow as fast as the average through the year 2008. There are several hundred thousand people employed in the United States in these positions. Newly degreed environmental scientists will be needed as workers retire and as new specialties arise, and to take new discoveries in environmental technology to their next stage of development.

STRATEGY FOR FINDING THE JOB

If you would like to obtain employment as an environmental scientist, be ready to find relevant summer employment while obtaining your degree, develop effective communication skills, and practice being a strong team player. The following three sections provide more detail for you to use in your job search.

Get Summer Experience Working as an Environmental Scientist

While researching jobs for the environmental sciences career path we came across many part-time and temporary job listings that were ideal for gaining the needed experience required for full-time positions. There was an ad for a summer full-time temporary research assistant for a local natural history area. Job requirements included outdoor field work measuring goldenrod plants and recording the data. A sustainable organic farm advertised for a forest resource assistant. They were willing to work with the student's college to get internship credit. They offered housing and a small weekly salary. These are just a few of the many, many job listings that are out there. The Environmental Careers Organization (environmentalnetwork.com/WIP/start1.htm) listed more than 650 paid internship opportunities on its website. Take advantage of them to obtain summer work or internships that will help you build the field work experience you'll need to get a job as an environmental scientist.

Even Scientists Need Effective Communication Skills

As we worked on the strategy section for each career path, the importance of possessing solid communication skills was repeated again and again. Look back at the job listings included in this chapter and you'll see direct references to the requirement for these skills: "must be excellent communicator," "good written/verbal communication skills," "exceptional written communication skills." You'll also see advertisements that list duties that require these skills but that don't directly state the need for them: "writing newsletters," "speaking at intense public meetings," "write reports," "maintain communications with federal and state agencies and other conservation groups." Environmental scientists must share important information! So work on developing and enhancing these communication skills in the classroom, on the job, and in other settings whenever the opportunity presents itself.

Know How to Work as a Team Member

Success is rarely achieved by an individual working alone. Environmental scientists often depend on others, including lab technicians, database developers, cartographers, and field work supervisors, for the data they need to do their work. And others within the organization need the analyses and the information provided by the scientist to develop policies, to share information with stakeholders, or to apply for grants that fund part of the operation of the organization. Effective teamwork creates synergy, meaning that the whole is greater than the sum of its parts. As an environmental scientist you can be the linchpin in your organization by acting as a role model: trusting and respecting those you work with, working efficiently, and communicating thoughtfully. Create a synergy in your workplace and just see what environmental problems you and your coworkers can resolve!

POSSIBLE EMPLOYERS

Environmental scientists work for a variety of employers. Governments regulate activities that help insure that certain elements of the environment are not degraded further, for example, air and water quality. In addition, governments set the rules for environmental cleanup and remediation. Larger companies in private industry have in-house scientists who insure compliance with regulations and undertake activities to prevent industrial activity and accidents that would degrade the environment. Some companies are not large enough to justify employing an environmental scientist, so they utilize the services of environmental consultants to undertake this work for them. And nonprofit organizations undertake environmental cleanup and protection activities that are not being addressed by regulated activities. In addition, some nonprofits help identify gaps in regulated activities. They also serve as watchdogs to make sure that government, industry, and consultants are all adhering to the current set of rules and regulations.

Federal Government

Probably the most obvious job you first think about when considering working for the federal government is that of an environmental protection specialist at the EPA. In this entry-level position you would provide support and assistance with respect to environmental policies and plans, and interact with all entities within the larger environmental network (e.g., other federal agencies and state and local governments). The Bureau of Land Management is another federal agency that hires environmental protection specialists. You could also work as an environmental specialist for the Department of the Interior, Bureau of Reclamation. This position involves preparing and processing environmental impact statements, environmental assessment and commitment plans, and other documents required by the Division. But wait! You could also work for the Office of the Secretary of the Army's Field Operating Office as a biological sciences environmental manager. And the Army Corps of Engineers hires civilians to work as biologists, botanists, ecologists, environmental resources specialists, geologists, geophysicists, and physical scientists, each of whom plays a role in positively impacting the environment.

Help in Locating These Employers. Graduates with a bachelor's degree in any number of disciplines can expect to start in a General Schedule (GS) position of 5 or 7. Visit the U.S. Office of Personnel Management's website (usajobs.opm.gov) and select the Entry Level Professional option. In the pull-down menu of job types, you will see "physical and biological sciences." Simply highlight this job type, enter the keyword *environment,* select a geographic area you'd like to search, and then submit your request. When we undertook this selection, almost fifty jobs were available for review. When the keyword was removed and the search resubmitted, 235 listings were shown. Depending on your major, you may also want to undertake a search using the "social science and welfare" or "legal, investigative, law enforcement and safety" options.

Also use this site to navigate to job listings published by the various agencies such as the U.S. Army Corps of Engineers.

State Government

A midwestern state's Department of Transportation recently advertised a position for an environmental planner to help prepare NEPA documentation, undertake wetland assessments and mitigations, and complete transportation plans. A southeastern state was looking for a waterfowl project leader who would implement waterfowl management and research activities. A water management district in a southern state was seeking to hire an environmental scientist to undertake the river channel vegetation component of a river restoration evaluation program. A western state's Department of Transportation posted a job listing for an environmental program coordinator. These are just a few of the hundreds of job listings that entry-level environmental scientists might want to investigate.

Help in Locating These Employers. One useful website that highlights state jobs is environmentalcareer.com/states.htm. It has a U.S. map and you can review jobs by state. Another site, called Environmental Career Opportunities (ecojobs.com), lists some state government environmental scientist jobs. Also be sure to visit the website for a state's employment office. Appendix A shows a list of these sites. Then work through the site's instructions for reviewing state employment listings. State positions are also advertised in area newspapers. Or visit or call your state's employment office to find out how to obtain listings of open positions.

Private Industry

You could work as a geologist for a large corporation assisting field crews in daily production, managing personnel within the field crew, and communicating with engineers and project managers. Or you might be employed as a technical support specialist who assists field sales representatives/customers and provides lab support activities. You could work as a project leader for a geographic data manufacturing company and coordinate the production of a product line that serves the telecommunications industry. The list could go on and on.

Help in Locating These Employers. Three websites that link to hundreds of jobs are Environmental Expert Web Resources (environmental-expert.com), Environmental Health and Safety Network (ehsnetwork.com), and Pollution Online Marketplace for Industry Professionals (pollutiononline.com). The primary purpose of these sites is to promote services and products, but each includes a job search option. If you're willing to take the time to explore all the various search options available on these sites, your time will be rewarded because you'll uncover many, many job leads. And be sure to look at the websites listed under the other employer categories detailed for this career path. Many of them also include job postings in private industry.

Once you get a better sense for the kinds of companies that hire environmental scientists, and the associated job titles, review the yellow pages for similar companies that are operating in the geographic locations where you'd like to work. And review newspaper classifieds and look for the job titles you've found.

Environmental Consulting Firms

Literally hundreds of environmental consulting firms currently operate in the United States and Canada. Some consist of a director and a handful of employees, while others employ dozens of engineers, geologists, hydrologists, planners, technicians, environmental scientists, support staff, and lawyers. Some specialize in the cleanup of brownfield sites and petroleum spills and the removal of chemical contaminants. Other firms concentrate upon the design and maintenance of systems to reduce emissions that might impact the hydrology of an area or the atmosphere. Yet some companies have a very different approach to consulting; they provide services such as the development of risk management plans, compliance with air and water pollution regulations, pollution prevention, and help with obtaining operating permits from governmental regulating agencies. Some specialize in the mitigation of air or water quality problems, while others offer services that involve planning and risk management.

Technical staffing agencies work to match temporary employment opportunities with environmental scientists. Recently one agency was looking for a wetland scientist to send to a company that wanted to undertake wetland delineation, assessment, mitigation design, and monitoring activities. A consulting firm was looking for a wetland biologist to coordinate activities with a regulatory agency and to write technical reports. An environmental specialist was needed for the natural resources division of a Houston, Texas, consulting firm. Another consulting company wanted to hire a habitat assessor who would undertake field work, technical writing, and leading field crews. Yet another engineering consulting firm that got a contract with FEMA to support the national flood insurance program, wanted someone to interpret maps, write reports, and interact with clients. An ecological risk assessor was needed by a consulting firm to manage eco-risk assessments required under the CERCLA and RCRA federal mandates and state programs, and to complete NRDAs.

Help in Locating These Employers. Two websites to start with include nerdworld.com/nw9274.html, which lists environmental consultants, and environmentalnetwork.com, which lists lead inspectors and risk assessors, lead abatement contractors, asbestos inspectors and asbestos abatement contractors, environmental consulting firms, and environmental training providers. This site covers both the United States and Canada.

In addition, the National Society of Professional Engineers lists engineering firms by state on their website (nspe.org/firms-pepp/ef-home.asp). There are links to each company and most include job listings. They do list jobs for nonengineers, including environmental scientists. Other good websites to visit include Earthworks (earthworks-jobs.com), Environmental Careers Bulletin Online (ecbonline.com), and Professional Outlook (professionaloutlook.com).

Nonprofit Organizations

Nonprofit organizations, such as The Nature Conservancy, hire environmental scientists to help them monitor activities that are a part of their mission. This organization was recently looking to hire a biohydrologist to assist in implementing conservation strategies for freshwater biodiversity in a four-state area. Another nonprofit, a foundation that allocates funds for education and the environment, was looking to hire a program assistant. Don't let this job title fool you. A bachelor's degree was required, along with very strong computer and communication skills, and the starting salary was $35,000.

Help in Locating These Employers. A number of excellent websites include job listings posted by nonprofit organizations. Be sure to go to ecojobs.com.

This site links you to jobs in conservation and natural resources, environmental science and engineering, outdoor and environmental education, and international environmental jobs. Another useful site is The Environmental Career Center (environmentalcareer.com). This site organizes jobs into several categories, including one entitled "nongovernmental/nonprofit organization jobs." A third site to check out belongs to the Environmental Health and Safety Network (ehsn.com/jobs). Lots of different employers advertise here, including nonprofit organizations.

Higher Education

Recently a midwestern university's River Studies Center advertised a position for a photo interpreter. This job called for mapping vegetation using aerial photographs, stereoscopes, and national vegetation classification standards. A West Coast university was looking for a research assistant/pesticide specialist to work assisting a national pesticide network housed at the school. The mission of the organization is to deliver objective, science-based information about pesticide-related issues to the public and professionals. They were looking for someone with a B.S. in toxicology, environmental chemistry, biotechnology, agricultural sciences, public health, or a closely related area. If you enjoy the academic environment and you want to be a part of it after graduation, don't overlook colleges and universities as potential employers.

Help in Locating These Employers. *The Chronicle of Higher Education* is a primary source for finding jobs in higher education. College libraries and departmental offices often have copies of this weekly publication. Or you can check their website at chronicle.com. Additionally, the Environmental Health and Safety Network website (ehsn.com/jobs) lists some positions in higher education as does Earthworks (earthworks-jobs.com) and the Environmental Career Opportunities website (ecojobs.com).

POSSIBLE JOB TITLES

Throughout this chapter we've provided job titles associated with working as an environmental scientist. Review the list shown here for additional selections as you begin your job search, and add to the list as you go. You'll find no dearth of titles for this career path.

Air quality scientist	Environmental specialist
Airphoto interpreter	Geographer
Biohydrologist	Geologist
Biologist	Geophysicist
Biotechnologist	Geoscientist
Chemist	GIS specialist
Conservation scientist	Hydrogeologist
Ecological risk assessor	Land steward
Ecologist	Natural resources specialist
Environmental associate	Project leader
Environmental biologist	Research supervisor
Environmental consultant	Researcher
Environmental field scientist	Resource assistant
Environmental geographer	Staff scientist
Environmental geologist	Wetland biologist
Environmental program coordinator	Wetland scientist
Environmental scientist	

RELATED OCCUPATIONS

There will be a variety of related occupations for you to consider, and the job titles will depend on the specific degree you achieved. Just a few of the many related job titles are shown here.

Cartographer	Salesperson (environmental equipment, supplies)
Horticulturist	Salesperson (medical supplies, pharmaceuticals)
Life scientist	Surveyor
Medical scientist	

PROFESSIONAL ASSOCIATIONS

The associations listed in this section are just a few of the many that exist to support environmental scientists working in government, industry, environmental consulting, nonprofits, and education. The website links that have been listed throughout this chapter will take you to other sites that can provide additional useful information for your job search.

Canadian Environment Industry Association, Ontario
2175 Sheppard Ave. E, Ste. 310
Toronto, ON M6H 1P7
Canada
Members/Purpose: Private sector, not-for-profit association dedicated to promoting the economic health of environment business, thereby strengthening its domestic and international competitiveness.
Training: Annual meeting, workshops, conferences, seminars, and online training opportunities
Journals/Publications: Monthly newsletter
Job Listings: None
Website/E-mail: ceia.on.ca; info@ceia.on.ca

Environmental Assessment Association
8383 E. Evans Rd.
Scottsdale, AZ 85260-3614
Members/Purpose: Environmental inspectors, lenders, remediation firms, and government agencies. Purpose is to provide members in the real estate industry with information about environmental inspection, testing, and hazardous waste removal.
Training: Many online courses
Journals/Publications: *The Environmental Times,* a bi-monthly newspaper; booklets; monographs; and manuals
Job Listings: None
Website/E-mail: iami.org/eaa.html; eaa@iami.org

Environmental, Health & Safety Auditing Roundtable
15111 N. Hayden Rd., Ste. 160355
Scottsdale, AZ 85260-2555
Members/Purpose: Environmental risk auditors; a professional organization dedicated to the development and practice of environmental health and safety auditing.
Training: Annual meetings
Journal/Publications: Newsletter, online bookstore, links to environmental health and safety websites
Job Listings: Links to job listings available online
Website: auditear.org

Environmental Law Institute
1616 P St. NW, Ste. 200
Washington, DC 20036

Members/Purpose: Environmental professionals in government, industry, the private bar, public interest groups, and academia. Convenes diverse constituency to work cooperatively in developing effective solutions to pressing environmental problems.
Training: Offers seminars, courses, and special events
Journals/Publications: *The Environmental Law Reporter; The Environmental Forum; National Wetlands Newsletter*
Job Listings: Links to sites that include job listings
Website: eli.org

Environmental Services Association of Alberta
10303 Jasper Ave., #1710
Edmonton, AB T5J 3N6
Canada
Members/Purpose: Environmental industry association; not-for-profit association dedicated to development of a strong environmental services industry by facilitating leadership, improvements in technology, and market development.
Training: Offers courses ranging from introductory to advanced levels
Journals/Publications: *Directory and Buyer's Guide*
Job Listings: None
Website/E-mail: esaa.org; info@esaa.ccinet.ab.ca

Institute of Professional Environmental Practice (IPEP)
333 Fisher Hall
600 Forbes Ave.
Pittsburgh, PA 15282
Members/Purpose: Certification organization for environmental professionals.
Training: Examination guides, links to review course
Journals/Publications: None
Job Listings: None
Website/E-mail: ipep.org; ipep@duq.edu

Northwest Environmental Business Council (NEBC)
P.O. Box 672
Portland, OR 97207
Members/Purpose: Environmental industry; acts as an information clearinghouse for environmental businesses.
Training: Annual meeting

Journals/Publications: Directory/resource guide
Job Listings: None, but has links to many environmental organizations that do list job openings
Website: nebc.org

Society for Ecological Restoration
1955 W. Grant Rd., #150
Tucson, AZ 85745
Members/Purpose: Individuals, academics, and environmental organizations. International nonprofit that promotes sensitive repair and management of ecosystems.
Training: Conference, workshops
Journals/Publications: Newsletter, online directory
Job Listings: Online links
Website/E-mail: ser.org; info@ser.org

13

PATH 4: ENVIRONMENTAL TECHNOLOGY

Y our mailbox is packed with a few advertisements, a friendly reminder from the Department of Campus Safety to pay a parking ticket, a note from Mom accompanied by a check. And something you've really been waiting for, a reply from a potential employer in response to myriad letters of interest and résumés that you've sent out over the past few months. This one is different, though. An environmental consulting firm wants you to interview at their facility. Your hands are shaking as you peruse the page and realize that they will fly you to their office in St. Louis, show you their facilities, let you observe the lab routine, and have you accompany a team to a local site to observe field procedures. This is the payoff after four years of tough chemistry, math, geology, and biology classes; tons of homework; countless hours in labs; uncountable lab and field reports; and weekends spent off campus on field trips. You have every right to be excited because this is your first step toward beginning an exciting and useful career!

The environmental technology career path describes jobs that are more technical in nature than either the environmental education or environmental policy, planning, and management career paths. An individual pursuing a career in environmental technology can present any one of a number of relevant degrees as an educational credential, but a certain core of knowledge will be required.

DEFINITION OF THE CAREER PATH

Environmental technologists support the work of environmental engineers, environmental biologists, and environmental planners in a variety of settings.

They often begin their careers performing routine laboratory and field data-gathering tasks. Later, with experience, they move up the ladder into more demanding positions, with broader responsibilities and more diverse assignments.

Job settings in this category range widely, from those where most work is done in the laboratory to those where most of the work is performed outside. Some jobs would entail both gathering and processing samples. Tasks might range from soil and water field sampling to lab testing of various types of materials. Some jobs would involve the collection of hazardous materials and their testing for concentrations of toxic substances. Others involve sampling and testing of materials at construction sites to ensure that soil and bedrock can support loads. Others are focused in the biologic arena, where field identification, recording, and testing of organisms is the most important task. Other environmental technologists sample emissions from industrial stacks in the field and determine in the lab the air quality of such emissions.

Many government agencies, notably the Environmental Protection Agency (EPA), employ large numbers of these field and lab technicians. Additionally, many environmental technologists are employed at the state level. And government entities as small as municipalities also have a need for these workers at water or waste disposal treatment plants. Environmental consulting firms both small and large employ people with environmental technology skills. These consulting firms sometimes rely upon outside, independent labs to test their samples instead of performing analyses in-house. Therefore, independent testing labs too are a source of jobs. Some larger nonprofit organizations hire environmental technicians for their staffs. Finally, chemical and other manufacturers hire environmental technicians.

Environmental Technologists and the Skills They Need

This career path covers a broad range of jobs, so the skill set that an employer might require is equally diverse. There is, however, a core set of skills and experience that is needed. Before we go into detail, let's look at several recent job listings.

Environmental Technician. (broad-based consulting firm) seeks individuals to support staff on various projects for client companies. Firm provides manufacturers with environmental, health & safety services. Undertake field sampling, lab work, and documentation of results. Qualifications include computer spreadsheet experience & advanced math skills. Successful candidate will be a self-starter, with an environmental or related degree and possess a strong background in chemistry and math.

Lab Technician. Full-time position at new cutting-edge recycling engineering lab. Perform engineering testing for geotechnical lab focusing on recycled construction materials. Will train to perform a variety of engineering test procedures related to soil, asphalt, concrete, and other materials. Work on QC and R&D projects using recyclable materials in various construction products. Research projects with industry and universities. Hands-on work at both the laboratory and project sites. Work around heavy equipment; requires lifting. Science major with strong geotechnical background preferred; chemistry knowledge a plus. Benefits include health insurance, vacation, 401(k) retirement plan, plus more.

Environmental Technician. Environmental firm has full-time & part-time entry-level positions in bioassay lab. Duties include conducting bioassays & routine chemical analyses, field sampling, sample pickup & delivery, & maintenance of aquatic cultures. Must be willing to share weekend coverage, as required. College degree in aquatic biology or related field preferred. Prior experience in a lab setting or culturing saltwater/freshwater fish is desirable.

Aquatic Technician, (state chapter of national nonprofit organization). Requires sampling fish and macroinvertebrates in the field, then sorting and identifying specimens. Develop and maintain records of specimens. B.S. in aquatic ecology or fisheries and wildlife.

Air-Monitoring Field Technician. Individuals responsible for testing air quality of emission stacks across the nation, primarily in the western region. Also includes processing some results in the lab & compiling results. No experience necessary. Must have a B.S. degree in hard science area such as chemistry, engineering, physics, or earth science, with very good math skills. Must love the outdoors and be able to lift 50 pounds above your head. The perfect candidate will be familiar with spreadsheets and be able to troubleshoot analyzers and laptop components.

What do all of these jobs have in common? Each advertisement emphasizes field data gathering, laboratory testing, and the processing of the results. There is little reference to presentation of these data in either written or verbal form. These sorts of jobs emphasize the technical aspects of the environmental sciences and place much less emphasis on those communication skills than we have encountered in each of the other environmental studies career paths. There is less expectation for report writing and presentations to various sorts of groups. This aspect of the environmental technician might appeal to you. But not all job descriptions in this category involve merely gathering, processing, and analyzing samples. Some additional skills are sometimes required. Let's examine a job listing that calls for additional capabilities.

Environmental Technician. An established and respected geotechnical/ environmental company is seeking highly motivated and investigative technicians to join their team of superstars. Candidate will learn how to do soil collection, compaction, and testing for strength and erosion. Candidate will write reports based on their findings. Candidate will be traveling to different sites throughout the area, working outdoors, and interacting with clients. If you like the outdoors and travel, and don't mind getting dirty, then this is the opportunity for you to learn new skills, work for a great company, and advance your career.

Here, a broad range of skills and expectations are emphasized. Obviously, the person who lands this job is going to be outdoors and doing hands-on types of work, but she or he will also be assembling reports and working with clients.

We also place those trained in Geographic Information Systems (GIS) and Global Positioning Systems (GPS) in the environmental scientist category as well. The following are typical of ads for those who have training in these areas.

GIS Specialist. Entry level. Typical projects involve working on environmental impact statements, resource management plans, habitat studies, reclamation & mitigation plans, and other natural resource and cultural resource assessments. Direct involvement with data capture/conversion of coverages, data format conversion, digital orthophotography, GPS collection/post-processing/projection, and data reconciliation. Software: ArcView 3.2 on Windows platform. Extensive knowledge of CadReader, GeoProcessing, and Projector extensions necessary. Knowledge of Spatial Analyst and 3-D Analyst extensions helpful, but not necessary.

GIS Analyst. Responsible for development and maintenance of Environmental Planning Checklist GIS analysis tools. Primary responsibility: work closely with environmental professionals to develop automated spatial analysis functions used to support project planning/environmental compliance on a navy installation. Other duties: gathering & developing spatial data required for the application, writing the code in an existing ArcView application for the analysis and the training (group and one-on-one) of application users. Requires: B.S. geography or related field; experience utilizing ArcInfo for data development of vector data; analysis and knowledge of modeling; comprehensive working knowledge of ArcView application;

experience programming with Avenue; knowledge of ArcSDE from a user's perspective and basic knowledge of SQL; ability to work in a team environment; and ability to communicate with customers and end users to define requirements. Experience with ArcInfo 8 a plus.

WORKING CONDITIONS

Environmental technicians perform a vital role in the organization with which they are affiliated. Without their contribution, there would be no hard data upon which administrative decisions could be made. However, many of these positions are challenging jobs, and challenging in a number of different ways. Let's examine some of these.

Travel

Travel is required of many environmental technicians. Field sampling requires site visits; for example, visits to locations in need of remediation. Data must be collected for testing at construction sites, and projects involving water quality require on-site collection of water samples. Consulting firms often are called upon to install monitoring wells at compromised sites. Water and gas samples must be continually collected, requiring visits and revisits. Guess who will perform most of the data gathering. Will it be the supervisor with 14 years of experience? Will it be the owner of the firm? Not likely. The environmental technician, you, will be doing a lot of field travel. Sometimes these sites are within a short drive, while other jobs require air travel to distant destinations and involve overnight stays away from home. This is the reality of entry-level positions. You will have to decide if extensive travel fits into your lifestyle. Some people welcome the opportunity to travel extensively, while others have no interest at all. Keep this in mind as you review job listings.

Routines and Repetition

Some people love knowing exactly how their day will play out, while others look forward to facing the unknown each day. A number of laboratory personnel perform repetitive analytical tasks. Sometimes, especially since much of this analysis is automated today, these tasks are mechanical and redundant. Make a conscious decision about whether you are the right kind of person to undertake lab work. Keep in mind, though, that lab training can be an important stepping-stone. As a trained environmental scientist, you will have opportunities to move up and out of the lab and into other kinds of situations if you want to. This lab work can be viewed as a period where you gather experience and learn the ins and outs of the institution where you work.

Hazardous Materials

For some people, an especially challenging aspect of this profession is reconciling working with hazardous materials. Some positions require that the worker come into contact with all sorts of "nasty" substances, such as synthetic organic chemicals, hydrocarbons, inorganic chemicals, pathogens, and radionuclides. This is just a sampling of the environmental "beasts" residing in surface water, groundwater, and soils. Many advertisements for job openings that we encountered refer to removal of petroleum wastes and asbestos, for example. But there are many other toxins out there. In a textbook that focuses upon contaminant hydrogeology, for instance, a table in Chapter 1 that lists possible toxic substances in groundwater continues for eight full pages! Of course, if you are expected to deal with these materials, you will be given training in proper handling, be provided with appropriate equipment to ensure that you avoid direct contact, and be closely supervised, at least initially.

Each environmental technology position requires you to complete challenging tasks and provide real solutions to important environmental problems. In some of these jobs, you will be making a significant contribution to environmental cleanup and awareness. Society in the twenty-first century depends upon people like you to work in this arena!

TRAINING AND QUALIFICATIONS

Since the types of jobs that fall into the environmental technician career path are so varied, training and qualifications also vary correspondingly. The basic educational requirement is a Bachelor of Science degree. If you have a degree in chemistry, microbiology, vertebrate or invertebrate biology, botany, hydrology, soil science, earth science, ecology, geology, geography, or fisheries and wildlife, just to name a few, you can consider a career in environmental technology. For those who didn't major in chemistry, chemistry coursework is a must. Additionally, a solid core of physics and math courses will be required for many of these positions.

What common demands are made of students who graduate in these majors? They have to identify and classify; understand laboratory procedures and instruments; be knowledgeable about field techniques; be conversant in research design, sampling, and statistics; understand data processing techniques; be familiar with a range of computer hardware and software; and possibly possess a working knowledge of other instrumentation.

Identify and Classify Using Procedures and Equipment

Some lab and field technicians identify and classify organisms down to the species level. Others, for example soil scientists, learn to identify soil textures in the field, and determine bulk density of soils, moisture content, and fertility in the lab. Both of these jobs require that the worker be comfortable and familiar with quite a number of laboratory procedures and instruments. Geologists have very similar demands made of them. They take a number of chemistry classes, learn laboratory and field sampling and data-processing techniques, and become familiar with the operation of a variety of instruments. Fisheries and wildlife majors develop strong laboratory and field data collection skills. They are also prepared to operate a plethora of instruments and computer software packages. The point is that students in many of these environmental disciplines receive training and gain experience in a variety of skill areas.

You may not have become comfortable with each and every lab technique and instrument and every field procedure, but you were introduced to the basic concepts and you were taught how to learn. Many skills that you picked up are transferable; you can take a technique that you learned in one area and slightly modify it to be appropriate for another instrument or procedure. You can apply this ability to learn to any situation!

Use Math, Chemistry, and Computer Science Knowledge

Quite a few opportunities require that candidates have strong backgrounds in math and chemistry and some experience in computer science. Soil scientists, geologists, geomorphologists, fisheries and wildlife majors, and foresters all have taken a number of courses in chemistry, math, and computer science and have the basic preparation for many of these environmental technician job opportunities.

Understand Statistics for Research Design and Sampling

You might be asked to assist in research design, including determining sampling methodologies and statistical treatments of the data that were gathered for a project. For example, you could participate in a project that focuses upon biodiversity in the watershed of a small glacial lake in northern Wisconsin. A solid background in statistics would be a very valuable asset to an employer that undertakes work like this. Not only will you be prepared to choose the statistical treatment for this project's data, but you will know how to interpret the data and draw conclusions from your interpretation.

Harness the Power of Computer Hardware and Software

The need for computer skills in the area of environmental studies almost goes without saying. At a very basic level, you must be comfortable with a significant number of software programs including word processing, spreadsheets, and databases. Some jobs will require additional software knowledge, including Geographic Information Systems (GIS) software. The candidates with strong skills in these areas will have a greater variety of jobs to choose from.

Field Techniques

Many environmental technician jobs require field work. Completion of field work requires you to be physically able to complete the task. Some jobs may involve hiking long distances over rough terrain. Others involve field work in exposed settings such as in the hot sun or the bitter cold. You must be prepared to undertake field visits during adverse weather, and you might be required to spend long days in the field.

Jobs involving field work may begin at any time of year and have deadlines that require site visits under less than ideal conditions. Field work is expensive for the employer. Therefore, it must be completed efficiently and quickly. Travel to and from remediation sites or data-gathering locales requires lots of commuting time, overnight stays, and meals away from home. If you love being outdoors, then assignments such as these will not be a problem for you. Just be sure that you have a clear understanding about the demands of the job.

SOME JOBS ARE NOT FOR THE FAINT OF HEART

Aside from a B.S. degree that includes chemistry course work and training in lab and field data gathering, sampling techniques, and statistical analysis, quite a number of the job opportunities in this career path require training in the handling of hazardous materials. The Occupational Safety and Health Administration (OSHA) requires a forty-hour training class that prepares graduates for treatment, disposal, storage, and emergency responses involving hazardous materials. This course is called Hazardous Waste Operations and Emergency Response, also known as the forty-hour HAZWOPER. Students learn the proper selection and use of protective gear, hazard assessment techniques, principles of air monitoring, steps for site decontamination, properties of hazardous materials, planning for response, regulations, and permitting.

This course is available at a number of sites; several universities offer this training as well as private companies that specialize in similar training programs. Some employers expect that you've already received this instruction, but others will enroll you as part of the on-the-job training process. The point of this discussion is twofold: first that you might be expected to have or develop these skills, and second that you might be in a situation to need them. Some jobs have an expectation that you will be exposed to or be handling various sorts of hazardous materials, including nuclear materials. Completion of this training and eight-hour updates over time, is a valuable addition to your "skills package." You will be worth more to your employer and future employers if you have a solid understanding of how toxic substances behave in the environment, and the proper means of their handling and disposal. This training is a significant asset to many people working in the environmental studies fields. It is also valuable on a personal level because you will be able to work on environmental problems with the confidence that you know the proper procedures and behaviors around such materials.

The following is a sampling of job advertisements that require this and similar training.

Sampling Technician. A reputable, very large national environmental consulting firm, whose focus is upon underground storage tanks, has openings for candidates to do groundwater and soil sampling. The job requires travel 70% of the time around the state. Candidate will need to have a 40-hour HAZWOPER certificate.

Hazardous Materials/Waste Specialists. B.S./B.A. Environmental Science/Studies, Chemistry, or related. 0–2 years' experience handling chemicals and familiarity with RCRA and DOT regs. Must be able to lift 50 lbs and be willing to work in the field. 40-hour OSHA training cert. required.

Environmental Geologists/Field Scientists. B.S./B.A. Geology, Geological Engineering, Hydrogeology, or related. 1–6 years' exp. with groundwater, wastewater, and soil sampling. Site drilling oversight experience & UST/LPST experience a plus. Report preparation & environmental site assessments involved. 40-hour OSHA HAZWOPER training cert. preferred.

Environmental Cleanup Technicians. Perform tasks relating to sampling and cleanup of hazardous materials and/or wastes. Related degree required. Must have completed OSHA 29 CFR 1910.210 (40-hour training). Experience a plus. Must be willing to travel. Excellent wages/benefits.

EARNINGS

Environmental technicians work for government agencies at the federal, state, and local levels; environmental consulting firms; independent testing laboratories; nonprofit organizations; and manufacturers.

Salary information for federal and state government positions is usually posted in the job advertisement. Federal workers employed at the General Schedule (GS) 5–7 level can expect a starting salary in the range of $21,947–$27,185, although GS pay is adjusted geographically and the majority of jobs pay a higher salary. State job salaries for similar job titles will vary by region. A recently advertised environmental specialist I job in Colorado had a starting salary of $39,600, while a similar environmental scientist I position in Alabama would pay $26,400 to start. Local government starting salaries will vary by the size of the governmental unit. For example, the City of Miami, Florida, would offer a starting salary that would be very similar to a state government position, while a much smaller local government would start you at a salary as low as $21,900.

Environmental consulting firms and independent testing labs both tend to offer modest salaries. These employers would offer something in the range of $25,350. The reason: some environmental lab technician jobs are advertised as requiring only an Associate of Science degree. This degree, though exceedingly useful, is vocational. As a result of enhanced technology, some of the thought process involved in testing is now automated. Some testing systems require minimal sample preparation, and a printout relates the results to an environmental scientist for interpretation. Don't overlook these jobs. They can be a great way to begin a career. Once you've gotten in the lab, you will show employers that you offer a wider range of skills than those individuals who possess an associate's degree, and you will find that you will quickly be called upon to undertake more challenging work that has a higher level of pay associated with it.

Nonprofit organizations are most likely to provide the lowest salaries. The larger the nonprofit, though, the better your chances are for a higher salary in this sector. If you are interested in working for a smaller nonprofit, you can expect to start in the low $20,000s. These organizations count on their low salaries being offset by providing workers the opportunity to make a difference in the earth's environment.

Manufacturers that hire environmental technicians who hold a bachelor's degree in chemistry start these workers at approximately $31,500.

One of the many useful salary websites is http://careerbuilder.salary.com. The site allows you to select a position title and geographic region, and an average salary figure will be calculated. Remember, though, these are average salaries for all workers with the given job title, not starting salaries. You can expect to earn something less than the "low" salary figure shown. You can also link to related salary surveys, but often these are one to three years old. At the time of publication a conservation technician in the Columbus, Ohio, region, for example, would expect to earn something less than $28,750.

CAREER OUTLOOK

The U.S. Department of Labor, Bureau of Labor Statistics reports that employment of science technicians, including environmental technicians, is expected to grow more slowly than average through the year 2008. *The U.S. Industry and Trade Outlook,* published by the Department of Commerce and McGraw-Hill, corroborates this expectation. Large private firms hire approximately 20 percent of environmental technicians, and the level of business for these firms is based on federal and state regulations as well as industry efforts for gains in efficiency. Environmental technologies and services is viewed as a maturing industry given the shift of "activities making up for the past to one dominated by preparations for the future." So you'll need to expect to compete for these 230,000+ jobs. The following section highlights some actions you can take that will insure you'll be in the running for environmental technology jobs.

STRATEGY FOR FINDING THE JOB

There are six key tactics you can undertake to be successful in your job search. They include: knowing the laws and regulations that will guide your work, getting related job experience, achieving HAZWOPER certification, generalizing your lab training, developing software proficiencies, and enhancing your communication skills.

Know the Environmental Laws and Regulations

Although the activities of this sector of the economy are transitioning from reacting to laws and regulations that force cleanup, remediation, and prevention to proactively increasing operational efficiency, you'll need to know about the laws currently in place that affect the kind of work you want to do. Your course work provided an introduction to this subject, but you'll want to be well versed in it.

Knowledge of various regulations was specifically mentioned in some job advertisements. Some of these regs, such as the Resource Conservation and Recovery Act (RCRA), Clean Air Act, the Worker's Right to Know Law, and the Toxic Substances Control Act, may have been covered in courses you completed. But there are many, many more regs to know about. A good place to start learning is the Environmental Protection Agency's website (epa.gov). And be sure to read professional journals related to the specific area you're interested in (air, water, hazardous materials, etc.) so that your knowledge is current and you're ready to speak knowledgeably during the interview process. The Professional Associations section of this chapter highlights many relevant journals.

Get Some Environmental Technician Job Experience

While writing this book we found many, many summer job listings that were perfect résumé builders. One job was advertised by a consulting firm that was conducting wetland delineations, and botanic and exotic species surveys. They were looking for someone to work in Florida. Another position involved collecting point data in a National Forest in Idaho. Technicians who hiked trails and bushwhacked through the woods located stock watering troughs in remote areas. The exact location of the hydrologic point was determined with a Global Positioning System (GPS) and recorded. Back at the lab, these data were downloaded into a large database.

If you want to be competitive in the marketplace when you graduate, you should plan to spend at least one summer in a "résumé building" job. Utilize the resources listed throughout this chapter to find the kind of summer job that will help you build the experience you need to get the job you want.

Consider HAZWOPER Certification

HAZWOPER stands for Hazardous Waste Operations and Emergency Response. The Occupational Safety and Health Administration (OSHA) requires a forty-hour training session for anyone working at treatment, storage, and disposal facilities and at hazardous waste cleanup sites. The training is also required for those persons responding to emergencies involving hazardous materials. Course content includes an overview of federal regulations, toxicology, hazard communication, site management, air monitoring, site characterization, operating procedures, safety, spill cleanup, and more. Many position listings require this training. The course is offered at colleges and universities across the country, and through private companies whose mission is to deliver health and safety training programs. You can access dates and locations of these offerings on the Internet by searching for "HAZWOPER Training Courses."

Generalize Your Limited Lab Training

In your lab courses you learned how to use various instruments and equipment to process and complete certain tests. Employers are likely to have more up-to-date labs than those you learned in. They will also require the use of equipment you've never seen before. So be sure to highlight your ability to adapt to new situations and quickly master the use of equipment. You can communicate this in your cover letter and résumé and also during interviews.

Develop Software Proficiencies

Employers expect their workers, irrespective of job title or position within the organization, to know how to use E-mail, word processing, spreadsheet, database, and Internet navigation software. If you did not learn to use all these types of software while obtaining your degree, be sure to take a short course and learn how to use them now.

Learn to Communicate Clearly

Whenever you have an opportunity to enhance your communication skills, either in your course work or on the job, take advantage of it. These skills are important as you embark upon the job search and again as you begin your career in environmental technology. As has been mentioned, you will face competition for these types of jobs. Candidates who are most effective at communicating their knowledge, abilities, and skills will be given more serious consideration than those who are not as practiced. Many of the job listings we reviewed specifically mentioned the need for communication skills. Just a sampling includes: interacting with coworkers, clients, or customers; working in a team environment; writing reports based on findings; or training applications users. Even environmental technicians need to have skills in these areas, especially if advancement is important to you!

POSSIBLE EMPLOYERS

Governments (federal, state, and local), consulting firms, independent testing labs, nonprofit organizations, and manufacturers are the primary employers of environmental technicians. A profile and tips for finding job listings are shown for each category of employer.

Federal Government

There are quite a few federal agencies that hire environmental technicians, but look through all the various federal job titles even if the words *environmental technician* are not given. Examples include: biological sciences environmental manager, environmental scientist, environmental protection specialist, environmental resource specialist, and physical science technician. Agencies to investigate include: Army Corps of Engineers, Bureau of Indian Affairs, Bureau of Land Management, Bureau of Reclamation, Department of Energy, Department of the Interior, Department of Defense, Environmental Protection Agency, Fish & Wildlife Service, Forest Service, Geological Survey, Minerals Management Service, National Park Service, Natural Resources Conservation Service, NOAA/National Marine Fisheries Service, U.S. Department of Labor's Occupational Safety and Health Administration, and Office of Surface Mining, Reclamation, and Enforcement.

Help in Locating These Employers. The best way to find out about openings with the federal government is to go online and look at the U.S. Office of Personnel Management's Current Job Openings site (usajobs.opm.gov). Using either the Entry Level Professional option or the Agency option, you can review current job openings. Or check out *The Book of U.S. Government Jobs: Where They Are, What's Available, and How to Get One,* published by Bookhaven.

State Government

Selected state government agencies hire environmental technicians. Among the agencies that had posted job openings at the time this book was written were the Massachusetts Department of Fisheries, Wildlife, and Environmental Law Enforcement; Oregon Department of Natural Resources; Connecticut Department of Natural Resources, and many others.

Help in Locating These Employers. State government job listings can be found on official state websites like Nevada's (state.nv.us/personnel/) or North Carolina's (ncgov.com/asp/basic/employee.asp) and in larger newspapers published in a given state, such as the *Denver Post* (denverpost.com) or the *Chicago Tribune* (chicagotribune.com). State employment offices will also have job listings posted on site. State governments may also advertise jobs with selected professional associations, so reviewing their websites and professional journals will reveal additional jobs. The American Institute of Professional Geologists (aipg.org) and the American Water Resources Association (awra.org) may post state government jobs.

Local Government

Local governments operate water treatment plants, solid and liquid waste disposal facilities, and recycling centers. As a result, facilities such as these require employees with a comprehensive understanding of the water treatment and wastewater disposal process, and techniques involved in recycling of all sorts of materials discarded by society. Additionally, municipalities require people trained in health and safety and air and water sampling.

Help in Locating These Employers. Some local governments are very large while many are fairly small. The city of Detroit, Michigan, would advertise much differently than Plymouth, New Hampshire. Detroit maintains a website and lists jobs there, in addition to advertising in the area's large metropolitan newspapers. On the other hand, Plymouth might advertise in a regional paper that is published once a week. Start your search by getting on the Internet and looking for websites for the local governments for whom you'd like to work. If you don't find job listings there, contact the local governmental unit directly to find out how and where it advertises open positions. The American Water Works Association (awwa.org) as well as other professional associations post links to hundreds of jobs, including local government jobs.

Consulting Firms

Environmental technicians work for environmental services firms, hazardous materials consulting firms, environmental consulting firms, and special disposal consulting firms, just to name a few. These consulting firms work with clients doing business in various sectors of the economy, including waste management, information technology, soil and groundwater, and health and safety. Some of the job titles you'll see advertised include: environmental field technician, OSHA technician, engineering technician, environmental technician, air monitoring field technician, aquatic technician, entry-level geologist, geotechnician, air and ground sampling technician, soils technician, and environmental scientist. Be sure to review the complete list of job titles shown later in this chapter. If this sector of the economy or this type of job interests you, keep reading!

Help in Locating These Employers. A good website to start with is Abracat Jobs (abracat.com). A search using the keywords *environmental technician* identified consulting firm jobs in Alabama, Connecticut, Montana, New Jersey, Florida, and Pennsylvania, just to name a few. Additionally, the American Society for Testing and Materials (astm.org) has an online listing of scientific and technical consulting firms. There are twenty-three categories of environmental engineering and management consulting firms to choose from. There are links to the companies' websites and access to the jobs listed online. And the American Indoor Air Quality Council (http://iaqcoun cil.org) also lists job openings on their website. Be sure to look at the listings for professional associations at the end of the chapter for other sites that include job listings.

Independent Testing Laboratories

If you are interested in working indoors in a laboratory, this is the type of employer you will want to check on. If you're interested in wet chemistry procedures, x-ray diffraction systems, fiber microscopy, organics prep, semivolatiles analyses, GCMS instrumentation, ICP, GFAA, FLAA and Cold Vapor technologies, or analysis of organic compounds, these are just a few of the many activities undertaken by testing labs.

Help in Locating These Employers. The American Society for Testing and Materials (astm.org) has an online listing of testing labs organized by geographic region and subject area. Some subject areas that may be of interest are biological, chemical and geotechnical, nondestructive evaluation, and surface analysis testing. More than 250 labs were found for the keyword *environment*. You can link to these companies' websites, and many of them list job openings and internship opportunities. The American Association for Laboratory Accreditation's website (a2la.org) contains a link to accredited environmental labs, and some of the labs post job openings on their own websites. A general Internet search using the keywords *testing laboratories* resulted in more than 350,000 hits. After reviewing the first 100 entries, this search was considered a successful effort in identifying potential employer websites.

Nonprofit Organizations

Imagine working as an ecosystem metabolism research technician collecting algae samples for a water research center. Or, being employed by a national nonprofit organization as an environmental database developer. Or, finding a job as a Research Assistant for a Natural History Area. These are just a few of the many jobs available in the nonprofit sector.

Help in Locating These Employers. The Environmental Yellow Pages (envi royellowpages.com) contains links to a variety of job advertisements, including many posted by nonprofit organizations. The Water Environment Federation (wef.org) website links to dozens of job listings. Or review *The Complete Guide to Environmental Careers in the 21st Century,* published by Environmental Careers Organization. It describes careers in fishery and wildlife management; parks and outdoor recreation; air and water quality management; education and communications; hazardous waste management; land and water conservation; solid waste management; and forestry, planning, and energy. Other books include: *Careers in the Environment,* published by VGM Professional Careers Series; *Sunshine Jobs: Career Opportunities Working Outdoors,* published by Live Oak Publishing; and *Outdoor Careers: Exploring Occupations in Outdoor Fields,* published by Stackpole Books.

Manufacturers

Most environmental technicians working in manufacturing are employed in the chemical industry. Their work can involve testing packaging to insure safe transport to market. They can also insure the integrity of the chemicals that are manufactured, and help determine the environmental acceptability of chemical products.

Help in Locating These Employers.
Several resources that you will find in your college or local library include *Standard and Poor's Industry Surveys, Moody's Industrial Manual,* and *Ward's Business Directory.* Use these references to identify companies that manufacture chemicals, and then review those companies' websites. If you don't find job vacancies listed online, contact the companies using the information provided in the printed references or online. In addition, two other websites will be useful as you look for environmental technician positions with chemical manufacturers. The American Chemistry Council (cmahq.com) site links to several organizations that list positions online. The American Chemical Society (acs.org) offers comprehensive career information via their website, but you must be a member of the organization to access this information.

POSSIBLE JOB TITLES

Usually you will find the word *technician* in the position title for jobs associated with this career path. Don't let that be your sole guide, though. Read through the job duties and you'll see that environmental technicians are also called scientists, researchers, officers, analysts, and more. The list shown below is a good guide as you begin your search.

Air monitoring field technician	GIS analyst
Aquatic technician	GIS specialist
Compliance officer	Hazardous materials/waste specialist
Conservation technician	Inspector
Environmental cleanup technician	Laboratory scientist
Environmental field scientist	Laboratory technician
Environmental geologist	OSHA technician
Environmental safety professional	Research assistant
Environmental specialist	Research technician
Environmental technician	Researcher
Environmental technologist	Sampling technician
Field technician	Sanitarian

RELATED OCCUPATIONS

Other positions that are practically oriented and that use scientific theories and principals as well as mathematics to solve problems are shown below. Add to the list as you work through your job search.

Agricultural technician	Forestry technician
Aviation safety inspector	Health inspector
Bank examiner	Mine safety inspector
Biological technician	Nuclear technician
Chemical technician	Park ranger
Consumer safety inspector	Petroleum technician
Engineering technician	Public health officer
Equal opportunity specialist	Science technician
Food inspector	

PROFESSIONAL ASSOCIATIONS

Air and Waste Management Association
One Gateway Center, Third Fl.
Pittsburgh, PA 15222

Members/Purpose: The Air & Waste Management Association (A&WMA) is a nonprofit, nonpartisan professional organization that provides training, information, and networking opportunities to 12,000 environmental professionals in sixty-five countries. The association's goals are to strengthen the environmental profession, expand scientific and technological responses to environmental concerns, and assist professionals in critical environmental decision making to benefit society.
Training: Offers conferences, workshops, and continuing education courses
Journals/Publications: *The Journal of the Air & Waste Management Association; EM, a Magazine for Environmental Managers; A&WMA News*
Job Listings: Jobs are posted online, but only association members can access them
Website/E-mail: awma.org; jdee@awma.org

American Association for Laboratory Accreditation (A2LA)
5301 Buckeystown Pike, Ste. 350
Frederick, MD 21704
Members/Purpose: Individuals, institutions, and corporations interested in achieving customer satisfaction through meeting the needs of both laboratories and their users for competent testing; improving the quality of laboratories and the test data they produce; and increasing acceptance of accredited laboratory test data to facilitate trade.
Training: Offers periodic public training courses
Journals/Publications: *A2LA News,* periodic newsletter; annual report; membership directory
Job Listings: Links to accredited labs' websites, including environmental labs. Some websites list job openings.
Website: a2la.org

American Chemical Society
1155 16th St. NW
Washington, DC 20036
Members/Purpose: Individual membership organization; provides a broad range of opportunities for peer interaction and career development.
Training: Hosts meetings and advertises training opportunities; website offers comprehensive career information
Journals/Publications: Publishes a large number of journals and magazines
Job Listings: Available on their website to members
Website: acs.org

American Indoor Air Quality Council
P.O. Box 11599
Glendale, AZ 85318-1599
Members/Purpose: A nonprofit association for indoor air quality
professionals and technicians. The council promotes awareness, education,
and certification in the field of indoor air quality through sharing, learning,
and networking.
Training: None
Journals/Publications: None
Job Listings: Lists job openings on their website
Website/E-mail: http://iaqcouncil.org; info@iaqcouncil.org

American Institute of Professional Geologists
8703 Yates Dr., Ste. 200
Westminster, CO 80031
Members/Purpose: Professional geologists, academics. Purpose is to
support working geologists, advocate, and provide professional certification.
Training: Annual meeting, workshops
Journals/Publications: *The Professional Geologist;* various handbooks and
brochures
Job Listings: Online for members
Website/E-mail: aipg.org; aipg@aipg.org

American Society for Testing and Materials
100 Barr Harbor Dr.
West Conshohocken, PA 19428-2959
Members/Purpose: Develops and provides voluntary consensus standards,
related technical information, and services having internationally recognized
quality and applicability that (1) promote public health and safety, and the
overall quality of life; (2) contribute to the reliability of materials, products,
systems, and services; and (3) facilitate national, regional, and international
commerce.
Training: Offers environmental continuing technical education programs
for industry and government
Journals/Publications: *Cement, Concrete & Aggregates; Geotechnical Testing
Journal; Journal of Composites Technology and Research; Journal of Forensic Sciences; Journal of Testing and Evaluation; Standardization News* (monthly),
Annual Book of ASTM Standards
Job Listings: Links to hundreds of labs and consulting firms that list jobs
and internships online
Website: astm.org

American Water Resources Association
4 W. Federal St.
P.O. Box 1626
Middleburg, VA 20118-1626
Members/Purpose: Individuals, corporations, universities, governmental agencies, and nonprofit institutions interested in any aspect of water resources
Training: Offers conferences, symposia, and short courses
Journals/Publications: *Journal of the American Water Resources Association; Impact* magazine
Job Listings: Links to almost one hundred job listings
Website/E-mail: awra.org; info@awra.org

American Water Works Association
6666 W. Quincy Ave.
Denver, CO 80235
Members/Purpose: Individuals, environmentalists, plant operators, manufacturers, academics interested in the improvement of water supply quality and quantity
Training: Offers publications, online resources, and symposia
Journals/Publications: *Journal of the American Water Works Association; MainStream; Opflow; Waterweek*
Job Listings: Links to hundreds of jobs online
Website/E-mail: awwa.org; E-mail for various individuals available at website

Association for Environmental Health and Sciences
150 Fearing St.
Amherst, MA 01002
Members/Purpose: Professionals concerned with the challenge of soil protection and cleanup; facilitates communication and fosters cooperation
Training: None
Journals/Publications: *Soil & Sediment Contamination: An International Journal; International Journal of Phytoremediation; Human and Ecological Risk Assessment; Environmental Forensics; The Matrix Newsletter*
Job Listings: None
Website/E-mail: aehs.com; info@aehs.com

Association of Engineering Geologists
c/o Department of Geology & Geophysics
Texas A&M University

MS 3115
College Station, TX 77843-3115
Members/Purpose: Academics, students, engineering professionals; provides leadership in the development and application of geologic principles to problems of remediation, city planning, and natural hazard risk reduction.
Training: Annual meetings, symposia
Journals/Publications: *Environmental and Engineering Geosciences; AEG News;* symposia proceedings; books; online publications
Job Listings: Online for members
Website: aegweb.org

Institute of Hazardous Materials Management
11900 Parklawn Dr., Ste. 450
Rockville, MD 20852
Members/Purpose: Professional hazardous waste handling firms; purpose is to certify hazardous waste managers.
Training: Offers accredited training for Certified Hazardous Materials Manager
Journals/Publications: *Handbook on Hazardous Materials Management*
Job Listings: None
Website/E-mail: ihmm.org; ihminfo@ihmm.org

National Ground Water Association
601 Dempsey Rd.
Westerville, OH 43081
Members/Purpose: To provide and protect our groundwater resource.
Training: Numerous conferences, many custom training opportunities, safety courses, lecture series
Journals/Publications: *Ground Water; Ground Water Monitoring and Remediation; Water Well Journal;* numerous handbooks
Job Listings: Online links
Website/E-mail: ngwa.org; ngwa@ngwa.org

Society of Environmental Toxicology and Chemistry (SETAC)
1010 N. 12th Ave.
Pensacola, FL 32501-3307
Members/Purpose: Academics, professionals in business and government; purpose is to provide a forum for discussion of environmental issues.
Training: Annual meeting

Journals/Publications: *Environmental Toxicology and Chemistry, SETAC Globe Newsletter,* many books, technical papers
Job Listings: Online links
Website/E-mail: setac.org; setac@setac.org

Water Environment Federation
601 Wythe St.
Alexandria, VA 22314-1994
Members/Purpose: Various water professionals. Purpose is to preserve and enhance the global water environment.
Training: Numerous conferences and workshops
Journals/Publications: *Water, Environment and Technology; Water Environment Federation Industrial Wastewater; Water Environment Federation Research; Water Environment Federation Reporter; Utility Executive; Water Environment Regulations Watch; Watershed and Wet Weather; Water Environment Federation Highlights;* technical bulletins, and books
Job Listings: Online links to dozens of job listings
Website/E-mail: wef.org; E-mail for various branches and individuals available at the home page

14

PATH 5:
ENVIRONMENTAL ENGINEERING

R emember back to your first semester of college when you had physics, calculus, chemistry, English composition, and, perhaps, a history class? You probably felt like you were never going to get out from underneath all of those assignments. Sometimes it seemed like you had a quiz in one class or another every day, and either a paper due or a book to read in history and English each week. And you felt like you were living in the lab. Engineering is one of the most difficult academic majors, regardless of the college or university. Lots of students start out in programs with tough requirements like those you faced, but a much smaller number of students actually go on to finish. Congratulations! You are one of them.

Now you have a chance to be rewarded for all of your hard work. A very high percentage of environmental engineering graduates land a job in their field within six months of graduation, or they are admitted to graduate school. Additionally, they command some of the highest starting salaries among college graduates.

EVOLUTION OF ENVIRONMENTAL ENGINEERING

Environmental engineering evolved from the chemical and civil branches of the discipline, and only recently emerged as a distinct discipline. Though Purdue University established its major in 1943, many additional programs emerged in the late 1960s and 1970s. The University of Delaware, as a matter of interest, established its program as recently as 1995. As we discussed in the introduction to the book, the environmental movement gained a great deal of momentum during the 1970s, and public awareness of environmental problems increased tremendously at this time. Students demanded courses that focused upon solving these problems, and so courses with an environmental theme became very popular. Eventually, these classes were merged into academic minors and following that, many institutions created majors in various areas of environmental studies, including engineering.

Environmental engineering is both interdisciplinary and exceedingly technical. Environmental engineers prepare for their profession with classes in chemistry, physics, engineering drafting, engineering principles, and math. But, depending upon the specialty within the field that is chosen, courses in geology, hydrology, geomorphology, soil science, and even biology can be elected. In order to design systems to protect and clean up the environment, engineers must also understand the mechanics of the atmosphere, lithosphere, and biosphere. Environmental engineers working for private industry; industrial plants; environmental consulting firms; and federal, state, and local governments provide services that lead to safe drinking water, proper disposal of solid and liquid wastes, clean air, and remediated sites that were contaminated by hazardous wastes.

INTERTWINING THE NATURAL AND SOCIAL SCIENCES

Many college and university academic programs emphasize the fact that training in the human dimension is as important as the natural sciences for environmental engineering careers. Course work emphasizes conservation, reuse, and pollution prevention in order to manage the environment. Political and economic issues are given consideration as well, because the reality is that political and economic conditions affect how environmental engineers go about solving the problems they face.

ENVIRONMENTAL ENGINEERS AT WORK

The American Academy of Environmental Engineers rewards innovative design for various projects annually. In a recent year, these important projects and programs were wide ranging in scope. Read through them to gain a better understanding of the kinds of activities you can get involved in as an environmental engineer.

- Noteworthy was the project for removal of nitrogen from very warm industrial wastewater outflow in Virginia. Nitrogen increases the chance for algal blooms in watercourses, which in turn negatively impacts biological oxygen demand. Another hydrological example in California was a program devised to remove silica from water associated with oil drilling. Silica fouls reverse osmosis treatment, requiring time-consuming removal from the filter membranes. Its elimination allows for the use of 25 billion barrels of water that otherwise would require disposal.

- In Alaska, solid waste handling is very difficult owing to subzero temperatures and seismic activity. Household and commercial waste freezes during transport. The freezing problem was reduced by routing vehicle exhaust through truck beds, effectively warming the debris. And geotechnical engineering helped reduce the seismic risk associated with storage of hazardous chemicals.

- A cryptosporidium outbreak in Wisconsin a number of years back has been countered with a process to introduce ozone, an effective remedy for such bacterial contamination, into the municipal water stream. This process was less expensive and required a small-scale modification of the water purification equipment already in place.

- In Wisconsin, nearly three and one-half tons of solvents were removed from clay soils at a tiny site that was near a shopping center and residential area. Removal of these compounds could have been a very disruptive process for both residents and shopping center customers. Negative impact was minimized by employing a technique that introduced high temperature steam into the soil through boreholes. The steam vaporized the solvents, which were subsequently captured by onsite catalytic oxidation. Excavation, removal, and truck transport of the contaminated soil was remarkably reduced by this new process.

Each of these innovations was directed by a team of project engineers whose task was to research and analyze the problem, design a system to solve it, and manage the outcome. Not every project is as remarkable as these examples, but you can quickly see that such innovations do help society, they have a positive impact on the environment, and they are cumulative. Not only has increasing technology set a cascade of environmental problems in motion, it has provided solutions to these problems as well.

NOW YOU'RE PART OF THE SOLUTION

The literature put out by one of the top rated engineering programs suggests that "graduates in this field have a significant opportunity to make an impact on the quality of life for people." Not every career offers this same opportunity. Environmental engineers develop the "tools" to solve environmental problems. Taken individually, these environmental solutions might be regarded as fairly insignificant. Collectively, they reduce or mitigate the effect of human activity upon the earth's ecosystems. Now you will be able to claim that you are part of the solution!

DEFINITION OF THE CAREER PATH

Environmental engineering can be separated into three principal sets of tasks: problem analysis, system design, and management and administration. Various combinations of duties lead to lots of different kinds of jobs for you to choose from. First we'll discuss the three task groupings, and then we'll show you the jobs that result from different combinations.

Problem Analysis

Engineers receive lots of training in the problem-solving process. They learn to break a situation down into a series of components, and devise steps to arrive at a solution for the overall situation. An example might include the creation of a new process for the disposal of solid waste, perhaps by introducing bacteria into the waste stream in order to break down materials into by-products such as water and carbon dioxide.

System Design

Environmental engineers employed by firms that specialize in the design of wastewater disposal systems often work closely with mechanical engineers to produce an entire wastewater treatment plant. Other projects might include a large-scale system to handle recycling of refuse, including plastics, metals separation, or papers. Environmental engineers may develop strategic plans for the protection of municipalities from hazardous waste emergencies.

Management and Administration

Some environmental engineers may serve as water treatment or municipal water plant managers. In order to properly manage such a system, the supervisor must know how every component of the plant operates. In other work settings, environmental engineers are called upon to write and administer regulations to protect the public and the environment. Their interdisciplinary training provides them with the experience to be able to understand the science behind environmental regulations.

Research

Environmental engineers also undertake research in order to develop methods and procedures, systems, and devices to reduce air and water emissions, clean up toxins, and improve site restoration techniques. Law firms, advocacy groups, governmental bodies, and consulting firms utilize environmental engineers to produce white paper reports for legislative bodies and lawsuits, to assemble background data for lobbyists, and to summarize research findings for commercial clients. Engineering graduates possess the technical background, the scientific foundations, and the human dimensions of environmental issues needed for research given their interdisciplinary training.

You will discover from the examples shown here the diversity of opportunities for environmental engineers and the wide-ranging set of skills and tasks expected for various jobs. Some require field work and sampling, others call for technical writing, many request that the successful candidate be very familiar with computer hardware and software, and some require travel to distant sites and the ability to deal with rugged terrain. Now let's look at some recent job advertisements:

Environmental Engineers. Innovative environmental firm working to provide solutions to environmental problems has attractive opportunities for engineers in a number of our offices. Reqs: 6 months to 7 years' previous environmental experience. B.S. or M.S. in Environmental Engineering. May require field work and travel.

Groundwater Modeler (CO). Entry level, degree required. Full-time. Excellent opportunity for advancement. Work on small team of modelers on simple to complex groundwater modeling studies in U.S. & overseas. Occasional travel & extended workweeks necessary. Requirements: Bachelor's in geological engineering required. Course work in the following areas of study or achievement: Hydrogeology and/or groundwater modeling; Mathematics through partial differential equations; Application of MODFLOW or other relevant groundwater simulation codes; Mathematical, numerical, or computer modeling desirable. Computer programming experience/studies desirable. Nonacademic-related experience relevant to groundwater modeling or hydrogeology desirable. Required proficiency in WinNT/Win2000, Excel, Access, and Surfer. Proficiency in ArcInfo/ArcView, AutoCAD, or other GIS-type software desirable.

Engineer. (national environmental consulting firm) with capabilities of resolving full range of environmental issues has great opportunity for engineer with 0–5 years' experience in environmental field. Candidate will work on wide range of challenging projects. Responsibilities include conducting Phase I & Phase II environmental site assessments, test borings, monitoring well installations, remediation activities, & technical report writing. Qualifications: B.S. in engineering, strong academic background, excellent writing skills, 40-hour OSHA training & HAZWOPER preferred. Compensation: competitive benefits package & friendly work environment.

Engineers (civil or environmental) (large consulting firm). Offer excellent opportunity to work on a wide spectrum of projects including Phase I real estate assessments, Phase II investigations, industrial compliance audits, stormwater planning, underground storage tank (UST) management, remediation design and oversight (soil and groundwater), voluntary cleanup program (VCP/brownfields) site investigations/closure, RCRA/Superfund remedial investigations (RI), and engineering design and oversight (landfills, remediation, and wastewater treatment). Qualifications: B.S. degree in engineering. At least one year of experience with an environmental consulting and/or engineering firm (including work as a co-op) highly preferred.

Environmental Engineer/Consultant. Environmental Services divisions in Boston and Edison have openings for environmental engineers/consultants. Involves selecting & coordinating contractors, collecting samples (soil, groundwater, wastewater, air/gas, solid waste, and other media of concern), data interpretation, proposal development, & the preparation of technical reports. Additional responsibilities include: prepare written correspondence/reports in a timely manner, review correspondence/reports for technical and editorial merit, control project costs & stay within budget, and maintain a current awareness of environmental regulations and technical developments. The position requires a self-motivated, resourceful individual with the ability to work under pressure and meet deadlines. The position also entails extensive travel in the tri-state area and occasional air travel within the continental U.S.

Environmental Engineers (CA). Need experience in environmental investigation, site remediation, & field data collection. Openings exist for junior, mid, and senior level positions. All positions require a B.S. degree and strong technical and writing skills. Company is employee-owned & offers competitive salary and benefits. Diversified client base in the municipal, federal, and industrial sectors.

Entry-Level Engineers (OR). Must have B.S. degree in engineering. Experience with water, wastewater, and environmental projects a plus. Relevant engineering project experience also a plus. Entry level through senior level résumés accepted.

Environmental Engineer—Jr. Level Position. Perform data collection & review, field work, and technical writing. B.S. in engineering, 0–3 years' experience, knowledge of NEPA, wetlands training/experience.

Entry-Level Engineers. Positions include groundwater modeling, remediation projects, assisting in preliminary assessments, field engineering evaluations, supervision of monitoring well installations, soil and groundwater sampling, aquifer testing, and oversight of remedial activities. Bachelor's degree required.

Engineers-in-Training (EITs). Currently have positions for Environmental Engineering in all offices. Qualified candidates must possess: B.S. in Engineering, and from entry-level to 3 years' experience.

Environmental Engineer Internship (environmental consulting firm specializing in wetlands and natural resource consulting). Seeking qualified candidate to fill summer position in Indianapolis office. Must be ambitious, self-motivated, & reliable. Must possess B.S. in engineering. Must have strong background in hydrology, chemistry, & wastewater treatment. Engineering focus will be on design of natural treatment systems and hydraulic computer modeling.

What characteristics do all of these job descriptions have in common? Many share a number of expectations. The ability to work as a member of a team appears in many job descriptions. Travel and field work are often components of a new engineer's job description as they travel to distant sites to evaluate, collect data, and plan and design solutions to problems. Technical skills are assumed; these are learned in the core engineering courses. But many jobs also require some expertise in GPS, GIS, and facility with computer hardware and modeling software. Additionally, knowledge of environmental regulations is expected.

Teamwork

In every work setting you will be expected to work on a team. Faculty are continually asked by employers to be sure to assign group projects so that graduates are accustomed to and prepared for work in teams. Belonging and contributing to a team is a skill that takes some time to develop. You have to learn to deal with diverse personalities and different work habits; like speed, attention to detail, and punctuality; and accept the consequences from your peers of being a poor contributor. Teamwork involves communication, both written and verbal. Even though you pursued an engineering program while at college, with lots of math, physics, and chemistry, you are still expected to be able to effectively handle all sorts of communication and "people" issues.

Travel and Field Work

Travel and field work is another expectation. Entry-level engineers will be expected to travel to distant sites to gain experience, learn to supervise data collection, install monitoring devices, scope situations, perform field analyses, and sometimes to simply visit with and reassure clients.

Well-Developed Technical Skills

Most all these position descriptions request a person with well-developed technical skills. You may not have been introduced to every possible technique or instrument while receiving your engineering training, but you were taught how to learn; that is what is important. You can figure out how to operate equipment and work your way through unfamiliar software.

Knowledge of Environmental Regulations

Many of the job advertisements we reviewed, and several of those listed, required knowledge of current environmental regulations. There is a lot of lingo, like UST, VCP/brownfields, RCRA, NEPA, and RI, that potential employers will expect you to know. Chapter 12 goes into detail about these terms, so it will be worth your time to review that information.

WORKING CONDITIONS

As with any entry-level position, you will be expected to gain experience before you are assigned projects of your own. Whether you accept an offer from a small municipality, an agency of the federal government, or an environmental consulting firm, you will be mentored. You might be assigned to a team or you may work under the direction of an experienced, licensed engineer or project manager. You will assist in any way possible as you learn the business. This mentorship might last for a year or two before you receive your own assignments. After you are working on your own, you can still expect assistance from other members of the team or department.

Typically, employers provide benefits such as paid holidays; two weeks of paid vacation; health, dental, and vision coverage; and a retirement package.

When working at the office you would likely have an office or cubicle that might be shared and, of course, a computer. When you're on the road, you'll likely share accommodations with coworkers. Your employer will reimburse you for specific expenses as outlined in the company policy.

Attire will probably be casual as you may spend time outdoors each day, checking on the progress of the various projects you're involved in, or working in the lab.

TRAINING AND QUALIFICATIONS

To qualify as an environmental engineer, you will have to present credentials for a Bachelor of Science degree in environmental or civil engineering. Some employers may expect that you've completed the OSHA forty-hour HAZWOPER training program, or that you are willing to complete it early in their employ. See Chapter 13 for more information about this training.

Lifelong education and professional development are expected of professionals working in environmental engineering. There are myriad short courses and institutes that your employer is likely to ask you to attend. A sampling of environmental consulting firm staff qualifications confirms that key personnel have taken many of these classes in order to become familiar with new techniques and processes, and to remain abreast of continually changing regulations and safety standards. Training might take one of three forms: on site, off site, or on the job.

- **On-site training.** Sometimes a training company will be employed by a firm to conduct a formal short course for staff members on any one of a number of topics, such as safety standards or hazardous materials handling. Some firms provide their own in-house training sessions. One company that we contacted suggested that informal "lunch and learn" sessions were conducted frequently.

- **Off-site training.** Your employer might, however, send you to a college or university to take classes for which you will be reimbursed.

Continuing education is expected of you in order to keep abreast of changes in technology and changes in your field. And professional associations like those listed at the end of this chapter offer ongoing training at their major annual conferences and at regional conferences. Once you join an association or two, you will begin receiving mailings about training programs that are offered.

▪ **On-the-job training.** Much of your training will be conducted "on the job" under the direction of a mentor. You will learn informally by observing and then assisting with subtasks. As your confidence grows and as your mentor's confidence in you blossoms, more exciting and comprehensive tasks and assignments will become the norm.

Licensure

Though licensure is not required at the entry level, most practicing engineers will work toward and achieve certification because it is necessary to advance at their organization and within the field. Most states regulate the licensing and registration of engineers and Engineers-in-Training (EITs). In Indiana, for example, the State Board of Professional Engineers requires the following for registration: (1) graduation from an approved four-year engineering curriculum, (2) four years of experience in engineering work, or eight years or more of engineering education and work experience, (3) successful completion of a sixteen-hour written exam, and (4) payment of fees for applications and exams. Engineers-in-training status demands are similar with the exception that the exam is eight hours in duration. Both exclude those persons convicted of a felony.

EARNINGS

In comparison with the other four paths described in this book, environmental engineers can expect to earn the highest starting salary. According to the American Academy of Environmental Engineers (aaee.net), Bachelor of Science degree engineers can demand a starting salary in the $36,000–$42,000 range. Once you become licensed (a minimum four-year process) and have five years of experience, your salary can jump into the $50,000–$60,000 range.

CAREER OUTLOOK

As has been discussed previously in this book, governmental policies, laws, and regulations are driving forces behind the need for environmental professionals, including engineers, working in the United States. Historically, there have been more jobs than workers in this field. The *U.S. Industry and Trade Outlook,* published by McGraw-Hill, portrays environmental engineering as a mature industry in terms of the effects that laws and regulations have on the industry. In other words, it appears that the expected implementation of new laws and regulations that affect the industry has peaked. So additional growth in the industry and the need for environmental engineers will come from one of two types of opportunities: (1) equipment and processes that provide economic savings to the various kinds of industries that have been discussed and (2) in the expansion of operations abroad on the part of U.S. companies hiring environmental engineers. At the time of publication, both of these types of activities are keeping the need for environmental engineers growing as fast as the average for all workers.

STRATEGY FOR FINDING THE JOB

The requirements listed in many, many job advertisements include knowledge of equipment and software, the ability to relate to clients and those affected by environmental problems by using effective communication skills, and knowledge about laws and regulations. Read on to learn more about how to be a contender as you undertake your job search.

Specifically Describe Your Expertise in Equipment and Software

One of the top schools offering a program in environmental engineering brags about the equipment it has in its lab. The equipment includes a gas chromatograph, total organic carbon analyzer, atomic absorption analyzer, pH meters, centrifuges, constant-temperature water baths, ovens, exhaust hood, various mixing devices, and pumps. You will have gained experience using at least some of this equipment and possibly most. So be sure to highlight your capabilities in this area as you begin talking with potential employers.

As you read this chapter, you saw references to lots of different software. Included were modeling software, word processing, spreadsheet and database software, and geographic information system software (GIS). As with equipment, no employer will expect you to know all the software in use at its company. But be sure to talk about the specific proficiencies you do possess, and your willingness to learn to use other tools as you begin your work.

Don't Forget the Human Element

Environmental engineers bridge the gap between technology and the people and societies the technology serves. Understanding the interplay between the two will be critical to your success in this field. So be sure to highlight your studies in the humanities, political science, and psychology in your résumé or cover letter, and talk about it during your interviews.

Hone and Highlight Your Communication Skills

Environmental engineers interact with lots of different people. You will encounter people with varying levels of education, people who may be either happy to see you or not, and people who have a high level of technical expertise or none at all. Your ability to communicate effectively will play an important role in your success. Prepare to be successful by taking appropriate course work and taking advantage of every opportunity to practice both the verbal and written communication skills you learn. You will be demonstrating these skills beginning with the presentation of your résumé and cover letter and then in your interviews. Be prepared to communicate effectively!

Keep Up on Current Affairs That Affect the Environmental Industry

If you haven't yet learned much about the laws and regulations that will affect your work as an environmental engineer, visit the Environmental Protection Agency's website (epa.gov) and read as much as you can. This site presents overviews and very detailed information that is critically important to the work of environmental engineers. Then share your knowledge and talk about your willingness to learn as you prepare for and engage in interviews.

Sustaining a career in environmental engineering may involve shifting your expertise over the years. You need to be committed to lifelong learning. Show your willingness to do so by reading appropriate professional journals (see the associations and the journals they publish that are listed at the end of the chapter) and by keeping up on current affairs that relate to the environmental industry. For example, know the latest status of projects the World Bank (worldbank.org) is funding. Firms you hope to work for may be involved in completing these projects.

POSSIBLE EMPLOYERS

There are several major types of environmental protection efforts, including air pollution control, industrial hygiene, radiation protection, hazardous waste management, toxic materials control, storm water management, solid waste disposal, public health, and land management. As an environmental engineer you will have a variety of employment settings to choose from.

Consulting Engineering Firms

Recently the top-ranked hazardous waste services consulting firm was advertising a position for an environmental engineer. They were providing an opportunity for a newly degreed engineer to learn task and project management skills through experience and training they were expecting to provide. They were looking for someone who would investigate hazardous waste sites, remediate contaminated soil and groundwater, create environmental plans, and ensure environmental compliance. If this kind of work interests you, keep reading!

Help in Locating These Employers. Using your favorite search engine on the World Wide Web and the keywords *consulting engineering firms,* you can bring up a wonderful selection of links to industry information and to the home pages of quite a variety of companies. Many of these companies post job openings on their website. In addition, the American Society of Civil Engineers' website (asce.org) also contains a list of job openings. Begin your exploration this way if you have access to the Web. Otherwise, work with the librarian at your college or local library to use resources such as *Moody's* to review listings of consulting firms. These references will contain contact information for the company. And if you're looking for employment in the area where you currently live, don't forget to check yellow page listings for categories such as environmental and ecological products and services, engineers-consulting, or engineers-environmental.

Testing Laboratories

In the environmental technology career path, we discussed testing laboratories as one of the major employers for technologists. They also employ environmental engineers to oversee and work with environmental technologists. If you like working in a lab environment and analyzing the results of tests that others conduct, this may be the type of employer for you.

Help in Locating These Employers. SuperPages.com (http://yp.super pages.com) has online yellow pages listings that you can search by topic and by state. A search on the category "environmental" for the State of New York showed a total of 3,089 listings, some of which were environmental testing labs. Or visit the website for the American Society for Testing and Materials (astm.org). It has an online listing of testing labs organized by geographic region and subject area.

Federal Government

Environmental engineers are hired by many federal agencies including the Environmental Protection Agency (EPA), Health and Human Services (HHS), U.S. Army, U.S. Navy, Interior, and Transportation. The Indian Health Service, an arm of HHS, was recently looking for a sanitary engineer to work in Arizona to design plans and prepare documents for construction of individual home water supply and wastewater disposal systems, community potable water supply and treatment systems, and community wastewater collection and treatment systems. Recently, the EPA was looking for an environmental engineer to work in the Waste Management Division, Underground Storage Tanks Program Office in San Francisco to review alleged violations of Underground Storage Tank (UST) program requirements (RCRA Subtitle I).

Help in Locating These Employers. Graduates with a bachelor's degree in engineering can expect to start in a General Schedule (GS) position of 5 or 7. Visit the U.S. Office of Personnel Management's website (usajobs.opm.gov) and select the Professional Career option. In the menu of job types, the first item you will see is "engineering, architecture, and transportation." Simply highlight this job type, enter the keyword *environment,* select the job experience/education option for GS-5/GS-7, select the salary range for a GS-5/GS-7, select a geographic area that you'd like to search, and then submit your request. When we undertook this selection, more than thirty jobs were available for review. Removing the keyword and resubmitting the search brought up more than 350 listings. Some of the civil engineering positions listed might be of interest to an environmental engineer.

State employment offices also list federal jobs available in that state. And you may also find federal positions listed in metropolitan newspapers. Review *The Directory of Federal Jobs and Employers,* put out by Impact Publications, and similar books on federal employment for additional information.

State Government

The District of Columbia advertised a position for an environmental engineer to develop and implement the District's water pollution control and storm water programs. One of the largest cities in California was recently looking for an assistant engineer—storm water, to perform professional storm water engineering work in the design, investigation, and construction of public works. Others include the design and supervision of regional solid waste disposal systems and recycling center design and operation. These are just a few of the many, many state jobs available to environmental engineers.

Help in Locating These Employers. State jobs can be found online at a variety of sites. One site, called Environmental Career Opportunities (ecojobs.com), lists some state government engineering jobs. The two jobs listed above came from the nonsubscription list available to the public at that site. You can subscribe to get a complete list available through this organization. If you aren't interested in paying to see the full list, be sure to visit the website for a state's employment office. Appendix A shows a list of state employment office websites. Then work through the site's instructions for reviewing state employment listings. State positions are also advertised in area newspapers. Be sure to visit or call your state's employment office to find out how to obtain listings of open environmental engineering positions.

Local Government

Most environmental engineering jobs available with local governments are in the areas of storm water and wastewater treatment and disposal, water treatment, solid waste disposal, and recycling. Larger local governments hire their own engineers to do this work. If you're interested in helping solve environmental problems that local governments face, there are jobs and careers available to you.

Help in Locating These Employers. Larger local governments will advertise their job openings in area newspapers, on their own websites, and also on websites of professional associations like the American Society of Civil Engineers. Be sure to review the list of associations at the end of this chapter for additional sources that list local government engineering positions.

Corporations

Nearly every company in every industry, from natural resources and energy to construction, industrial materials to production and manufacturing equipment, and information and communications to transportation, undertakes activities to avoid polluting and creates plans to respond to emergency situations. These activities lead to a need for in-house environmental engineers at the larger companies. General Motors, an automobile manufacturer, hires environmental engineers. The work at this company involves management of waste reduction, wastewater discharge, air discharge, and waste from manufacturing operations and processes. The Abu Dhabi National Oil Company's Environment, Health & Safety Division recently advertised a position for an environmental team leader that required an engineering degree. The successful candidate would help develop policies and strategies relating to the company's oil and gas exploration and production operations. Environmental engineers are needed all around the world!

Help in Locating These Employers. The range of potential corporate employers is so wide it would be difficult to detail how to find all of the relevant job listings. Appendix B contains a list of the major North American Industry Classification System sectors. Once you have identified the names of industry categories that interest you, use your favorite Internet search engine and enter individual industry names as keywords. For example, when the keywords *chemical manufacturers* were entered, a link took us to the American Chemistry Council site, which in turn led us to a list of member companies. There was a link to each company's website, and each site that we checked included job listings for environmental engineers. Conduct a similar search for an industry that interests you.

POSSIBLE JOB TITLES

Most of the job titles for environmental engineers will have that keyword, *engineer,* in the title. But don't overlook other job titles such as designer, manager, or regulator. Review the list shown below and use it as a starting point as you look for job listings in environmental engineering.

Assistant engineer	Environmental regulator
Associate engineer	Environmental researcher
Civil engineer	Environmental scientist
Designer	Geological engineer
Environmental designer	Hydrological engineer
Environmental engineer	Pollution control engineer
Environmental planner	Pollution control facility operator
Environmental program manager	Sanitary engineer

RELATED OCCUPATIONS

Environmental engineers use their science and math knowledge to solve specific problems. Those same skills are useful in other engineering jobs and in a variety of other occupations. Some representative job titles are shown below.

Architect	Life scientist
Chemical engineer	Mechanical engineer
Computer information systems manager	Natural scientist
Computer systems analyst	Physical scientist
Geographer	Pollution liability claims adjuster
Geologist	Science technician
Hydrologist	

PROFESSIONAL ASSOCIATIONS

The professional associations listed below are specifically related to engineering. Be sure to review the lists of professional associations at the end of the other chapters, too. Many of the websites associated with these other organizations will list job openings for environmental engineers.

American Academy of Environmental Engineers
130 Holiday Court, Ste. 100
Annapolis, MD 21401
Members/Purpose: Students, academics, and professional engineers. AAEE is dedicated to improving the practice, elevating the standards, and advancing the cause of environmental engineering to ensure public health and safety and to enable people to live in harmony with nature.
Training: Certification organization; links online to publications, conferences with workshops, and training sessions
Journals/Publications: *Environmental Engineer,* journal; online bookstore
Job Listings: None
Website/E-mail: aaee.net; E-mail available from home page

American Institute of Chemical Engineers (AIChE)
3 Park Ave.
New York, NY 10016-5991

Members/Purpose: Students, academics, and professional engineers. AIChE is a professional organization whose purpose is to provide leadership in advancing the chemical engineering profession. Members are creative problem-solvers who use scientific and technical skills to develop processes and design and operate plants to assure the safe and environmentally sound manufacture, use, and disposal of chemical products.
Training: Conferences, including student conferences; training modules; many professional and technical courses
Journals/Publications: *Chemical Engineering Progress,* journal; CD-ROMS; training modules; technical reports, online catalog of videos, books, journals, and journal articles; trade publications and software
Job Listings: Many online postings and job search tools
Website/E-mail: aiche.org; xpress@aiche.org

American Society of Civil Engineers

1801 Alexander Bell Dr.
Reston, VA 20191
Members/Purpose: Professional engineers, students, and academics. Purpose is to develop leadership, advance technology, advocate for lifelong learning, and promote the profession.
Training: Many opportunities
Journals/Publications: Online access to twenty-nine related journals; online bookstore, manuals, technical reports, conference proceedings
Job Listings: Online search
Website/E-mail: asce.org; E-mail available to various offices at home page

American Society of Safety Engineers

1800 E. Oakton St.
Des Plaines, IL 60018-2187
Members/Purpose: Academics, students, and professional engineers, EIT. Members manage, supervise, and consult on safety, health, and environmental issues for industry, insurance, government, and education.
Training: Annual conference, on-site seminars, symposia, professional development, professional certification
Journals/Publications: Online bookstore, technical publications, online book reviews
Job Listings: Online job bank for members, résumé posting
Website/E-mail: asse.org; customerservice@asse.org

Association for Facilities Engineering (AFE)
8180 Corporate Park Dr., Ste. 305
Cincinnati, OH 45242
Members/Purpose: Professional organization with student, academic, corporate, and professional members. Purpose is to support facility professionals by improving productivity and profit and providing opportunities to learn, lead, and influence.
Training: Certification programs, conferences with workshops and seminars
Journals/Publications: *Facilities Engineering Journal;* books and videos available online
Job Listings: Online link to a jobs website
Website/E-mail: afe.org; mail@afe.org

National Society of Professional Engineers
1420 King St.
Alexandria, VA 22314-2794
Members/Purpose: Represents individual engineering professionals and licensed engineers (PEs) across all disciplines. Promotes engineering licensure and ethics, enhances the engineer image, and advocates and protects PEs' legal rights at the national and state levels. Has fifty-three state and territorial societies and more than 500 chapters.
Training: Provides continuing education opportunities
Journals/Publication: *Engineering Times;* online *U.S. Engineering Press Review;* monthly E-mail *NSPE Update*
Job Listings: None
Website: nspe.org

INTERNET RESOURCES

This appendix lists, for each state, the Internet address of the state's

- official website,

- employment website,

- related environmental, and

- environmental agency website

If you are interested in working at the state government level, this information will help you locate the available jobs and the application procedures you'll need to follow.

State	Official Website
Alabama	state.al.us
Alaska	state.ak.us
Arizona	http://azportal.clearlake.ibm.com/webapp/portal
Arkansas	state.ar.us
California	ca.gov/state/portal/myca_homepage.jsp
Colorado	state.co.us/demp.html
Connecticut	state.ct.us/home.asp
DC	washingtondc.gov
Delaware	delaware.gov
Florida	myflorida.com/myflorida/copyright.html
Georgia	state.ga.us
Hawaii	hawaii.gov
Idaho	accessidaho.org/index.html
Illinois	state.il.us
Indiana	ai.org
Iowa	state.ia.us
Kansas	http://accesskansas.org
Kentucky	kydirect.net
Louisiana	state.la.us
Maine	state.me.us
Maryland	state.md.us

State	Official Website
Massachusetts	state.ma.us
Michigan	michigan.gov
Minnesota	state.mn.us
Mississippi	state.ms.us
Missouri	state.mo.us
Montana	state.mt.us
Nebraska	state.ne.us
Nevada	http://silver.state.nv.us/main.htm
New Hampshire	state.nh.us
New Jersey	state.nj.us
New Mexico	state.nm.us
New York	state.ny.us
North Carolina	ncgov.com
North Dakota	http://discovernd.com
Ohio	state.oh.us
Oklahoma	state.ok.us
Oregon	state.or.us
Pennsylvania	state.pa.us/PAPower
Rhode Island	state.ri.us
South Carolina	myscgov.com/SCSGPortal/static/home_tem1.html
South Dakota	state.sd.us
Tennessee	state.tn.us
Texas	state.tx.us
Utah	utah.gov
Vermont	state.vt.us
Virginia	state.va.us
Washington	http://access.wa.gov
West Virginia	http://wvweb.com/www/government/government_homepage.html
Wisconsin	wisconsin.gov/state/home
Wyoming	state.wy.us

State	Employment Website
Alabama	personnel.state.al.us
Alaska	http://notes.state.ak.us/wa/mainentry.nsf/?OpenDatabase
Arizona	hr.state.az.us/employment
Arkansas	arstatejobs.com
California	spb.ca.gov
Colorado	gssa.state.co.us/announce/Job+Announcements.nsf/$about?OpenAbout
Connecticut	state.ct.us/general.htm#Employment

State	Employment Website
DC	washingtondc.gov/gov/jobs.htm
Delaware	state.de.us/spo/howto.htm
Florida	myflorida.com/myflorida/employment/search/jobjobsearch.html
Georgia	dol.state.ga.us/eshtml/eshtml02.htm
Hawaii	hawaiigov.org/working/html/resources.html
Idaho	accessidaho.org/working/employment.html
Illinois	ides.state.il.us/general/jobs.htm
Indiana	IN.gov/jobs/stateemployment/jobbank.html
Iowa	iowaccess.org/jobs
Kansas	accesskansas.org/working/employment-opportunities.html
Kentucky	http://web.state.ky.us/KyHome/TransferShortCut.asp?LKSYSID=6
Louisiana	state.la.us/employ_statejobs.htm
Maine	state.me.us/statejobs
Maryland	http://dop.state.md.us/nowopen.html
Massachusetts	http://ceo.hrd.state.ma.us
Michigan	state.mi.us/mdcs
Minnesota	doer.state.mn.us/stf-bltn/jobs2/i
Mississippi	spb.state.ms.us
Missouri	conservation.state.mo.us/about/careers
Montana	discoveringmontana.com/doa/spd/index.htm
Nebraska	wrk4neb.org
Nevada	state.nv.us/personnel
New Hampshire	http://webster.state.nh.us/das/personnel/index.html
New Jersey	state.nj.us/personnel/vacancy/vacancy.htm
New Mexico	state.nm.us/spo
New York	dec.state.ny.us/website/career/index.html
North Carolina	ncgov.com/asp/basic/employee.asp
North Dakota	state.nd.us/cpers
Ohio	stateofohiojobs.com/applicant/index.asp
Oklahoma	state.ok.us/~opm
Oregon	hr.das.state.or.us/Jobs
Pennsylvania	scsc.state.pa.us
Rhode Island	det.state.ri.us/webdev/JobsRI/statejobs.htm
South Carolina	state.sc.us/jobs
South Dakota	state.sd.us/denr/denr_jobs.htm
Tennessee	state.tn.us/environment/jobs.htm
Texas	tnrcc.state.tx.us/admin/employ/index.html
Utah	dhrm.state.ut.us/employment/bulletin.htm
Vermont	state.vt.us/pers/recruit/howto.htm
Virginia	dpt.state.va.us

State	Employment Website
Washington	http://hr.dop.wa.gov/statejobs/index.htm
West Virginia	dep.state.wv.us/jobs
Wisconsin	wisconsin.gov/state/app/employment
Wyoming	http://wydoe.state.wy.us/doe.asp?ID=4

State	Related Environmental Agency Name
Alabama	Department of Environmental Management
Alaska	Department of Environmental Conservation
Arizona	Department of Environmental Quality
Arkansas	Department of Environmental Quality
California	California Environmental Protection Agency
Colorado	Department of Natural Resources
Connecticut	Department of Environmental Protection
DC	None available
Delaware	Department of Nat. Resources and Environmental Control
Florida	Fish and Wild. Conservation Commission
Georgia	Department of Natural Resources
Hawaii	Department of Lands and Natural Resources
Idaho	Department of Environmental Quality
Illinois	Department of Natural Resources
Indiana	Department of Natural Resources
Iowa	Department of Natural Resources
Kansas	Department of Wildlife and Parks
Kentucky	Natural Resources and Environmental Protection
Louisiana	Department of Wildlife and Fisheries
Maine	Department of Inland Fisheries and Wildlife
Maryland	Department of the Environment
Massachusetts	Department of Environmental Protection
Michigan	Department of Environmental Quality
Minnesota	Department of Natural Resources
Mississippi	Department of Wildlife, Fisheries, and Parks
Missouri	Department of Conservation
Montana	Department of Environmental Quality
Nebraska	Department of Environmental Quality
Nevada	Department of Conservation and Natural Resources
New Hampshire	Department of Environmental Services
New Jersey	Department of Environmental Protection
New Mexico	Energy, Minerals, and Resources Department
New York	Department of Environmental Conservation

State	Related Environmental Agency Name
North Carolina	Department of Environment and Natural Resources
North Dakota	Department of Game and Fish
Ohio	Department of Natural Resources
Oklahoma	Department of Wildlife Conservation
Oregon	Department of Environmental Quality
Pennsylvania	Department of Conservation and Natural Resources
Rhode Island	Department of Environmental Management
South Carolina	Department of Natural Resources
South Dakota	Department of Environmental and Natural Resources
Tennessee	Department of Environmental Conservation
Texas	Natural Resource Conservation Commission
Utah	Department of Natural Resources
Vermont	Agency of Natural Resources
Virginia	Secretary of Natural Resources
Washington	Department of Natural Resources
West Virginia	Department of Environmental Protection
Wisconsin	Department of Natural Resources
Wyoming	Department of Environmental Quality

State	Related Environmental Agency Website
Alabama	adem.state.al.us
Alaska	state.ak.us/local/akpages/ENV.CONSERV/home.htm
Arizona	adeq.state.az.us
Arkansas	adeq.state.ar.us
California	calepa.ca.gov
Colorado	dnr.state.co.us
Connecticut	http://dep.state.ct.us/rec-nat.htm
DC	None available
Delaware	dnrec.state.de.us/dnrec2000
Florida	http://floridaconservation.org
Georgia	dnr.state.ga.us
Hawaii	state.hi.us/dlnr/Welcome.html
Idaho	state.id.us/deq
Illinois	http://dnr.state.il.us
Indiana	IN.gov/dnr
Iowa	state.ia.us/government/dnr
Kansas	kdwp.state.ks.us
Kentucky	nr.state.ky.us/nrepc/jobs/listing.htm
Louisiana	wlf.state.la.us/apps/netgear/page1.asp

State	Related Environmental Agency Website
Maine	state.me.us/ifw/index.html
Maryland	mde.state.md.us
Massachusetts	state.ma.us/dep/dephome.htm
Michigan	deq.state.mi.us
Minnesota	dnr.state.mn.us
Mississippi	mdwfp.com
Missouri	conservation.state.mo.us
Montana	deq.state.mt.us
Nebraska	deq.state.ne.us
Nevada	state.nv.us/cnr
New Hampshire	des.state.nh.us
New Jersey	state.nj.us/dep
New Mexico	emnrd.state.nm.us
New York	dec.state.ny.us
North Carolina	enr.state.nc.us
North Dakota	state.nd.us/gnf
Ohio	dnr.state.oh.us
Oklahoma	wildlifedepartment.com
Oregon	deq.state.or.us/about/index.htm
Pennsylvania	dcnr.state.pa.us
Rhode Island	state.ri.us/dem
South Carolina	dnr.state.sc.us
South Dakota	state.sd.us/denr/denr.html
Tennessee	state.tn.us/environment
Texas	tnrcc.state.tx.us
Utah	nr.utah.gov
Vermont	anr.state.vt.us
Virginia	snr.state.va.us
Washington	wa.gov/dnr
West Virginia	dep.state.wv.us
Wisconsin	dnr.state.wi.us
Wyoming	http://deq.state.wy.us

APPENDIX B

NORTH AMERICAN INDUSTRY CLASSIFICATION SYSTEM

The North American Industry Classification System provides common industry definitions for the United States, Canada, and Mexico and replaces the countries' separate classification systems with one uniform system. For more information, visit the U.S. Census Bureau website at census.gov/epcd/naics02/naicod02.htm.

Code	Sector
11	Agriculture, forestry, fishing, and hunting
21	Mining
22	Utilities
23	Construction
31–33	Manufacturing
42	Wholesale trade
44–45	Retail trade
48–49	Transportation and warehousing
51	Information
52	Finance and insurance
53	Real estate and rental and leasing
54	Professional, scientific, and technical services
55	Management of companies and enterprises
56	Administrative and support, waste management, and remediation services
61	Education services
62	Health care and social assistance
71	Arts, entertainment, and recreation
72	Accommodation and food services
81	Other services
92	Public administration

INDEX